电子商务专业英语教程
（第3版）

张强华　司爱侠　编著

U0360800

清华大学出版社
北京

内 容 简 介

本书是电子商务专业英语教材，选材广泛，覆盖电子商务软件与硬件、网络技术、网络营销和物流等方面，同时兼顾发展热点。本书分为 10 个单元，内容涉及电子商务基础、B2B、B2C、建立虚拟商店、数字钱包、密码术、数字证书、安全电子交易、电子支付以及电子商务的未来等。每单元包含以下部分：课文、单词、词组、习题、阅读材料、参考译文和难点脚注，有的单元还给出了缩略语。附录 A"词汇总表"既可用于复习和背诵，也可作为小词典供学习时查阅。附录 B"电子商务英语新词的构成与词汇翻译"揭示新词的构成方法并提供翻译技巧。

本书可以支撑备课、教学、复习及考试各个教学环节，有配套的 PPT、参考答案、参考试卷等。

本书既可作为本、专科院校电子商务相关专业的专业英语教材，也可供电子商务从业人员自学或作为培训班教材。

图书在版编目（CIP）数据

电子商务专业英语教程/张强华，司爱侠编著. —3 版. —北京：清华大学出版社，2023.8
高等学校电子商务专业教材
ISBN 978-7-302-64306-7

Ⅰ. ①电…　Ⅱ. ①张… ②司…　Ⅲ. ①电子商务－英语－高等学校－教材　Ⅳ. ①F713.36

中国国家版本馆 CIP 数据核字（2023）第 139212 号

责任编辑：白立军　战晓雷
封面设计：常雪影
责任校对：申晓焕
责任印制：沈　露

出版发行：清华大学出版社
　　　网　　　址：http://www.tup.com.cn，http://www.wqbook.com
　　　地　　　址：北京清华大学学研大厦 A 座　　　　　　邮　　　编：100084
　　　社 总 机：010-83470000　　　　　　　　　　　　邮　　　购：010-62786544
　　　投稿与读者服务：010-62776969，c-service@tup.tsinghua.edu.cn
　　　质量反馈：010-62772015，zhiliang@tup.tsinghua.edu.cn
　　　课件下载：http://www.tup.com.cn，010-83470236
印 装 者：三河市龙大印装有限公司
经　　　销：全国新华书店
开　　本：185mm×260mm　　　　　印　　张：17　　　　　字　　数：406 千字
版　　次：2012 年 7 月第 1 版　2023 年 9 月第 3 版　　　印　　次：2023 年 9 月第 1 次印刷
定　　价：59.00 元

产品编号：098730-01

前　言

电子商务已经进入高速发展期，从业人员众多，覆盖范围广阔。它以低廉的交易成本以及突破时间与空间限制的特性引领了经济的发展。电子商务的高速发展要求从业人员及时掌握国际新技术、新方法，因此对专业英语水平要求较高。具备相关职业技能并精通外语的人往往能赢得竞争优势，成为职场中不可或缺的核心人才与领军人物。

本书的特点与优势如下：

（1）选材全面，包括电子商务软件与硬件、网络技术、营销和物流系统，同时兼顾发展热点。许多内容非常实用，具有广阔的覆盖面。作者对丰富的课文素材进行了严谨推敲与细致加工，使其具有教材特性。本次修订删除了部分过时的内容，增加了人工智能和大数据在电子商务中的应用、电子商务法规以及直播电商等新内容。

（2）内容全面，包括电子商务基础、电子商务的类型、网上购物、建立网络商店、电子商务网站设计、撰写产品介绍、客户服务、电子商务 CRM、在线支付和移动支付、移动电子商务、供应链管理、物流及其管理、跨境电子商务、电子商务系统安全、电子商务常见风险与规避、电子商务法规、人工智能在电子商务中的应用、智能推荐系统、电子商务聊天机器人、大数据在电子商务中的应用以及直播电子商务等。

（3）体例创新，非常适合教学，与课堂教学的各个环节紧密切合，支持备课、教学、复习及考试各个教学环节。每单元包含以下部分：课文——选材广泛、风格多样、切合实际的两篇专业文章；单词——给出课文中出现的新词，读者由此可以积累电子商务专业的基本词汇；词组——给出课文中的常用词组；习题——既有针对课文的练习，也有一些开放性练习；阅读材料——进一步扩大读者的视野；参考译文——让读者对照理解和提高翻译能力；难点脚注——即时讲解，视野宽广，具有开放性。有的单元还给出课文中出现的、业内人士必须掌握的缩略语。

（4）习题量适当，题型丰富，难易搭配，便于教师组织教学。

（5）附录 A"词汇总表"既可用于复习和背诵，也可作为小词典供学习时查阅。附录 B"电子商务英语新词的构成与词汇翻译"，揭示新词的构成方法、提供翻译技巧,对读者"破译"新词大有裨益。

(6) 教学支持完善,有配套的 PPT、参考答案、参考试卷等。

(7) 作者有近 20 年 IT 行业英语图书的编写经验。在作者已出版的图书中,3 部入选普通高等教育"十一五"国家级规划教材,1 部成为全国畅销书,1 部获得华东地区教材二等奖。作者已经出版了 3 部电子商务专业英语教材,以前的经验有助于本书的完善与提升。

在使用本书过程中有任何问题,都可以通过电子邮件与我们交流,我们一定会给予答复。邮件标题请注明姓名及"索取电子商务英语参考资料"字样,教师也可在清华大学出版社网站(http://www.tup.com.cn)免费下载课件。

作者恳请大家不吝赐教。让我们共同努力,使本书成为一部符合学生实际、切合行业实况、知识实用丰富、严谨开放创新的优秀教材。

作　者
2023 年 8 月

C O N T E N T S

目　录

C O N T E N T S

C O N T E N T S

C O N T E N T S

C O N T E N T S

Unit 1

Text A

E-commerce

1 What Is E-commerce?

E-commerce simply means selling goods，services，information，or whatever over the Internet.

How do you get your share of the action? That's easy. You create a website that promotes your products，obtain an Internet address，hire space on a web-hosting company，upload your pages，add a payment system and then use various promotion services to get your site noticed.

2 Building the Website

You'll be familiar with websites—collections of HMTL pages grouped around some URL like http://www.companyname.com. Websites can be very ambitious，with stunning graphics，animation，sound，database search systems，customer recognition and a good many other features. But they don't need to be. Many successful e-commerce sites are half a dozen pages extolling the virtues of the product. More can be less，and "wow" sites will only hinder customers getting to your products，and make promotion more difficult.

But your site still needs to look professional. How do you create something convincing? You can：

（1）Hire a web design company. Thousands exist，conveniently collected into directories.

（2）Build your own pages using HTML-editing software. Easy-to-use editors exist for all pockets，some of them are shareware① or even free.

（3）Purchase an out-of-the-box shopping cart program that builds the whole site for you，including an online catalogue with payment facilities in place.

---

① Shareware is software that is distributed free on a trial basis with the understanding that the user may need or want to pay for it later. Some software developers offer a shareware version of their program with a built-in expiration date（有效期）. Other shareware is offered with certain capabilities disabled as an enticement to buy the complete version of the program.

共享软件的原创作者持有版权,但允许他人自由复制并收取合理注册费用。使用者可在软件规定的试用期限内免费试用,再决定注册购买与否。

(4) Rent space on a web-hosting company offering site build online. Much like the out-of-the-box solution, the hosting company gives you templates and wizards to create a distinctive and professional-looking site.

3   Finding an URL or Internet Domain

The URL (Uniform Resource Locator) is your address or domain on the Internet. You'll want something that identifies your company and possibly your line of business. How do you get a domain?

You visit an online company offering domains for sale. As you're a commercial concern, you'll go for a dot-com, or possibly a dot-biz domain. You'll try possible names in the search box provided until you find a suitable one available.

Suppose your company is Acme Diving Equipment Ltd. You find that acme.com has been taken, and so has diving.com, both a long time ago. But acme-diving-equipment.com is still free, and you therefore take that domain for a few dollars a year. An online credit card facility accepts your order, and an email a few minutes later confirms the purchase. Just as soon as ownership is recorded by the relevant authorities, usually within a couple of days, the domain is yours.

4   Hosting Your Site

You're halfway there. You have the site built, and a domain name to host it under. Now you have to upload the site to a web-hosting company that will display it on the Internet, 24 hours a day, seven days a week. Thousands of such web-hosting companies exist, and there are now web-hosting directories that enable you to select by cost, platform type, facilities, etc. You make your choice of hosting company, click through to their site, pay their hosting fee, and can then upload your site to that company's server. The hosting company will explain how. It's very simple, but you'll need a cheap or free piece of software called an FTP program. You can obtain it from any software supplier, and use it to maintain your site thereafter. Once uploaded, your site goes 'live'. You're on the Internet.

Of course if your site has been built by a web design company, then they'll upload it for you. And if you've built your site online, then all you need to do is email the hosting company that you're ready to start trading.

5   Taking the Money

In selling something you'll want to be paid as quickly, safely and painlessly as possible.E-commerce now has many options. Starting with the simplest, you can:

(1) Display your goods online, but take payment off-line—by check, bank transfer, credit card details given over the phone.

（2）Display your goods online and take payment online through some simple wallet system.

（3）Display and take payment online，but employ a payment service provider①. A link to your shopping cart or catalogue will seamlessly transfer the customer to the payment provider for immediate card processing，transferring the customer back for you to handle the purchase. You can use your online merchant account if you possess one，but that is not required. The payment service provider will verify the credit card purchase，collect the payments，deduct the commissions，and send you the balance，usually by bank transfer monthly.

（4）Display and take payment online，but use your own online merchant account，which you have obtained from your local bank or from a Merchant Account Provider②.

Wondering how to link your site to the payment process? Links will be built in automatically if you use an out-of-the box shopping cart，employ a web design company，or rent space on an online e-commerce-hosting site. Otherwise—if you've built your own site—you'll have to add code to the pages concerned. With payment service providers that's fairly easy：they'll supply a snippet of code for you to paste in. Using your own merchant account will require liaison with the credit card processing company and good programming experience，particularly if you're hosting the site on your own server. You'll probably have to employ a professional.

6　Promoting Your Site

With hundreds of new E-commerce sites appearing every day on the Internet，it's getting mighty crowded out there. How is your site going to be noticed?

（1）Getting out a press release.

（2）Featuring in business directories，in online and off-line versions.

（3）Submitting to the search engines，perhaps employing a site optimization company to get a high ranking.

（4）Using the pay-per-click③ search engines，which charge a few cents to a few

---

①　A payment service provider（PSP）offers merchants online services for accepting electronic payments by a variety of（多种）payment methods including credit card，bank-based payments such as direct debit，bank transfer，and real-time bank transfer based on online banking.

②　Merchant account providers give businesses the ability to accept debit and credit cards in payment for goods and services. This can be face-to-face（面对面），on the telephone，or over the Internet.

③　Pay per click（PPC）is an Internet advertising model used on websites，where advertisers pay their host only when their ad is clicked. With search engines，advertisers typically bid（竞价）on keyword phrases relevant to their target market（目标市场）. Content sites commonly charge a fixed price（固定价格）per click rather than use a bidding system.

点击付费广告是大公司最常用的网络广告形式，比如百度竞价、搜狐和新浪首页上的 banner 广告。这种方法费用很高，但效果很好。这种形式的广告是这样收费的：起价＋点击数×每次点击的价格。越是著名的搜索引擎起价越高，最高可达数万元甚至数十万元。

dollars for each visitor that clicks through to your site with a particular search phrase.

(5) Signing up other sites as affiliates, paying them a commission on the sales they achieve for you.

(6) Using search engine ads.

(7) Persuading other sites to link to yours, possibly through a reciprocal links directory.

(8) Winning awards for your site.

(9) Offering online competitions, introductory deals and promotions.

(10) Providing free and helpful information on your site.

(11) Advertising off-line in newspapers and specialist magazines.

7 Will the Business Be Successful?

Now the vital question. Having followed these steps faithfully, you can surely expect your site to be successful?

Possibly—if you're in an especially favourable position. You're the sole suppliers of spare parts for some particular machinery. Or yours is the only guest house in a popular tourist area. Yes, in those cases, free information may be all you need. Similarly if you have only an academic interest in commerce, and are not running an e-business yourself.

But in all other cases we have to issue this stark warning.E-commerce is not easy, and if you follow the blandishments of advertising and e-commerce journalism it's unlikely that you'll even get your expenses back.

The early e-business casualties believed otherwise, of course, and there are still many sites, books and e-books that assure you that e-commerce is entirely a matter of following certain procedures. It isn't, and you can readily see why.

(1) E-commerce is an extremely crowded marketplace. In many areas you'll need a well-researched strategy backed by a large marketing budget.

(2) It's easy to get locked into the wrong goal or business model—as the spectacular dotcom failures discovered.

(3) You've built a site and then think about promoting it. Wrong. Your site has to be a selling machine, which means, from the very first, designing around some well-honed selling proposition. That in turn calls for careful thought, competitor research and detailed analysis.

(4) The number of e-commerce products and services is immense, and all are heavily promoted. Without specialist advice you'll make the wrong choice, which is costly in time and money.

(5) E-commerce has its own inside knowledge, which sets newcomers at a disadvantage. You need to look beyond the *"How I made a fortune and so can you"* sort of guides, which generally enrich their authors more than purchasers.

New Words

e-commerce	[iˈkɒmɜːs]	n.	电子商务
website	[ˈwebsaɪt]	n.	网站
promote	[prəˈməʊt]	vt.	促销,推销
obtain	[əbˈteɪn]	vt.	获得,得到
upload	[ˌʌpˈləʊd]	v.	上载
payment	[ˈpeɪmənt]	n.	付款,支付
various	[ˈveərɪəs]	adj.	不同的,多方面的,多样的
notice	[ˈnəʊtɪs]	v.	注意到
		n.	通知,布告,注意
collection	[kəˈlekʃn]	n.	收集,收藏品
ambitious	[æmˈbɪʃəs]	adj.	有雄心的,野心勃勃的
stunning	[ˈstʌnɪŋ]	adj.	极好的
graphics	[ˈgræfɪks]	n.	图形
animation	[ˌænɪˈmeɪʃn]	n.	动画
recognition	[ˌrekəgˈnɪʃn]	n.	承认,识别
extol	[ɪkˈstəʊl]	v.	赞美
virtue	[ˈvɜːtʃuː]	n.	优点,长处
hinder	[ˈhɪndə]	vt.	阻碍
conveniently	[kənˈviːnjəntli]	adv.	便利地
directory	[dəˈrektəri]	n.	目录
editor	[ˈedɪtə]	n.	编辑器
pocket	[ˈpɒkɪt]	n.	衣袋,口袋
online	[ˌɒnˈlaɪn]	n.	联机,在线式
catalogue	[ˈkætəlɒg]	n.	目录
rent	[rent]	vt.	租赁
facility	[fəˈsɪləti]	n.	设备,工具
solution	[səˈluːʃn]	n.	方案
template	[ˈtempleɪt]	n.	模板
wizard	[ˈwɪzəd]	n.	向导
concern	[kənˈsɜːn]	n.	(利害)关系,关心,关注
		vt.	涉及,关系到
suitable	[ˌsuːtəbl]	adj.	适当的,相配的
confirm	[kənˈfɜːm]	vt.	确定,批准
purchase	[ˈpɜːtʃəs]	vt. & n.	买,购买
relevant	[ˈreləvənt]	adj.	相关的,有关的
stage	[steɪdʒ]	n.	阶段,时期

halfway	[ˌhɑːfˈweɪ]	adj. 中途的,部分的,不彻底的
		adv. 半路地,在中途,在半途
maintain	[meɪnˈteɪn]	vt. 维护,维修
thereafter	[ˌðeərˈɑːftə]	adv. 其后,从那时以后
painless	[ˈpeɪnləs]	adj. 愉快的,轻松的,不难的
option	[ˈɒpʃn]	n. 选项,选择权
check	[tʃek]	n. 支票
employ	[ɪmˈplɔɪ]	vt. 使用;雇用
seamlessly	[ˈsiːmləsli]	adv. 无缝地
commission	[kəˈmɪʃn]	n. 佣金,手续费;委托
balance	[ˈbæləns]	n. 结余,余额,资产平稳表
		v. 结算
code	[kəʊd]	n. 代码,编码
		v. 编码
snippet	[ˈsnɪpɪt]	n. 小片,片断,摘录
liaison	[liˈeɪzn]	n. 联络
submit	[səbˈmɪt]	vt. 提交,递交
optimization	[ˌɒptəmaɪˈzeɪʃn]	n. 最佳化,最优化
affiliate	[əˈfɪlieɪt]	v. (使…)加入,接收…为会员
reciprocal	[rɪˈsɪprəkl]	adj. 互惠的,相应的
faithfully	[ˈfeɪθfəli]	adv. 忠诚地,如实地
favorable	[ˈfeɪvərəbl]	adj. 有利的,赞许的,良好的
academic	[ˌækəˈdemɪk]	adj. 学术的,学院的,理论的
stark	[stɑːk]	adj. 刻板的,十足的
		adv. 完全地
blandishment	[ˈblændɪʃmənt]	n. 奉承,哄诱,甜言蜜语
expense	[ɪkˈspens]	n. 费用,开支,损失,代价
spectacular	[spekˈtækjələ]	adj. 引人入胜的,壮观的
advice	[ədˈvaɪs]	n. 忠告,建议
newcomer	[ˈnjuːkʌmə]	n. 新来者,新手

Phrases

be familiar with	熟悉
web design company	网站建设公司
out-of-the-box shopping cart program	开箱即用的购物车程序
hosting company	托管公司
software supplier	软件提供商
go for	适用于;选择,想要获得;喜爱

search box	搜索框
be ready to	预备,即将
wallet system	电子钱包系统
payment service provider	支付服务提供商
online merchant account	在线商家账号
merchant account provider	商家账号提供商
local bank	本地银行
bank transfer	银行转账
crowd out	挤出,推开,驱逐
press release	新闻稿
search engine	搜索引擎
sign up	注册,签约
site optimization company	网站优化公司
reciprocal links directory	互惠链接目录

Exercises

【Ex1】 **Answer the following questions according to the text.**

1. What does e-commerce simply mean?

2. What will "wow" sites do?

3. How can you create a convincing site?

4. What does URL stand for? What is it?

5. What do you have to do after you have the site built, and a domain name to host it under?

6. And if you've built your site online, what will you need to do?

7. What are the options listed in the passage if you'll want to be paid as quickly, safely and painlessly as possible?

8. How to link your site to the payment process?

9. Do you have a web site of your own? If yes, tell us something about it.

10. How are you going to get your site noticed?

【Ex2】 **Translate the following terms or phrases from English into Chinese or vice versa.**

1. bank transfer   1. _____

2. online merchant account   2. _____

3. payment service provider   3. _____

4. wallet system   4. _____

5. search engine   5. _____

6. *n*. 付款,支付   6. _____

7. *n*. 选项,选择权   7. _____

8. *n*. 支票　　　　　　　　　　8. _____

9. *vt*. 确定,批准　　　　　　　9. _____

10. *vt*. 促销,推销　　　　　　10. _____

【Ex3】 Fill in the blanks with the words given below.

fact	platform	quantity	receive	public
involve	without	purchase	exchanging	bid

E-commerce Definition and Types of E-commerce

E-commerce or electronic commerce, a subset of e-business, is the purchasing, selling, and _____1_____ of goods and services over computer networks (such as the Internet) through which transactions or terms of sale are performed electronically. Contrary to popular belief, e-commerce is not just on the Web. In _____2_____, e-commerce was alive and well in business to business transactions before the Web back in the 70s via EDI (Electronic Data Interchange) through VANs (Value-Added Networks). E-commerce can be broken into four main categories: B2B, B2C, C2B, and C2C.

B2B(Business-to-Business)

Companies doing business with other such as manufacturers selling to distributors and wholesalers selling to retailers. Pricing is based on _____3_____ of order and is often negotiable.

B2C(Business-to-Consumer)

Businesses selling to the general _____4_____ typically through catalogs utilizing shopping cart software. By dollar volume, B2B takes the prize, however B2C is really what the average Joe has in mind with regards to e-commerce as a whole.

Having a hard time finding a book? Need to _____5_____ a custom, high-end computer system? How about a first class, all-inclusive trip to a tropical island? With the advent e-commerce, all three things can be purchased literally in minutes _____6_____ human interaction. Oh how far we've come!

C2B(Consumer-to-Business)

A consumer posts his project with a set budget online and within hours companies review the consumer's requirements and _____7_____ on the project. The consumer reviews the bids and selects the company that will complete the project. Elance empowers consumers around the world by providing the meeting ground and _____8_____ for such transactions.

C2C(Consumer-to-Consumer)

There are many sites offering free classifieds, auctions, and forums where individuals can buy and sell thanks to online payment systems like PayPal where people can send and _____9_____ money online with ease. eBay's auction service is a great example of where person-to-person transactions take place everyday since 1995.

Companies using internal networks to offer their employees products and services online—not necessarily online on the Web—are engaging in B2E (Business-to-Employee) e-commerce.

G2G (Government-to-Government), G2E (Government-to-Employee), G2B (Government-to-Business), B2G (Business-to-Government), G2C (Government-to-Citizen), C2G (Citizen-to-Government) are other forms of e-commerce that ___10___ transactions with the government—from procurement to filing taxes to business registrations to renewing licenses. There are other categories of e-commerce out there, but they tend to be superfluous.

【Ex4】 **Translate the following passage from English into Chinese.**

Building an E-commerce Site

The things you need to keep in mind when thinking about building an e-commerce site include:

- Suppliers. This is no different from the concern that any normal store or mail order company has. Without good suppliers you cannot offer products.
- Your price point. A big part of e-commerce is the fact that price comparisons are extremely easy for the consumer. Your price point is important in a transparent market.
- Customer relations. E-commerce offers a variety of different ways to relate to your customer. E-mail, FAQs, knowledge bases, forums, chat rooms... Integrating these features into your e-commerce offering helps you differentiate yourself from the competition.
- The back end: fulfillment, returns, customer service. These processes make or break any retail establishment. They define, in a big way, your relationship with your customer.

Text B

E-commerce Business Model

1 Type of E-commerce Business Model

There are six major e-commerce business models.

1.1 Business to Consumer (B2C)

As the name implies, Business to Consumer (B2C) is the model that a company markets its products or services directly to end users. It is the most widely known form of commerce. B2C e-commerce is fairly straightforward.

In e-commerce，there are five different B2C business models：direct selling，online intermediaries，advertising-based，community-based，and fee-based models.

（1）Direct selling is the most common model. It means consumers buy products from online retailers.

（2）Online intermediaries are online businesses that bring sellers and consumers together and take a cut of each transaction made.

（3）In the advertising-based model，information is given away for free and money is made from advertising on the site.

（4）Facebook is an example of a community-based model that makes money from targeting ads to users based on their demographics and location.

（5）Finally，the fee-based model involves companies that sell information or entertainment to consumers for a fee，like Netflix or subscription-based newspapers.

In recent years，online B2C sales have been trending upward. Many traditional brick-and-mortar retailers have either been closing，or pivoting and adding in digital channels to their strategy as shoppers go online for the things they need.

This hybrid approach means that companies have both a traditional brick-and-mortar presence and an online shopping platform. Many companies integrate these approaches with an omnichannel e-commerce strategy to maximize the customer experience. For example，some companies now let you order your products online and pick them up at one of their local stores. Many companies also allow customers to return products they bought online to local stores for a quick and easy refund or exchange.

1.2　Business to Business（B2B）

In Business to Business（B2B）model，a company markets its products or services directly to other businesses. B2B e-commerce can be broken down into two methodologies，vertical and horizontal.

Vertically oriented businesses sell to customers within a specific industry. With a horizontal approach，you are selling to customers across a myriad of industries. Each approach has their own pros and cons，such as industry expertise and market depth（vertical）versus wide-spread market coverage and diversification（horizontal）.

They both can be a lucrative pathway，but your strategy will depend on your products and customers，so consider them carefully.

1.3　Business to Government（B2G）

Business to Government（B2G）means a company markets its products and services directly to a government agency. In B2G，companies typically bid on projects when governments announce Requests For Proposals（RFPs）.

A local government agency can，for example，place an order directly from an e-commerce company for a part to repair a piece of equipment. It depends on a variety of factors including the size of the agency and the need.

1.4 Business to Business to Consumer (B2B2C)

In B2B2C e-commerce, a company sells products to another company which then sells the products to consumers. An example of B2B2C is a wholesale distributor sells merchandise to retail stores, then the retail stores sell the merchandise to end users. The B2B2C model is comprised of three parts: the first business (the business of product origin), an intermediary, and the end user.

There are several different ways the B2B2C model can be used in e-commerce applications. For example, a company can partner with another company to promote its products and services, giving the partner a commission for each sale.

The primary advantage of the B2B2C business model for e-commerce companies is the acquisition of new customers. This is an important consideration for new e-commerce companies that need a way to rapidly grow their customer base.

1.5 Consumer to Business (C2B)

In the C2B e-commerce business model, individuals sell goods and services directly to companies. We see this most commonly in websites that allow individuals (contractors or freelancers) to share work or services they're skilled in. Often, businesses will put in a request or a bid for that person's time and will pay the person through that platform.

One of the most recognizable examples of a C2B business is Upwork, a freelancing platform that connects organizations directly with talent. It's marketed as a "marketplace for work" and gives businesses the ability to find and source project support, ranging for anything from software development and content creation to UX design and even financial needs for things like bookkeeping or filing tax returns.

One of the key benefits of this business model is that it allows consumers to set their own price and it can also often help expand their individual reach by giving more visibility.

1.6 Consumer to Consumer (C2C)

Another model most people don't typically think of is the consumer to consumer business model. The rise of the digital landscape has really enabled the concept to take off, with companies like eBay, Craigslist, and Esty leading the way.

In C2C e-commerce, consumers sell goods or services directly to other consumers. This is most often made possible by third-party websites (such as the examples we previously mentioned) or marketplaces, which facilitate transactions on behalf of the buyers and sellers.

These e-commerce marketplaces allow smaller businesses, or even hobbyists, to sell their products at their own pricing without having to maintain their own online storefront.

2　How to Choose Your E-commerce Business Model?

Now that you've familiarized yourself with the various models and product management and delivery methods，you can start the groundwork for actually choosing your model. There are three key criteria that will impact how you move forward.

（1）Understand your customer. Who are they? What are their buying habits and purchasing behaviors? What are their pain points? Building your Ideal Customer Profile （ICP）with this information is the first critical step in choosing the right e-commerce business model.

（2）Understand your value proposition. What makes you different and in what areas do you exceed compared to the competition? Is it your pricing，customer service，or product selection? Also ask yourself，"What am I not doing well?" Understanding your strengths and weaknesses is vital to your business strategy. And being honest about it with potential customers will only built trust and brand loyalty.

（3）Sell your product in a way that makes sense for your customers. A good way to look at this is from the point of view of a manufacturer versus a distributor. If you create your own products then you'll probably want to consider wholesale or a subscription service. If you're selling someone else's goods，you'll need to focus more on building your brand and customer base.

Once you have identified your target market and the correct model you need to best serve your customer base，you can focus on building and optimizing your e-commerce infrastructure and marketing tactics to fine-tune your business and maximize revenue.

New Words

straightforward	[ˌstreɪtˈfɔːwəd]	adj. 简单明了的
intermediary	[ˌɪntəˈmiːdiəri]	n. 中间人；媒介
demographic	[ˌdeməˈɡræfɪk]	adj. 人口（学）的；人口统计（学）的
pivot	[ˈpɪvət]	vt. 以…为核心
hybrid	[ˈhaɪbrɪd]	n. 混合物
omnichannel	[ˈɒmnɪˈtʃænl]	n. 多渠道，全渠道
methodology	[ˌmeθəˈdɒlədʒi]	n. 一套方法；方法学；方法论
expertise	[ˌekspɜːˈtiːz]	n. 专门技术，专门知识
diversification	[daɪˌvɜːsɪfɪˈkeɪʃn]	n. 多样化；多种经营
lucrative	[ˈluːkrətɪv]	adj. 有利可图的，赚钱的
wholesale	[ˈhəʊlseɪl]	adj. 批发的
		adv. 用批发方式；以批发价
		n. 批发

distributor	[dɪˈstrɪbjətə]	n. 批发公司, 批发商; 分发者
contractor	[kənˈtræktə]	n. 承包商
freelancer	[ˈfriːlɑːnsə]	n. 自由职业者
third-party	[ˈθɜːdpɑːtɪ]	adj. 第三方的
hobbyist	[ˈhɒbiːɪst]	n. 沉溺于某种癖好者
storefront	[ˈstɔːfrʌnt]	n. 店面
groundwork	[ˈɡraʊndwɜːk]	n. 基础; 基本原理
fine-tune	[faɪn tjuːn]	vt. 调整
revenue	[ˈrevənjuː]	n. 收入, 收益

Phrases

end user	最终用户
direct selling	直销, 直接销售
advertising-based model	基于广告的模型
community-based model	基于社区的模型
fee-based model	收费模型
online shopping platform	网上购物平台
pick up	捡起; 获得
local store	本地商店
break ... down into	把…分为
vertically oriented business	面向垂直业务
bid on	投标承包(某项工程)
value proposition	价值主张, 价值定位

Abbreviations

B2C（Business to Consumer）	企业对消费者
B2B（Business to Business）	企业对企业
B2G（Business to Government）	企业对政府
RFP（Requests For Proposal）	需求建议书
B2B2C（Business to Business to Consumer）	企业对企业对消费者
C2B（Consumer to Business）	消费者对企业
C2C（Consumer to Consumer）	消费者对消费者
ICP（Ideal Customer Profile）	理想客户特征

Exercises

[Ex5] **Fill in the blanks with the information given in the text.**

1. As the name implies，Business to Consumer（B2C）is the model that _____ markets _____ or services directly to _____.

2. In e-commerce，there are five different B2C business models：_____，_____，_____，_____，and _____．

3. Vertically oriented businesses sell to customers _____．With a horizontal approach，you are selling to customers _____．

4. Business to Government（B2G）means _____ markets its products and services directly to _____．In B2G，companies typically _____ when governments announce Requests For Proposals（RFPs）．

5. The B2B2C model is comprised of three parts：_____，_____，and _____．

6. The primary advantage of the B2B2C business model for e-commerce companies is _____．This is an important consideration for new e-commerce companies that need a way to _____．

7. One of the most recognizable examples of a C2B business is _____，a freelancing platform that connects _____ directly with _____．

8. In C2C e-commerce，consumers sell goods or services directly to _____．This is most often made possible by _____（such as the examples we previously mentioned）or marketplaces，which facilitate transactions on behalf of _____ and _____．

9. Understanding _____ and _____ is vital to your business strategy. And being honest about it with potential customers will only built _____ and _____．

10. Once you have identified _____ and _____ you need to best serve your customer base，you can focus on building and optimizing your _____ and _____ to fine-tune your business and maximize revenue.

[Ex6] **Translate the following terms or phrases from English into Chinese or vice versa.**

1. direct selling
2. online shopping platform
3. end user
4. local store
5. vertically oriented business
6. *n*. 批发公司,批发商;分发者
7. *n*. 佣金,手续费
8. *n*. 多渠道,全渠道
9. *n*. 店面
10. *adj*. 批发的；*n*. 批发

1. _____
2. _____
3. _____
4. _____
5. _____
6. _____
7. _____
8. _____
9. _____
10. _____

Reading Material

E-commerce Strategy

1 Establish Your E-commerce Goals

The first step to your e-commerce strategy is to establish a set of goals. Whether your goal is to attract① a certain number of customers or to generate a certain amount of revenue within a specific time period，you'll be able to judge② the performance of your online store and the efforts of your e-commerce campaign with the set goals in place. Be sure to measure your goals against industry standards and set quantitative benchmarks③.

A good starting place would be to set objectives and key results. Objectives describe the goal while key results are the steps you take to get there. Look at the following example：

Objective Examples：Become a well-known and loved workout clothes company comparable④ to a brand like Lululemon.

Key Results：

- Attract x amount of qualified customers to our online store each quarter.
- Build a loyal fan base⑤.
- Delight customers with friendly，helpful and responsive customer service.
- Create a relatable and authentic⑥ social media presence to connect with target audience.

Use this as your framework for setting up and promoting your online store. What steps do you need to take to accomplish these key results? This is a great way to set your priorities and align your e-commerce strategy with your entire team.

2　Develop Your Buyer Personas⑦

Knowing who your target audience is will be critical to the success of your e-commerce strategy.

Take some time to identify your target audience by developing your buyer personas. Buyer personas are representations of your "perfect" customers that you can use to more effectively target potential customers. They're basically fictional⑧ characters created to develop real customers to help you focus your efforts. They're also a reflection of your company's goals and ideals.

Building out personas will help guide your marketing strategy while establishing the voice and tone for your online store. Marketing to the wrong audience will hurt⑨ your ability to generate sales as well as waste your time and money.

---

① attract [ə'trækt] v. 吸引。
② judge [dʒʌdʒ] v. 判断；估计；评价。
③ benchmark ['bentʃmɑːk] n. 基准；参照。
④ comparable ['kɒmpərəbl] adj. 类似的，可比较的。
⑤ fan base：粉丝群，粉丝团。
⑥ authentic [ɔː'θentɪk] adj. 真正的；真诚的；可靠的。
⑦ persona [pə'səʊnə] n. 人物角色。
⑧ fictional ['fɪkʃənl] adj. 虚构的。
⑨ hurt [hɜːt] v. 损害，危害。

You can start building your buyer personas by asking yourself the following questions：

- How well does this buyer know my product?
- What types of media do they consume?
- Are they using your products to solve problems?
- Does your product impact their overall life?
- What items are you better positioned to do than your competitors?
- Who influences their buying decisions?
- What communication channels do they prefer?

3　Identify Your Unique Value Proposition

Online customers tend to[①] do a lot of research before making the decision to purchase. This means that they will likely be comparing the products or services that you offer to those of your competitors.

Identify what your brand's unique value proposition is and make it clear to your potential customers. The value proposition[②] answers a crucial question that every e-commerce customer is asking："Why should I buy from you instead of your competitors?"

It details out how you solve customer pain points and how you improve their experience by adding value. It can refer to specific benefits like how your product is eco-friendly[③]，cost-effective，incorporates fast shipping，or is easier and more convenient.

Make sure to keep buyer personas' pain points，wants and needs in mind when determining your value proposition.

4　Create Effective Product or Service Descriptions

Write detailed descriptions of the products or services you're selling on your e-commerce page. These descriptions should highlight the benefits and features of your products or services and should be easy for customers to read. Equip[④] your customers with as much information as possible.

Don't forget to optimize your e-commerce store for SEO. Optimize your pages for short，product-driven keywords that include the name of the product. Make sure your page titles，headers，and image alt texts focus on the targeted keywords，so search engines know to show your e-commerce store for the right query.

---

① tend to：趋向；偏重。
② proposition [ˌprɒpəˈzɪʃn] *n*. 主张。
③ eco-friendly [ˌiːkəʊˈfrendli] *adj*. 对生态环境友好的，不破坏生态环境的。
④ equip [ɪˈkwɪp] *v*. 装备；使做好准备。

5   Delight Your Customers

There are so many different ways to delight your customers and build brand ambassadors①. Think of features that will make your customers' shopping experience as pleasant as possible. For example: offer free shipping, 15% off of their first order, express shipping on orders over $100, personalization on packaging, etc.

Expensive shipping is the primary reason shoppers abandon their carts. Offering free shipping on orders more than X amount will encourage customers to buy more of your products and make them feel like they are getting more value out of their purchase.

Chatbots are a good feature that you can pre-program to answer basic questions and provide basic information. Customers who have questions about a product or service can rely on your chatbot to answer their inquiries right away and when they're in the checkout process.

6   Optimize the Checkout Process

Optimize your checkout process to be as smooth of an experience as possible. A poorly implemented checkout process can lead to a high cart abandonment rate.

Here are some other ways to mitigate shopping cart abandonment:

- Provide a money-back guarantee.
- Implement a clear and simple return policy.
- Offer different delivery options.
- Include easy access to customer support.

7   Run Retargeting and Remarketing Campaigns

Many of the people who visit your online store will not make a purchase the first time they visit. In fact, 79% of people abandon their shopping carts while online shopping.

Run retargeting ads on other websites or on social media channels to showcase the products or services that they were previously looking at in order to recapture② their attention and remind them of their interest.

8   Establish Trust

Trust is absolutely essential in running an e-commerce store. After all, customers are providing you with sensitive information, so be sure to use HTTPS③ protocol to encrypt

---

① brand ambassador: 品牌大使。
② recapture [ˌriːˈkæptʃə] vt. 重新捕获；重温。
③ HTTPS (Hypertext Transfer Protocol Secure): 超文本传输安全协议。

all data that's transferred to and from your website.

Be very transparent about the costs of your products or services as well as shipping，tax expenses，and return/exchange policies. Add trust badges to your e-commerce pages，such as payment processor logos，SSL① certificates，security badges，and third-party endorsements②.

Text A 参考译文

电 子 商 务

1 什么是电子商务？

简单地说，电子商务就是通过因特网销售商品，提供服务和信息。

如何参与其中？容易。建立一个促销产品的网站，获得一个因特网地址，在提供网站托管的公司租用空间，上传你的网页，增加支付系统，然后使用多种促销服务方式使人们注意你的网站。

2 建立网站

你会熟悉网站——围绕在像 http://www.companyname.com 这样的 URL 周围的一组 HTML 页面。网站也可以非常出色，带有极佳的图片、动画、声音、数据搜索系统、用户识别及许多其他功能。但这并非必需的。许多成功的电子商务网站只有几个页面赞美产品的优点。还有更多的网站页面更少。"让人惊叹"的网站不仅妨碍客户得到产品，也更难以推广。

但你的网站必须看上去很专业。如何建立一个令人信服的网站？你可以：

（1）雇用一个网页设计公司。有数以千计的公司列在收集好的目录中。

（2）使用 HTML 编辑软件建立自己的网页。容易使用的软件包很多，一些是共享软件，还有一些甚至是免费的。

（3）购买开箱即用的购物车程序来建造完整的网站，包括带有支付功能的在线目录。

（4）从提供在线网站的网站托管公司租用空间。就像开箱即用的解决方案，托管公司可以给你提供模板和向导，帮助你建立有特色并且看上去很专业的网站。

3 寻找 URL 或域名

URL（统一资源定位符）是在因特网上的地址或域名。你需要用一个域名标识你的公司以及可能的业务线。怎样得到域名呢？

可以访问销售域名的在线公司。由于与商业有关，你需要努力找.com 或.biz 域名。在搜索框中输入可能的域名直到找到满意的为止。

假定你的公司是 Acme Diving Equipment Ltd.。你发现 acme.com 和 diving.com 都已

---

① SSL（Secure Sockets Layer）：安全套接字协议。
② third-party endorsement：第三方背书。

经被占用了。但 acme-diving-equipment.com 还空着,你就可以支付一点年费使用这个域名。在线信用卡机构接受你的订单,几分钟后向你发送电子邮件确认这次交易。一旦这个域名在相关机构记录,一般在几天之内它就归你使用了。

4　托管你的网站

你做了一半了。你已经建了网站而且拥有域名。现在需要把网站上传到网站托管公司,该公司在因特网上全天候地显示网站。这样的网站托管公司数以千计,可以按照价格、平台类型、便利性等加以选择。你可以选择托管公司,点击它们的网站,支付托管费用并把你的网站放到该公司的服务器上。托管公司会告诉你怎么做。非常简单,但你需要一个叫作 FTP 程序的廉价或者免费软件。它可以从任何一个软件提供商处获得,用来维护你的网站。一旦上传完成,你的网站就"诞生"了,你就在因特网上了。

当然,如果你的网站由一个网站设计公司建造,它会替你上传。如果你已经建立了在线网站,那么你要做的只是给托管公司发电子邮件,告诉它你要开始交易了。

5　收款

在销售货物后,希望尽可能快速、安全、轻松地收款。电子商务中有许多选择,从最简单的开始,你可以:

(1) 在线显示货物,但离线支付——通过支票、银行转账,用电话提供信用卡详细信息。

(2) 在线显示货物并通过一些简单的电子钱包系统在线支付。

(3) 在线显示货物并支付,但雇用一个支付服务提供商。购物车或目录的链接将把客户账单无缝传输到支付服务提供商,实现即时的银行卡操作,再把客户账单转给你,完成购买。如果你有在线商家账号,也可以使用,但这不是必需的。支付服务提供商将核对信用卡购物信息,收取费用,扣除佣金,把账单发送给你,通常每月结账一次。

(4) 在线显示和支付,但使用你自己的在线商家账号,该账号可以从本地银行或者商家账号提供商处获得。

怎样把你的网站链接到支付处理?如果你使用开箱即用的购物车软件、雇用网站设计公司或租用在线电子商务托管公司,会自动建立链接。另外,如果你自己建造了网站,必须在相关网页加上代码。如果有支付服务提供商,这就非常容易了,它们为你提供可以粘贴加入的代码段。使用你自己的商家账号需要联络信用卡业务处理公司并具有良好的编程经验,特别是当你在自己的服务器上托管网站时。或许必须雇用专业人士。

6　推广你的网站

在因特网上每天会出现数以百计的电子商务网站,那里已经拥挤不堪。怎样让你的网站引人注意?

(1) 发布公告。

(2) 在商务目录、在线和离线版本中展示特色。

(3) 提交到搜索引擎,也许可以雇用一个网站优化公司提高排名。

(4) 使用按点击付费搜索引擎,为每个访问者支付几分到几元的费用,这些访问者通过特定的搜索短语点击到你的网站。

(5) 签约其他网站成为会员,根据你实现的销售额向其支付佣金。

(6) 使用搜索引擎广告。

(7) 劝说其他网站链接到你的网站,可以通过互惠链接目录。

(8) 为你的网站赢得奖项。

(9) 提供在线竞争、介绍交易和促销。

(10) 在你的网站上提供免费并有用的信息。

(11) 做离线广告,在报纸和专业杂志上刊登广告。

7　商业会成功吗?

现在这真是一个重要问题。切实遵循了这些步骤,你敢保证你的网站就能成功吗?

也许——如果你占据十分有利的位置。你是某种特殊机器配件的唯一供应商。或者你是热门旅游区唯一的宾馆。是的,在这种情况下,你可能只需要免费信息。如果你只对商务有学术兴趣,而不是自己运行电子商务,情况是类似的。

但是在其他情况下,我们必须告诫你电子商务是不容易的,如果你听信广告,受电子商务杂志的引诱,你未必能够收回投资。

当然,早期的电子商务受害者不这么认为。如今仍然有许多网站、书籍和电子图书保证电子商务完全就是只执行几个步骤。实情并非如此,其原因如下:

(1) 电子商务是一个非常拥挤的市场。在许多领域,你需要有一个用大量的营销预算支持的深入研究的市场策略。

(2) 容易受制于错误的市场目标或商业模式——这是为数众多的失败的网络公司的发现。

(3) 你已经建立了一个网站,然后就要推广它。错误。你的网站必须是一个销售机器,这就是说从一开始就是围绕着某一深思熟虑的销售建议而设计。这就需要反复地认真思考、研究竞争者并分析细节。

(4) 电子商务的产品和服务数量巨大,而且都很依赖促销。不听取专家的告诫,你就会做出错误的选择,将付出时间和金钱的代价。

(5) 电子商务有其内在知识,这对新手不利。你不能只看"我怎样赚大钱,你也能"这类手册,它们通常只填满了作者的腰包而不是买家的。

Unit 2

Text A

Online Shopping

Online shopping is the process whereby consumers directly buy goods or services from a seller in real-time without an intermediary service over the Internet. If an intermediary service is present the process is called electronic commerce. An online shop, e-shop, e-store, internet shop, web-shop, webstore[①], online store, or virtual store evokes the physical analogy of buying products or services at a brick-and-mortar retailer[②] or in a shopping mall[③]. The process is called Business-to-Consumer (B2C) online shopping. When a business buys from another business it is called Business-to-Business (B2B) online shopping. Both B2C and B2B online shopping are forms of e-commerce.

1　Customers

In recent years, online shopping has become popular; however, it still caters to the middle and upper class. In order to shop online, one must be able to have access to a computer, a bank account and a debit card. Shopping has evolved with the growth of technology. According to a research found in the Journal of Electronic Commerce, if we focus on the demographic characteristics of the in-home shopper, in general, the higher the level of education, income, and occupation of the head of the household, the more favourable the perception of non-store shopping. An influential factor in consumer attitude towards non-store shopping is exposure to technology, since it has been demonstrated that increased exposure to technology increases the probability of developing favourable attitudes towards new shopping channels.

①　A webstore is a website that sells products or services and typically has an online shopping cart associated with it. With the popularity of the Internet rapidly increasing, online shopping became advantageous for retail store owners, and many traditional "brick and mortar" stores saw value in opening webstore counterparts.

②　Brick and mortar (B&M) refers to a company that possesses a building or store for operations. The name is a metonym derived from the traditional building materials associated with physical buildings—bricks and mortar—in contrast with online stores, which have no physical presence.

③　A shopping mall, shopping centre or shopping precinct is one or more buildings forming a complex of shops representing merchandisers, with interconnecting walkways enabling visitors to easily walk from unit to unit, along with a parking area—a modern, indoor version of the traditional marketplace.

Online shopping widened the target audience to men and women of the middle class. At first, the main users of online shopping were young men with a high level of income and a university education. This profile is changing. For example, in USA in the early years of Internet there were very few women users, but by 2001 women were 52.8% of the online population.

2 Logistics

Consumers find a product of interest by visiting the website of the retailer directly, or do a search across many different vendors using a shopping search engine.

Once a particular product has been found on the web site of the seller, most online retailers use shopping cart software to allow the consumer to accumulate multiple items and to adjust quantities, by analogy with filling a physical shopping cart or basket in a conventional store. A "checkout" process follows (continuing the physical-store analogy) in which payment and delivery information is collected, if necessary. Some stores allow consumers to sign up for a permanent online account so that some or all of this information only needs to be entered once. The consumer often receives an e-mail confirmation once the transaction is complete. Less sophisticated stores may rely on consumers to phone or e-mail their orders (though credit card numbers are not accepted by e-mail, for security reasons).

2.1 Payment

Online shoppers commonly use credit card to make payments, however some systems enable users to create accounts and pay by alternative means, such as:

- Debit card
- Various types of electronic money
- Cash on delivery[①](COD, offered by very few online stores)
- Check[②]
- Wire transfer[③]/delivery on payment
- Postal money order[④]
- Reverse message billing to mobile phones

---

① Collect on delivery or COD is a financial transaction（金融交易）where the payment of products and/or services received is done at the time of actual delivery rather than paid-for in advance（预先付费）.

② A cheque or check (American English) is a document that orders a payment of money.

③ Wire transfer or credit transfer（信用转账）is a method of electronic funds transfer（电子资金转账）from one person or institution（entity）to another. A wire transfer can be made from one bank account to another bank account or through a transfer of cash at a cash office.

④ A money order is a payment order for a pre-specified（预先指定）amount of money. Because it is required that the funds be prepaid（先付的）for the amount shown on it, it is a more trusted method of payment than a personal check（个人支票）.

- Gift cards[①]
- Direct debit in some countries

Some sites will not allow international credit cards and billing address and shipping address have to be in the same country in which site does its business. Other sites allow customers from anywhere to send gifts anywhere. The financial part of a transaction might be processed in real time (for example, letting the consumer know their credit card was declined before they log off), or might be done later as part of the fulfillment process.

2.2　Product delivery

Once a payment has been accepted the goods or services can be delivered in the following ways.

- Download: This is the method often used for digital media products such as software, music, movies, or images.
- Shipping: The product is shipped to the customer's address.
- Drop shipping[②]: The order is passed to the manufacturer or third party distributor, who ships the item directly to the consumer.
- Post: It can be also posted to any customer bypassing the retailer's physical location to save time, money, and space.
- In-store pickup: The customer orders online, finds a local store using locator software and picks the product up at the closest store. This is the method often used in the bricks and clicks[③] business model.
- In the case of buying an admission ticket one may get a code, or a ticket that can be printed out. At the premises it is made sure that the same right of admission is not used twice.

2.3　Shopping cart systems

- Simple systems allow the offline administration of products and categories. The shop is then generated as HTML files and graphics that can be uploaded to a webspace. These systems do not use an online database.
- A high end solution can be bought or rented as a standalone program or as an addition to an enterprise resource planning program. It is usually installed on the

---

① A gift card is a restricted (受限的) monetary equivalent or scrip (临时凭证) that is issued by retailers or banks to be used as an alternative to a non-monetary gift.

② Drop shipping is a supply chain management technique in which the retailer does not keep goods in stock (库存), but instead transfers customer orders and shipment details to either the manufacturer or a wholesaler (批发商), who then ships the goods directly to the customer.

③ Bricks-and-clicks is a business model by which a company integrates both offline (bricks) and online (clicks) presences. One example of the bricks-and-clicks model is when a chain of stores (连锁商店) allows the user to order products online, but lets them pick up their order at a local store.

company's own webserver and may integrate into the existing supply chain so that ordering, payment, delivery, accounting and warehousing can be automated to a large extent.

- Other solutions allow the user to register and create an online shop on a portal that hosts multiple shops at the same time.
- Open source[①] shopping cart packages include advanced platforms such as Interchange, and off the shelf solutions as Avactis, Satchmo, osCommerce, Magento, Zen Cart, VirtueMart, Batavi and PrestaShop.
- Commercial systems can also be tailored to one's needs so that the shop does not have to be created from scratch. By using a framework already existing, software modules for different functionalities required by a web shop can be adapted and combined.

2.4 Online Shopping Malls

Like many online auction[②] websites, many websites allow small businesses to create and maintain online shops, without the complexity that involved in purchasing and developing an expensive stand alone ecommerce software solutions.

3 Design

Why does electronic shopping exist? For customers it is not only because of the high level of convenience, but also because of the broader selection; competitive pricing and greater access to information. For organizations it increases their customer value and the building of sustainable capabilities, next to the increased profits.

3.1 Consumer expectations

The main idea of online shopping is not just in having a good looking website that could be listed in a lot of search engines or the art behind the site. Neither is it just about disseminating information, because it is also about building relationships and making money. Mostly, organizations try to adopt techniques of online shopping without understanding these techniques and/or without a sound business model. Rather than supporting the organization's culture and brand name, the website should satisfy consumer's expectations. A majority of consumers choose online shopping for a faster and more efficient shopping experience. Many researchers notify that the uniqueness of the web has dissolved and the need for the design, which will be user-centered, is very

---

① Open source describes practices in production and development that promote access to the end product's source materials.

② The <u>online auction</u>（在线拍卖）business model is one in which participants bid for products and services over the Internet. The functionality of buying and selling in an auction format is made possible through auction software which <u>regulates</u>（控制）the various processes involved.

important. Companies should always remember that there are certain things, such as understanding the customer's wants and needs and living up to promises, that never go out of style, because they give reason to come back. And the reason will stay if consumers always get what they expect. McDonaldization[①] theory can be used in terms of online shopping, because online shopping is becoming more and more popular and a website that wants to gain more shoppers will use four major principles of McDonaldization: efficiency, calculability, predictability and control.

Organizations, which want people to shop more online for them, should spend extensive amounts of time and money defining, designing, developing, testing, implementing, and maintaining the website. Also if a company wants their website to be popular among online shoppers, it should leave the user a positive impression about the organization so consumers can get an impression that the company cares about them. The organization that wants to be accepted in online shopping needs to remember that it is easier to lose a customer then to gain one. Lots of researchers hold that even though a site is "top-rated", it will go nowhere if the organization fails to live up to common etiquette, such as returning e-mails in a timely fashion, notifying customers of problems, being honest, and being good stewards of the customers' data. Organizations that want to keep their customers or gain new ones should try to get rid of all mistakes and be more appealing to and be more desirable for online shoppers. And this is why many designers of webshops consider research outcomes concerning consumer expectations.

3.2   User interface

It is important to take the country and customers into account. For example, in Japan privacy is very important and emotional involvement is more important on a pension's site than on a shopping site. Next to that, there is a difference in experience: experienced users focus more on the variables that directly influence the task, while novice users are focusing more on understanding the information.

When the customers go to the online shop, a couple of factors determine whether they will return to the site. The most important factors are the ease of use and the presence of user-friendly features.

3.3   The system itself

The Shopping Cart system works like the name suggests. Firstly, the customer must choose the product desired from the source. Once this step is done, an option to *add the product to the cart* will be given, this step will assure that the item you desire will be

---

① McDonaldization is a term used by sociologist George Ritzer in his book *The McDonaldization of Society* (1993). He explains it occurs when a culture possesses the characteristics of a fast-food restaurant (快餐店).

bought. Once the customer has finished browsing for other potential purchases and has decided that the product he chose previously is the one that he wants to buy, the user must then follow the steps provided by the website in order to fulfill the transaction. Lastly, the order will then be sent to the desired address at a predicted date.

New Words

brick-and-mortar	[brɪk ənd ˈmɔːtə]	n. 实体店,传统的实体企业
logistics	[ləˈdʒɪstɪks]	n. 物流;后勤
retailer	[ˈriːteɪlə]	n. 零售商人
characteristic	[ˌkærəktəˈrɪstɪk]	adj. 特有的,典型的
		n. 特性,特征
occupation	[ˌɒkjuˈpeɪʃn]	n. 职业,占有
perception	[pəˈsepʃn]	n. 理解,看法,见解
influential	[ˌɪnfluˈenʃl]	adj. 有影响的
attitude	[ˈætɪtjuːd]	n. 态度,看法,意见
probability	[ˌprɒbəˈbɪləti]	n. 可能性,或然性,概率
channel	[ˈtʃænl]	n. 渠道,通道
population	[ˌpɒpjuˈleɪʃn]	n. 人口
vendor	[ˈvendə]	n. 卖主
basket	[ˈbɑːskɪt]	n. 篮
confirmation	[ˌkɒnfəˈmeɪʃn]	n. 证实,确认,批准
download	[ˌdaʊnˈləʊd]	v. 下载
manufacturer	[ˌmænjuˈfæktʃərə]	n. 生产者,制造者,生产商
generate	[ˈdʒenəreɪt]	vt. 产生,发生
database	[ˈdeɪtəbeɪs]	n. 数据库,资料库
warehousing	[ˈweəhaʊzɪŋ]	n. 入库,仓库贮存,仓储配送
tailored	[ˈteɪləd]	adj. 订做的,剪裁讲究的
framework	[ˈfreɪmwɜːk]	n. 构架,框架,结构
module	[ˈmɒdjuːl]	n. 模块
functionality	[ˌfʌŋkʃəˈnæləti]	n. 功能性
sustainable	[səˈsteɪnəbl]	adj. 可持续的
disseminate	[dɪˈsemɪneɪt]	v. 传播,散布
satisfy	[ˈsætɪsfaɪ]	vt. 满足,使满意
notify	[ˈnəʊtɪfaɪ]	v. 通报
uniqueness	[juˈniːknəs]	n. 唯一性,独特性
dissolve	[dɪˈzɒlv]	v. 消失,消除
principle	[ˈprɪnsəpl]	n. 法则,定律,原则,原理
calculability	[ˌkælkjʊləˈbɪlɪti]	n. 可计算

predictability	[prɪˌdɪktəˈbɪləti]	n. 可预测性,预见性
spend	[spend]	v. 花费,消耗,用尽
etiquette	[ˈetɪket]	n. 礼节
honest	[ˈɒnɪst]	adj. 诚实的,正直的
steward	[ˈstjuːəd]	n. 管家
privacy	[ˈprɪvəsi]	n. 隐私
emotional	[ɪˈməʊʃnəl]	adj. 情绪的,情感的
involvement	[ɪnˈvɒlvmənt]	n. 包含
pension	[ˈpenʃn]	n. 养老金,退休金
variable	[ˈveərɪəbl]	n. 变量
		adj. 可变的,不定的
novice	[ˈnɒvɪs]	n. 新手,初学者
factor	[ˈfæktə]	n. 因素,要素
assure	[əˈʃʊə]	vt. 保证,担保

Phrases

online shopping	在线购物,网上购物
shopping mall	大型购物中心
cater to	迎合,为…服务
by analogy with	从…类推,根据…类推
conventional store	普通商店
debit card	借记卡
cash on delivery	货到付款,交货付现
wire transfer	电汇
delivery on payment	交货付款
postal money order	邮政汇票
gift card	礼品卡,赠卡
real time	实时
log off	退出,注销
digital media	数字媒体
drop shipping	工厂直接送货
third party distributor	第三方分销商
in-store pickup	实体店内取货
admission ticket	入场券
print out	(打)印出
high end	高端
multiple shop	连锁店,联营商店

open source	开放源代码
from scratch	从零开始,从无到有,白手起家
web shop	网络商店
making money	赚钱
brand name	商标,品牌
business model	商业模式
a majority of	大部分
live up to	实践,做到
positive impression	正面印象

Exercises

【Ex1】 **Answer the following questions according to the text.**

1. What is online shopping?

2. What must one be able to do in order to shop online?

3. What is an influential factor in consumer attitude towards non-store shopping?

4. Who were the main users of online shopping at first? What percentage did women take up of the online population by 2001 in USA?

5. Why do some stores allow consumers to sign up for a permanent online account?

6. What are some alternative means to make payment besides credit card?

7. What is download often used for?

8. What is in-store pickup?

9. Why do a majority of consumers choose online shopping?

10. What are the most important factors that determine whether the customers will return to the site?

【Ex2】 **Translate the following terms or phrases from English into Chinese or vice versa.**

1. delivery on payment	1. _____
2. drop shipping	2. _____
3. gift card	3. _____
4. in-store pickup	4. _____
5. business model	5. _____
6. *n.* 实体店,传统的实体企业	6. _____
7. *n.* 渠道,通道	7. _____
8. *n.* 构架,框架,结构	8. _____
9. *n.* 变量;*adj.* 可变的,不定的	9. _____
10. *n.* 唯一性,独特性	10. _____

[Ex3] Fill in the blanks with the words given below.

shipping	customers	database	online	manipulated
almost	rely	installed	accepts	basket

Shopping Cart Software

Shopping cart software is software used in e-commerce to assist people making purchases online, analogous to the American English term "shopping cart". In British English it is generally known as a shopping basket, ____1____ exclusively shortened on websites to "basket".

The software allows online shopping ____2____ to accumulate a list of items for purchase, described metaphorically as "placing items in the shopping cart". Upon checkout, the software typically calculates a total for the order, including ____3____ and handling (i.e. postage and packing) charges and the associated taxes, as applicable.

These applications typically provide a means of capturing a client's payment information, but in the case of a credit card they ____4____ on the software module of the secure gateway provider, in conjunction with the secure payment gateway, in order to conduct secure credit card transactions ____5____.

Some setup must be done in the HTML code of the website, and the shopping cart software must be ____6____ on the server which hosts the site, or on the secure server which ____7____ sensitive ordering information. E-shopping carts are usually implemented using HTTP cookies or query strings. In most server based implementations however, data related to the shopping cart is kept in the Session object and is accessed and ____8____ on the fly, as the user selects different items from the cart. Later at the process of commit, the information is accessed and an order is generated against the selected item thus clearing the shopping cart.

Although the simplest shopping carts strictly allow for an item to be added to a ____9____ to start a checkout process (e.g. the free PayPal shopping cart), most shopping cart software actually provides additional features that an Internet merchant uses to fully manage an online store. Data (products, categories, discounts, orders, customers, etc.) is normally stored in a ____10____ and accessed in real time by the software.

Shopping Cart Software is also known as e-commerce software, e-store software, online store software or storefront software and online shop.

[Ex4] Translate the following passage from English into Chinese.

Frequently Asked Questions about the Shopping Cart and Payment

1 What is the shopping cart?

This is an application that runs on your own web site that allows you to sell goods and services over the internet.

2　How much does the program cost?

The PayPal version of the program is free and there are no charges made by us, the suppliers of the shopping cart.

3　Are there any transaction charges?

For Credit Card processing we have integrated the store with PayPal who have their own transaction charges.

4　How am I paid?

Your customers payments are transferred directly to your PayPal account. These can then be transferred to your own bank account at your convenience. Payments are converted to the currency your account is held in.

5　How do I upload the store to my website?

The store contains it own inbuilt FTP program for transferring files. Alternatively you may use your own FTP program such as Cute FTP. FrontPage users should import the files first and then publish them to their web site.

Text B

Create an Online Shop

1　Benefits of Selling Online

Selling products and services online can have major advantages for businesses, leading to increased profitability and lower costs. Selling online has a number of advantages over selling by conventional methods, including:

- Making savings in set-up and operational costs. You don't need to pay shop assistants, rent high street premises, or answer a lot of pre-sales queries.
- Reducing order processing costs. Customer orders can automatically come straight into your orders database from the website.
- Reaching a global audience, thereby increasing sales opportunities.
- Competing with larger businesses by being able to open 24 hours a day, seven days a week.
- Being able to receive payment more quickly from online transactions.
- Attracting customers who would not normally have investigated your type of high street outlet.
- Improving your offerings using the data gathered by tracking customer purchases.
- Using your online shop as a catalogue for existing customers.

Online selling will work best if you have:

- well-defined products or services that can be sold without human involvement in the sales process.

- fixed prices for all types of potential customers.
- products or services that can be delivered within a predictable lead time.

Many businesses can run pilot e-commerce sites without significant investment. However, creating a fully automated online shop tailored to meet your precise requirements could be expensive.

Whatever form of online shop you choose, it's important to take a strategic view. If you launch a website that disappoints your customers or is overwhelmed by traffic, you risk damaging your reputation and losing sales.

2 A basic Online Shop

The requirements for building a basic online shop are fairly straightforward. A simple setup allows you to sell a small range of products, provide photos, descriptions and prices as well as accept orders online.

The equipment and facilities you need include a computer, internet access, email, a website and hosting services. Using a broadband connection as opposed to dial-up[①] will ensure fast connection to the internet. However, the "always-on" connection means you may be susceptible to unauthorized access. Having a firewall will prevent this occurring. A firewall is sometimes included as part of your operating system.

You will also need a hosting package for your shop. There are many e-commerce web-hosting specialists and it's worth shopping around for the best deal. While this service is not necessarily expensive, you tend to get what you pay for. It's important to study the service level agreement and the type of technical support on offer. You should be looking for round-the-clock support.

Most customers shopping online will want to pay by debit or credit card. You can create electronic mail-order forms, using one of the various web authoring software packages on the market.

These order forms let customers email their orders to be processed offline. If you already have a website, software can add e-commerce functionality.

A basic site is low cost and easy to create for a limited product range. However, be aware that the design and functionality may be restricted and it may be less secure than other more sophisticated options.

3 An Intermediate Online Shop

To create an intermediate level online shop you will need an e-commerce package.

---

① Dial-up Internet access is a form of Internet access that uses the facilities of the Public Switched Telephone Network (PSTN, 公用电话交换网) to establish a dialed connection to an Internet Service Provider (ISP) via telephone lines.

Facilities vary, but broadly you can expect catalogue management, enhanced order processing and a broader range of design templates.

Crucially, you can also expect encryption for secure ordering. Making sure checkout procedures are secure and user friendly are essential if customers are going to feel confident about ordering a product or service. Many people will abandon purchases at the checkout stage if the process is not quick and easy.

Using Secure Socket Layer technology to collect card details is key to encouraging online sales.

Some e-commerce packages offer a degree of back end systems integration, i.e. they connect to your product database and accounts systems, streamlining the order process and keeping the website up to date. If you update your site content regularly, you will encourage customers to come back to you rather than switch to a competitor.

If you use a broadband connection, you can also receive orders in real time and update your website automatically. Be aware that some Internet service providers offer combined web hosting and software packages, so it's worth doing some research.

An intermediate-level site can provide you with a professional looking design, full e-commerce and payment functionality and value-added features, e.g. account information, customer references and customer alerts. However, you should be aware that it may not suit you if you wish to offer more complex products and services.

4　A Sophisticated Online Shop

A sophisticated online shop offers a huge range of options, including cutting-edge design and functionality, personalized pages and product news. As such, it can provide your customers with a rich, interactive shopping experience.

However, customers should not have to navigate their way past distracting graphics and animations. If they do not find it quick and easy to buy your products and services, they will shop elsewhere. It's important not to ask for personal details too soon. Most customers will not be prepared to fill in forms until they are ready to buy.

Having a sophisticated online shop can also make the running of the business smoother. Software can be integrated to trigger order confirmations and automatically dispatch goods and replenish stocks.

You should be aware that you may need the help of a design and development company to define your technical requirements and integrate the website with your existing systems. This could take longer to create, lock you into one service provider and be very expensive.

Alternatively you may want to look at free, open source shopping cart software packages such as Zen Cart, OXID eShop Community Edition, osCommerce, OpenCart and PrestaShop. These programs enable you to set up a sophisticated e-commerce website that has a wide range of options, features and support, even if you have only basic computer skills.

5　Planning Your Online Shop

Before building your website, you must create the right processes and procedures to support it and put in place the resources to deal with orders.

You need to work out how to:

- deliver your products or services to fulfill customer orders.
- collect payments.
- maintain security and demonstrate this to the customer.
- let customers contact you.
- comply with relevant regulations.

You need to ensure that you can deliver goods or services in a reasonable time, ideally the next day. Your business should be ready to deal with calls, emails and queries about delivery.

Test your website and processes thoroughly. A soft launch will allow you to test it with perhaps just existing customers before giving it stronger marketing support. Find delivery methods that keep charges low.

Customers may be wary of paying online. However, you can encourage them by providing a secure area on your website for placing orders and giving debit and credit card details. This can prevent late payment problems and helps to safeguard your cashflow[①].

As well as online payments, you may wish to offer other payment methods to customers, such as invoicing, particularly if you're selling to businesses, or paying by debit or credit card over the telephone.

With the use of encryption technology, virus-scanning software and a "firewall", e-commerce transactions can be as secure as offline ones. It's important to create confidence in your shop. A professional-looking website with an explanation of your security precautions will help.

Consider how to:

- handle debit and credit card details safely.
- ensure that key information on your website cannot be defaced or altered fraudulently.
- preserve the confidentiality of customer data such as telephone numbers, addresses, etc.

---

①　Cash flow is the movement of cash into or out of a business, project, or financial product. Note that the word cash is used here in the broader sense, where it includes bank deposits（银行存款）.

现金流是指某一段时间内企业现金流入和流出的数量。

Customers will want to know that they can speak to a person if something goes wrong. Your website will therefore need a contacts page including:

- your business name, address, phone and fax numbers.
- an email address for enquiries or orders.
- the name of the person to contact in the first instance.

6 Helping Customers Find Your Website

For your online shop to be effective, customers must be able to find it easily. There are a number of things you can do to steer customers towards your website, including:

- Improving your website listing in search engine results.
- Getting your website listed prominently in web directories or through internet advertising.
- Using social media and online communities to engage with your customers, build a community around your brand and help improve online visibility for your product or service.
- Publicizing your site through related websites—many individuals go to sites after seeing a link, an advertisement or a mention on another site.
- Adding your website address to all emails, letterheads and other stationery and to your business vehicles.
- Mailing or emailing your customers with a newsletter.
- Getting into local online business directories, such as those produced by local Chambers of Commerce①—find Chambers of Commerce in your area on the Chamber Online website.

When you choose your internet address or domain name, try to make it simple and easy to remember so that customers will be more likely to go to your site rather than those of your competitors.

If you want to build your audience, it is essential that you are listed in web directories and search engines. This can be a time-consuming process but you can get your website listed or improve your search ranking by:

- Thinking about how people are going to find your site—pick key words and make sure they are in your page title and repeated further down the page. Ask friends and family to get involved with this for some objective feedback.
- Getting other websites to link to your site—many search engines rank sites according to how many other websites link to them. However, there are risks involved with this.

---

① A chamber of commerce (also referred to in some circles as a board of trade (同业公会)) is a form of business network, e.g., a local organization of businesses whose goal is to further the interests of businesses.

- Writing a description of your site and the services it offers and placing it prominently on your home page.

7   Pitfalls

Many e-commerce websites fail because of basic mistakes that are easily rectified. Customers will be put off by:
- out-of-date or incorrect information.
- difficult site navigation and purchasing processes.
- poor customer fulfillment and late delivery.
- lack of customer support.
- lack of business information.
- poor visual design.

So it is essential to:
- make sure all information on your website, especially on prices, is up to date.
- monitor the information you provide on a regular basis.
- make it easy to find and purchase products.
- make sure that resources and procedures are in place to support your website.
- ensure that orders can be processed promptly, emails can be responded to quickly and help lines are manned by the appropriate staff at reasonable times.
- have your website professionally designed.

Remember: when selling through an online shop, you don't normally have any personal contact with your customers, so you need to try harder to find and keep them.

There are further steps you can take to increase the chances of visitors placing an order and to make them feel more secure about buying from your site. These include:
- making your site easy to navigate and user friendly.
- giving a 100 per cent no-quibble money-back guarantee if they don't like or want the product.
- making sure photographic images on your site are accurate and show products in their best light.
- hiring a customer service representative who can give advice on the phone to customers on more complex or expensive products.
- making ordering procedures straightforward and quick.
- confirming orders immediately by email.
- being honest—e.g. telling the customer if you can't deliver on time.
- providing a way for customers to track down the progress and availability of their order.

New Words

investigate	[ɪnˈvestɪgeɪt]	v. 调查,研究
predictable	[prɪˈdɪktəbl]	adj. 可预言的
reputation	[ˌrepjuˈteɪʃn]	n. 名誉,名声
dial-up	[ˈdaɪəl ʌp]	v. 拨号(上网)
unauthorized	[ʌnˈɔːθəraɪzd]	adj. 未被授权的,未经认可的
restricted	[rɪˈstrɪktɪd]	adj. 受限制的,有限的
streamline	[ˈstriːmlaɪn]	v. 使(系统、机构等)效率更高
automatically	[ˌɔːtəˈmætɪkli]	adv. 自动地,机械地
trigger	[ˈtrɪgə]	vt. 引发,引起,触发
replenish	[rɪˈplenɪʃ]	v. 补充
cashflow	[ˈkæʃfləʊ]	n. 现金流
precaution	[prɪˈkɔːʃn]	n. 预防,警惕,防范
deface	[dɪˈfeɪs]	vt. 损伤…的外表(尤指乱涂、乱写)
confidentiality	[ˌkɒnfɪˌdenʃiˈæləti]	n. 机密性
steer	[stɪə]	v. 控制,引导
publicize	[ˈpʌblɪsaɪz]	v. 宣扬
letterhead	[ˈletəhed]	n. 信头
vehicle	[ˈviːəkl]	n. 交通工具,车辆;媒介物
rectify	[ˈrektɪfaɪ]	vt. 矫正,调整
promptly	[ˈprɒmptli]	adv. 敏捷地,迅速地
representative	[ˌreprɪˈzentətɪv]	n. 代表
progress	[ˈprəʊgres]	n. 进程;进步,发展

Phrases

operational cost	运营成本
online transaction	在线交易
fixed price	固定价格
lead time	订货至交货的时间
strategic view	战略眼光
be overwhelmed by	受不起,不敢当
be susceptible to	易受…感染的;易受…影响的
pay for	偿还,赔偿
round-the-clock support	全天候支持,连续不停地支持
design template	设计模板
checkout procedure	支付过程
cutting-edge design	最前沿的设计

take long	花费很多时间
late payment	逾期付款
in the first instance	首先, 起初
chamber of commerce	商会
search engines rank site	搜索引擎排名网站
be essential to...	对…必要的, 对…非常重要
track down	追踪

Exercises

【Ex5】 Decide whether the following statements are True（T）or False（F）.

1. Selling online has a few of advantages over selling by conventional methods.
2. Selling online can save operational costs, such as renting high street premises.
3. Creating a fully automated online shop tailored to meet your precise requirements is not expensive.
4. Having a firewall will prevent unauthorized access occurring.
5. A firewall is always included as part of your operating system.
6. Few customers shopping online will want to pay by debit or credit card.
7. Many people will not abandon purchases at the checkout stage if the process is quick and easy.
8. A sophisticated online shop offers a wide range of options, including cutting-edge design and functionality, personalized pages and product news.
9. You need to ensure that you can deliver goods or services in a reasonable time, ideally the same day.
10. If you want to build your audience, it is essential that you are listed in web directories and search engines, which can be a time-consuming process.

【Ex6】 Translate the following terms or phrases from English into Chinese or vice versa.

1. design template
2. fixed price
3. online transaction
4. track down
5. checkout procedure
6. *n*. 机密性
7. *adj*. 未被授权的, 未经认可的
8. *v*. 使（系统等）效率更高
9. *n*. 现金流
10. *v*. 补充

1. _____
2. _____
3. _____
4. _____
5. _____
6. _____
7. _____
8. _____
9. _____
10. _____

Reading Material
10 Tips for Selling on the Internet and WWW

Can you make money① on the Internet and the World Wide Web? Certainly. Thousands of other small business people are making money and saving money right now in this new communications medium.

But if you want to set up shop on the Net，it's important for you to be just as professional，businesslike②，and cautious③ as you would be in any other new venture. So I suggest taking time to get to know the Internet and to develop a strategy.

Here in this free report I'll clue you in on a few vital tips that will give you a good head start.

Tip ♯1：Get to know the Internet. Do plenty of exploring.

If you're already on the Net，you're way ahead of the pack. I've run into④ plenty of people who are gung ho⑤ to advertise on the Internet before they've even got their own account.

You need to know what you're getting into. Sure，you can hire someone to set up a Web site for you. Nothing is wrong with that. But this is your business，and you should have a good feel for how it's being promoted. You know your business better than anyone else. Because of that，you're going to find dynamite ways to put the Internet to work—ways that no consultant or presence provider could ever think of.

In most places，especially in the U.S. and Canada，you can get decent Internet access for about ＄25 a month. If by any chance you're reading this and you haven't already got an Internet account，here's my advice：Go do it. Join in some electronic discussion groups. Surf⑥ the World Wide Web. Start communicating by e-mail. Don't wait. Do it now.

Tip ♯2：Be a resource.

Internet users expect information.

So make sure your message is more than just hype⑦. Add value. Be an information provider.

Participate in online discussion groups，and be helpful. If you have a World Wide

---

① make money：挣钱。
② businesslike [ˈbɪznəslaɪk] *adj.* 有条理的，有效率的。
③ cautious [ˈkɔːʃəs] *adj.* 谨慎的，小心的。
④ run into：碰到，遇到。
⑤ gung ho：同心协力，合作。
⑥ surf [sɜːf] *v.* 冲浪。
⑦ hype [haɪp] *n.* 大肆宣传，大做广告。

Web site，provide useful background information about your industry，your specialties，your areas of expertise. You will become known as an expert on the Internet，and others—including potential customers—will be drawn to you.

Tip #3：Don't send out unsolicited① e-mail marketing messages.

This won't help your business and will just get recipients angry. There are much better ways to market your product or service.

Electronic mail is different from postal mail. For one thing，sending out a conventional direct mail package costs you，the sender. But often your electronic mail message will cost the recipient money!

If you become a regular user of e-mail，you'll see how annoying② it would be if your mailbox got filled up③ every day with e-mail advertising. There's nothing to be gained by this.

Tip #4：Use online discussion groups for "soft selling④".

Newsgroups and e-mail discussion groups can be fertile fields for marketing. But watch out. Most groups don't tolerate commercial postings.

Instead of barging in to hype your product，be a real participant. Lurk⑤ and listen. Answer questions and offer help. Include a "signature" block at the end of your postings to let people know how to get in touch with you. You'll be surprised how often this will bring in leads from potential clients or customers.

Tip #5：Check your e-mail regularly.

People on the Internet expect fast response. I recommend checking your e-mail messages twice a day. Respond as quickly as possible. This shows that you're serious⑥ about your Internet presence and that you care.

Tip #6：Beware of "creativity".

I'm talking particularly about your World Wide Web site，once you start setting one up. Because the Web allows graphical presentations，it's easy to get caught up in designing something you like—but that does nothing to sell your product.

Make sure your site communicates and offers value to the user. Make sure it's readable and that it's easy to get around.

Your Web site doesn't have to be boring. You can be clever and you can be visual. But just remember this favorite advertising maxim："If it doesn't sell，it isn't creative."

Tip #7：Keep your World Wide Web site changing，so people will come back.

---

① unsolicited [ˌʌnsəˈlɪsɪtɪd] *adj*. 主动提供的。
② annoying [əˈnɔɪɪŋ] *adj*. 恼人的，讨厌的。
③ got filled up：装满。
④ soft selling：软推销，说服式推销。
⑤ lurk [lɜːk] *n*.& *vi*. 潜藏，潜伏，埋伏。
⑥ serious [ˈsɪərɪəs] *adj*. 严肃的，认真的。

Repeat visitors are more likely to become clients or buyers, and they're more likely to recommend your site to others. To draw users back to your site, you need to keep it changing. Update your material. Take advantage of new technology as it appears. Add new features, new resources and new information.

Tip #8: Use correct spelling, punctuation, and grammar.

I'm surprised how much poorly written copy I see on the Internet. Project a professional image by correct writing. Even if it's a lowly e-mail message, double-check it for typos① or vague language.

Tip #9: Include a clear call to action in your message.

What do you want the user to do after he or she has followed your presentation? Purchase a product? Request a proposal and price quotation? Join a mailing list? Ask for more information?

Let them know what you want them to do, and ask them to do it in clear, direct terms. Make it easy for them to respond. Set up a response mechanism—a direct e-mail link, a form to fill out, a button to click. The more direct and immediate the better. A phone number, a fax number, or a postal mail address is a second choice but better than nothing.

Tip #10: Promote your Internet presence through offline channels.

Let your regular customers② and the public know about your Internet presence. Put your e-mail address and URL on your business cards, stationery③, ads, brochures④, packaging, signage—anything you can think of. Send out press releases. Get the word out.

Marketing over the Internet and the World Wide Web can bring results in the form of leads, direct sales, publicity, and image-boosting. Get to know the medium. Work up a sound strategy. Seek out appropriate online marketing methods that will get your selling message across while respecting other Internet users.

Text A 参考译文

在 线 购 物

在线购物就是通过因特网从销售者处直接、实时地购买产品或服务。如果在这个过程中出现了中介,就叫做电子商务。在线购物、电子商店、电子店铺、互联网商店、网点、网铺、在线商店或虚拟商店与在实体零售店或购物中心实际购买类似。这个过程叫做企业对消费者在线购物。当一个商家从另一商家处进行购买时,则叫做企业对企业电子商务在线购

---

① typos ['taɪpəʊs] n. 打字稿。
② regular customer：老主顾。
③ stationery ['steɪʃənri] n. 办公用品,文具,信纸。
④ brochure ['brəʊʃə] n. 小册子。

物。B2B 和 B2C 在线购物都是电子商务的形式。

1　客户

最近几年,在线购物开始流行,但依然是迎合中上阶层。要进行在线购物,必须有计算机、银行账号及借记卡。购物随着技术的进步而发展。根据《电子商务杂志》的研究,如果我们注意在家购物者的人口统计特性,一般来说,教育、收入水平越高,家庭主要成员的职业越好,就越喜欢非店面购物的感觉。影响客户非店面购物的主要因素是其接触的技术,因为已经证明接触新技术越多,越容易喜欢新购物渠道。

在线购物在中层人群中扩展了目标用户。起初,在线购物的主要用户是有较高收入并受过高等教育的年轻人。这方面正在改变。例如,早期美国因特网的女性用户很少,但2001 年已经占到了网民的 52.8%。

2　物流

客户通过直接访问零售商的网站寻找感兴趣的产品,或者使用购物搜索引擎搜索多个经销商。

一旦在零售商的网站上找到了特定的产品,大多数在线零售商就使用购物车软件使客户集中多个商品并修改数量,这与在普通商店中把货物放到购物车或购物篮中一样。如果必要,在收集了支付和送货信息后,紧接着就是一个结账过程(还是与实体店一样)。有些零售商允许客户签约一个永久在线账号,以便只输入一次必要的信息。一旦交易完成后,客户通常会收到一个确认电子邮件。一些不那么先进的商店可以接受电话或电子邮件订单(尽管出于安全考虑,不接受通过电子邮件发送的信用卡账号)。

2.1　付款

在线购物者通常使用信用卡付款,但是有些系统允许用户使用如下方法建立账号并支付:

- 借记卡。
- 各种电子货币。
- 交货付现(COD,采用的网店很少)。
- 支票。
- 电汇/交货时付款。
- 邮政汇票。
- 把记账信息发送给手机。
- 赠卡。
- 在有些国家使用直接借记。

有些网站不接受国际信用卡,并且收账单的地址和送货地址必须与网站在同一国家。其他一些网站允许世界各地的客户进行交易,把东西送到任何地方。交易的财务部分可以实时处理(例如,让客户在注销之前就知道他们的信用卡已经扣款),也可以作为交易过程中的一部分随后处理。

2.2 交货

一旦付款完成，就可以用以下方式交货：

- 下载：这种方法通常用于数字媒体产品，如软件、音乐、电影或图片。
- 运送：产品送到客户的地址。
- 厂家直接送货：订单送达厂家或第三方经销商，它们直接给客户送货。
- 邮递：绕过零售商的实际位置邮递给任何客户，以便省时、省钱和省地方。
- 到店自提：客户在线订货，用定位软件找到最近的本地店面，然后到最近的店面自提货物。这种方法通常使用在实体店开网店的商业模式中。
- 在购买入场票时，可以得到一个编码或者可以打印的票。前提是确保一张票只能用一次。

2.3 购物车系统

- 简单的系统允许离线管理产品和目录。随后就产生了商店，形式为可以上传到网络空间的 HTML 文件和图片。这些系统不能使用在线数据库。
- 高端的解决方案可以按独立的程序或企业资源计划的附加程序购买或租用。它通常安装在公司自己的网络服务器上或者整合到已经存在的供应链中，以便在很大的范围内自动实现订购、支付、交货、记账及入库。
- 一些解决方案让用户在同时托管了多个商店的门户网站注册并建立在线商店。
- 开放资源购物车软件包包括高级平台，如 Interchange，以及无须定制的解决方案，如 Avactis、Satchmo、osCommerce、Magento、Zen Cart、VirtueMart、Batavi 及 PrestaShop。
- 商业系统也可以按照用户的需求定制，这样就无须从头建立商店。使用已经存在的框架，网店所需的不同功能的软件模块可以改编与组合。

2.4 在线大型购物中心

与许多在线拍卖网站一样，许多网站允许小企业建立和维护在线商店，而无须购买或开发昂贵的独立电子商务软件方案。

3 设计

为什么电子购物会存在？对客户来说，这不仅因为比较便利，也因为选择的范围更广、有竞争力的价格和可以大量地获取信息。对组织而言，它不仅增加了利润，也提升了客户的价值，并具有可持续发展的能力。

3.1 客户期望

在线购物的主要观点是不仅仅是有一个漂亮的、在许多搜索引擎中列出的或者能够展示其网站背后的艺术的网站，也不仅仅是发布信息，因为它也建立关系并挣钱。通常，一些组织试图采用在线购物技术而不了解这些技术并/或没有一个良好的商业模式。网站应该满足客户的期望，而不是支持组织的文化和品牌。大多数客户为了体验快速和高效购物而选择在线购物。许多研究者声称网站的独特性已经消失并需要以用户为中心来设计，这是很重要的。公司应该始终记住几个问题,如了解客户需求并兑现承诺,因为这些可以使客户再次光临。如果客户总是能得到自己期望的东西,他们就会回来。麦当劳化理论也可以用于在线购物方面,因为在线购物日益流行,并且如果网站要获取更多的购物者,就需要使用麦当劳化的四个主要原则:效率、可计算、可预测及控制。

要让人们更多地在线购物的组织,应该在网站的定义、设计、开发、测试、实现和维护方面花费更多的时间和金钱。同样,如果一个公司的网站要在在线购物者中流行,它就应该给客户留下该公司的正面印象,这样客户就会觉得该公司关心客户。想在网上得到承认的公司要记住:与得到客户相比,失去客户更容易。许多研究者认为,即使一个网站是"最受好评的",如果该组织未能做到常规礼仪(如及时回电子邮件、向客户通报问题、诚实、管理好客户数据),那么它将没有前途。要保持客户并增加客户的公司应努力消除各种问题,并迎合在线购物者,使他们更满意。这也就是许多网站设计者考虑用户体验研究结果的原因。

3.2 用户界面

考虑国家和客户是很重要的。例如,在日本隐私是非常重要的,与购物网站相比,情感对养老金网站更重要。接下来,有不同的体验:有经验的用户更关注直接影响购物的变数,而新手则更关注了解信息。

当客户进行在线购物时,有一些因素决定他们是否会成为回头客。最重要的因素是易用和对用户友好。

3.3 系统本身

购物车系统的工作如其名所示。首先,客户必须从网上选择所期望的商品。这一步完成后,会出现"把商品加入购物车"选项,这一步将确保购买所需的商品。客户一旦完成了其他有潜在购买可能性的浏览并确定以前选择的产品就是要购买的商品,就必须接着执行网站提供的步骤以便实现交易。最后,在预定的日期商品将送往期望的地址。

Unit 3

Text A

E-commerce Website Design

Designing an e-commerce site is not just about building a website to sell products but designing a pleasant online shopping experience.

1　Design E-commerce for Trust and Security

First and foremost, it is important to design a website that shoppers feel they can trust. Most shoppers are concerned about privacy and whether the site will protect their personal data by providing a secure transaction. If the website does not feel trustworthy, they will simply choose to shop elsewhere. Here are some methods that will communicate trustworthiness:

- Include an overview of the business: Provide general information, contact information, links to social media and a Frequently Asked Questions (FAQ) page.
- Publish store policies and make sure they are not too difficult to find: Provide shipping and return policies, outline the returns process and what products can be returned, and provide easy access to a privacy policy that covers shoppers' personal and financial information (this is crucial).
- Write in plain language and avoid legal or internal policy jargon.
- Share product reviews. Provide product reviews to help shoppers understand more about the product. This will help alleviate any concerns they may have and provide great e-commerce UX. Take it a step further by offering product reviews along with additional information about the reviewers, or by summarizing the reviews. This step can help make it easier for shoppers to get the full benefit of others' opinions.
- Use a secure server. Shoppers expect that their personal information will stay secure while they purchase online. SSL (Secure Sockets Layer) certificates authenticate the identity of a website and encrypt information that needs to remain safe. It is an essential sign that indicates checkouts are secure. Assure shoppers that their data is protected by implementing SSL and displaying SSL certificate badges.

2　E-commerce UI Design Considerations

The look and feel of a website is the main driver of first impressions. Research concludes that people will determine whether they like a website or not in just 50 milliseconds.

Here are some essential UI design tips:

- Follow the brand identity. The branding should be apparent throughout the website. Choose colors that reflect the brand, and set the style in order to make clear what type of products are sold. Ensure brand experience is consistent across all channels—whether online, in-store, or on a mobile device. This will help build a strong brand-customer relationship.
- Adopt visual hierarchy. The most critical content should be displayed above the fold. In some cases, using less white space to bring items closer together is better than pushing critical content below the fold.
- Do not over design. Limit font formats such as font face, sizes, and colors. When the text looks too much like graphics, it will be mistaken for an ad. Use high-contrast text and background colors to make the content as clear as possible.
- Stick to known symbols. Use icons or symbols that are easy to identify. Unfamiliar icons will only confuse the shoppers.
- Avoid popup windows. Popup windows are a distraction.

3　The Importance of Frictionless E-commerce Site Navigation

3.1　Well-defined Product Categories

The top level of navigation should show the set of categories that the site offers. Group products into categories and subcategories that make sense. Category labels work best as single words that describe the range of products, so shoppers can scan through them and instantly understand what they represent. It's best to user-test site navigation as much as possible for great e-commerce UX as it's a key make-or-break feature of the site.

3.2　Product Search

Simply put, if shoppers cannot find the product, they cannot buy the product. So take the following actions to build a search function that helps them easily find what they are looking for:

- Make search omnipresent. Put the search box on every page and in familiar locations. The box should be visible, quickly recognizable, and easy to use. Standard positions to implement the search box are the top right or top center of the pages, or on the main menu.

- Support all kinds of queries. Searches need to support all types of queries such as product names，categories，and product attributes，as well as customer service related information. It's a good idea to include a sample search query in the input field to suggest the shoppers the use of the various functions.

- Have a search auto-complete functionality. Auto-complete functionality makes it easier for shoppers to find what they are looking for and increases sales potential by suggesting things within the area they are already searching.

- Allow sorting and filtering of results. Let shoppers sort search results based on various criteria（best sellers，highest or lowest price，product rating，newest item，etc.）as well as eliminate items that do not fit within a certain category. See Figure 3-1.

Figure 3-1　Sportsgirl allows sorting and filtering the search results

3.3　Filtering Products

The more choices given，the harder it is to choose. Help shoppers find the right products by implementing filters. It will help them narrow their choices and jump to their desired product range directly.

3.4　Product Quick View

A "quick view" reduces the time it takes for shoppers to find the right product by eliminating unnecessary page loads. Typically，the product details are displayed in a modal window[①] over the viewed page. Do not try to show all the product details，

---

　　① 　模态窗口（modal window），或者称为浮窗，一般用于在空间紧张的页面中展示额外信息。在模态窗口中，可以放置放大版的图像、额外内容、警告/提示信息、视频等。用模态窗口展示信息时，要同时明确地提示用户如何关闭它。同时，用于打开模态窗口的链接、缩略图、图标或者其他图形元素一定要保证与模态窗口要展示的内容有足够的关联。相似的图标、摘要、图形元素都能帮助用户建立原始链接与打开的模态窗口的联系。

instead, include a link to the full product page to view complete details. Also, be sure to include a prominently positioned "Add to Cart" button as well as a "Save to Wishlist" functionality. See Figure 3-2.

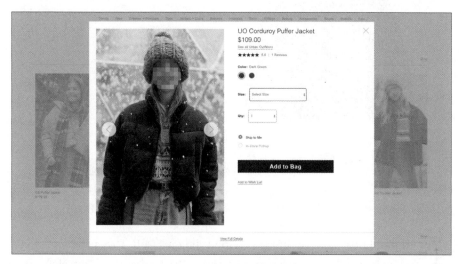

Figure 3-2　A "quick view" modal window from Urban Outfitters

3.5　Special Offers

Shoppers always look for special offers, discounts, or best deals. Make exclusive offers visible so shoppers know about them. Even if the price differences aren't that great, the psychological feeling of saving some money creates an illusion of having an upper hand.

4　E-commerce Product Page Design

Design a product page that creates an experience that is as similar to an in-person shopping experience as much possible by including lots of images, detailed descriptions and any other useful and related information about the product. Let's take an in-depth look at what this means.

4.1　Provide Great Product Images

With e-commerce, shoppers cannot touch, feel, or try out the product. Instead, everything depends on what they see online. This is why providing product images that clearly exhibit all aspects of the product is critical. See Figure 3-3. Here is a checklist for perfect product images:

- Use a white background. The background for product images should not distract or conflict with the product itself. A white background works best because it allows the product to stand out, and works with almost any style or color scheme.

Figure 3-3　Product images include a zoom feature and even a video

- Use high-quality，large images. Good images sell the product. High-quality images catch shoppers' interest and show them exactly what they are buying. Having large images lets shoppers zoom up and examine a product in fine detail. See Figure 3-4.

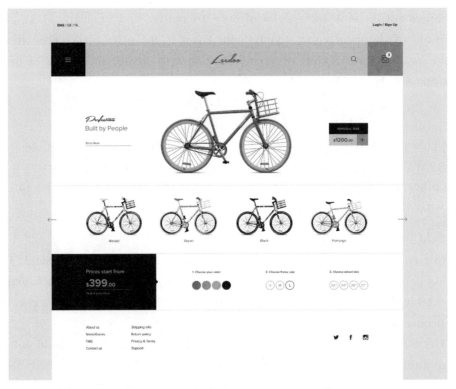

Figure 3-4　High-quality product images on a minimalist UI

- Use a variety of images. Display the product from a number of different angles and include close-ups in order to provide a more complete sense of the product. A 360-degree view, where they can move the product around, is a good way to provide an experience close to physically going into the store and engaging with it. VR e-commerce is the next wave of this experience.
- Use video. Videos have the ability to deliver a lot of information in a short amount of time. Use a video to show the product in use, and to provide as much functional information as possible.
- Be consistent. Use images that are consistent across multiple pages and are also in line with the look and feel of the rest of the website. This will keep everything looking clean and uncluttered. The main product image should be the same across all areas of the site, such as product highlights or in the featured items section.

4.2   Give Just the Right Amount of Product Information

Give shoppers detailed information about the product so they can make an informed purchase decision. Show availability, options for different sizes or colors, dimensions, a size chart, materials used, total cost, warranties, and more. The fewer remaining questions they have about a product, the more likely they are to make a purchase. See Figure 3-5.

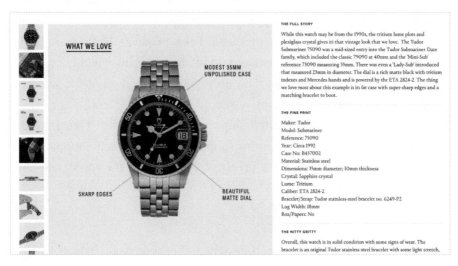

Figure 3-5   Detailed product information

4.3   Show Related and Recommended Products

Display similar products that shoppers might also like, or products that others have purchased. This can be displayed on a product detail page or in the shopping cart and will help guide shoppers to the products that meet their needs, potentially encouraging them to continue shopping—a great way to cross-sell related products.

5　Shopping Cart Design

The shopping cart is essential as it is where shoppers review their selected products，make the final decision，and proceed to checkout. The primary goal of the shopping cart is to lead shoppers to checkout. The following are tips on designing a shopping cart that is user-friendly，and will encourage shoppers to purchase further.

- Use a clear Call To Action（CTA）[①]. The primary call to action on the shopping cart page should be the checkout button. Use bright colors，plenty of clickable areas and simple language to make the checkout button visible，straightforward and easy to use.
- Provide adequate feedback. Make sure when a product is added to the shopping cart it is immediately and clearly confirmed. Shoppers get confused by inadequate feedback，such as showing inconspicuous confirmation text. A good idea is to use animations，as movement attracts the human eye.
- Use a mini cart widget. Allow shoppers to add products to their cart without leaving the page they are on by using a mini cart. It also allows them to navigate，discover，and add more products. Mini cart widgets should always link to the full page shopping cart.
- Display product details. Displaying details like product names，images，sizes，colors，and prices in the shopping cart helps the shoppers to remember each product as well as to compare products. Link products in the cart back to their full product pages，so shoppers can review more details when necessary.
- Make the cart easily editable. The ability to remove，save for later or change details like size，color，or quantity should be easy to access.
- Avoid the surprise of unexpected shipping costs and taxes. Unexpected shipping costs are one of the leading reasons shoppers abandon their shopping carts. Place shipping options and taxes with precise calculation of the costs，and an expected delivery date up front.

6　E-commerce Checkout Design

Here are a few ways to build a well-designed checkout page，which will contribute to a successful conversion：

- Offer various payment options. Different shoppers have different preferences when it comes to making payments. Provide as many payment options as possible

---

① 　A Call To Action（CTA）is a marketing term that refers to the next step a marketer wants its audience or reader to take. The CTA can have a direct link to sales. For example，it can instruct the reader to click the buy button to complete a sale，or it can simply move the audience further along towards becoming a consumer of that company's goods or services.

(contingent on the target audience) to expand the customer base, and to make it easy for shoppers to complete their order.

- Keep it simple. Minimize the number of fields and steps to complete the purchase. Using shipping address as billing address by default is a good way to minimize the number of fields—ideally, design a single page checkout where shoppers can view their cart and enter delivery and payment information.

- Make registration optional. Forcing shoppers to create an account prior to their first purchase will drive the shoppers away. Give them an option to register after the purchase is complete, and highlight the benefits of registration when asking them to register. Benefits include faster checkout thanks to personal information like saved shipping address or payment information and access to exclusive offers that are only available to registered members.

- Use clear error indications. There is nothing more frustrating than not being able to make a purchase or figure out why. Instead of showing the errors after a form is submitted, make error notifications come up in real time. Place clear and concise error messages directly above, or next to the item that requires correction, so shoppers will notice and understand them.

- Keep people on track. When using a multi-page checkout, include a progress bar that shows how many more steps are left to complete the purchase. This will eliminate any ambiguity, and assure shoppers they are on the right track. When the purchase is complete, display an order confirmation and order status with shipment tracking.

- Offer support. Include a live chat or contact number throughout the checkout process, so when shoppers have questions, they can quickly get answers rather than having to leave the site and go elsewhere.

7　Summary

All online shoppers expect frictionless experiences. When designing an e-commerce site, it is not just about building a website but creating an online shopping experience that will convert passive shoppers into paying customers.

New Words

pleasant	['pleznt]	adj. 令人愉快的;友好的
security	[sɪˈkjʊərəti]	n. 安全性
shopper	[ˈʃɒpə]	n. (商店的)顾客,买东西的人
transaction	[trænˈzækʃn]	n. 交易,业务,事务
trustworthy	[ˈtrʌstwɜːði]	adj. 值得信赖的,可靠的
link	[lɪŋk]	n.& v. 链接

return	[rɪˈtɜːn]	v. & n. 退货
policy	[ˈpɒləsi]	n. 政策;策略
share	[ʃeə]	v. 共享,分享
alleviate	[əˈliːvieɪt]	v. 减轻;缓解
opinion	[əˈpɪnjən]	n. 意见
server	[ˈsɜːvə]	n. 服务器
certificate	[səˈtɪfɪkət]	n. 证书
authenticate	[ɔːˈθentɪkeɪt]	vt. 证明是真实的、可靠的或有效的
encrypt	[ɪnˈkrɪpt]	v. 加密,将…译成密码
checkout	[ˈtʃekaʊt]	n. 结账
badge	[bædʒ]	n. 徽章;象征
identity	[aɪˈdentəti]	n. 身份;个性;一致
in-store	[in-stɔː]	adj. 商店内的
fold	[fəʊld]	n. 首屏
font	[fɒnt]	n. 字体;字形
ad	[ˌeɪˈdiː]	n. 广告
icon	[ˈaɪkɒn]	n. 图标
confuse	[kənˈfjuːz]	v. 混淆,使困惑
distraction	[dɪˈstrækʃn]	n. 使人分心的事
navigation	[ˌnævɪˈgeɪʃn]	n. 导航
make-or-break	[meik ɔː breik]	conj. 不成则败
search	[sɜːtʃ]	n. & v. 搜索
omnipresent	[ˌɒmnɪˈpreznt]	adj. 无所不在的
query	[ˈkwɪəri]	n. 查询,询问
auto-complete	[ˈɔːtəʊ kəmˈpliːt]	adj. 自动完成的
filter	[ˈfɪltə]	n. 过滤器;筛选(过滤)程序
load	[ləʊd]	v. 装载,加载
wishlist	[wɪʃlist]	n. 意愿清单,心愿单
psychological	[ˌsaɪkəˈlɒdʒɪkl]	adj. 心理的;心理学的
in-person	[ˈinˈpɜːsən]	adj. 亲自的,本人的;现场的
exhibit	[ɪgˈzɪbɪt]	v. 展览;表现
background	[ˈbækgraʊnd]	n. 背景;底色
distract	[dɪˈstrækt]	v. 分散注意力;使分心
video	[ˈvɪdiəʊ]	n. 视频
consistent	[kənˈsɪstənt]	adj. 一致的;连续的
unclutter	[ʌnˈklʌtə]	vt. 使整洁,整理
dimension	[daɪˈmenʃn, dɪˈmenʃn]	n. 尺寸;维度
material	[məˈtɪəriəl]	n. 材料;原料;布料

user-friendly	[ˌjuːzə'frendli]	adj. 用户友好的
clickable	['klɪkəbl]	adj. 可点击的
visible	['vɪzəbl]	adj. 可见的；明显的
inconspicuous	[ˌɪnkən'spɪkjuəs]	adj. 不明显的，不显著的
widget	['wɪdʒɪt]	n. 小器具，窗口小部件
compare	[kəm'peə]	v. 比较
editable	['edɪtəbl]	adj. 可编辑的
taxe	['tæks]	n. 税款
abandon	[ə'bændən]	v. 抛弃，舍弃，放弃
contribute	[kən'trɪbjuːt]	v. 增加，增进
conversion	[kən'vɜːʃn]	n. 转换
target	['tɑːgɪt]	n. 目标；对象
		v. 瞄准，面向
field	[fiːld]	n. 区域，字段
default	[dɪ'fɔːlt]	adj. 默认的
		n. 默认值；默认指令
registration	[ˌredʒɪ'streɪʃn]	n. 登记，注册
indication	[ˌɪndɪ'keɪʃn]	n. 表明；标示
notification	[ˌnəʊtɪfɪ'keɪʃn]	n. 通知；通知单；布告；公布
concise	[kən'saɪs]	adj. 简明的，简洁的
ambiguity	[ˌæmbɪ'gjuːəti]	n. 歧义；不明确，模棱两可
frictionless	['frɪkʃnləs]	adj. 无障碍的

Phrases

personal data	个人数据，个人资料
social media	社交媒体
returns process	退货步骤，退货过程
privacy policy	隐私政策
internal policy	内部政策
product review	产品评论
essential sign	基本符号，重要标志
first impression	第一印象，初步印象
in order to	为了…
mobile device	移动设备
high-contrast text	高对比度文本
background color	背景颜色
as clear as possible	尽可能清晰
stick to	遵守；保留；坚持

popup window	弹出式窗口
main menu	主菜单
quick view	快速查看
modal window	模态窗口
Add to Cart	添加到购物车
upper hand	优势,上风,有利地位
depend on	取决于;依赖于
stand out	突出;超群
zoom up	放大视图;推近
a variety of	各种各样的
size chart	尺码表
product detail page	产品详细信息页面
confirmation text	确认文本
mini cart	迷你购物车
full page	整个页面;整版
contingent on ...	视…而定
customer base	客户群
error message	出错信息
progress bar	进度条
order confirmation	确认订单,证实订单
order status	订单状态

Abbreviations

FAQ (Frequently Asked Questions)	常见问题
UX (User eXperience)	用户体验
SSL (Secure Sockets Layer)	安全套接层
UI (User Interface)	用户界面
VR (Virtual Reality)	虚拟现实
CTA (Call To Action)	行动召唤

Exercises

[Ex1] Answer the following questions according to the text.

1. What is it important first and foremost when designing a website? What are most shoppers concerned about?

2. What do SSL (Secure Sockets Layer) certificates do?

3. What are some essential UI design tips mentioned in the passage?

4. Why is it best to user-test site navigation as much as possible for great e-commerce UX?

5. What actions should the designer take to build a search function that helps shoppers easily find what they are looking for?

6. What does a "quick view" do? And how? Where are the product details displayed typically?

7. How can we design a product page that creates an experience that is as similar to an in-person shopping experience as much possible?

8. What is the checklist for perfect product images?

9. What are the tips on designing a shopping cart that is user-friendly, and will encourage shoppers to purchase further?

10. What are the ways to build a well-designed checkout page?

【Ex2】 **Translate the following terms or phrases from English into Chinese or vice versa.**

1. Add to Cart   1. _____

2. customer base   2. _____

3. mini cart   3. _____

4. order confirmation   4. _____

5. order status   5. _____

6. *n.* 证书   6. _____

7. *n.* 意愿清单,心愿单   7. _____

8. *adj.* 可点击的   8. _____

9. *n.* 结账   9. _____

10. *adj.* 用户友好的   10. _____

【Ex3】 **Fill in the blanks with the words given below.**

important	purchasing	orders	tracking	review
information	system	fulfillment	experience	customer

Three Reasons to Provide Order Tracking

1   Reduce costs

With e-commerce order tracking, there are significantly fewer inquiries. Once implemented, all the tracking _____1_____ is automatically provided to your customer. And if there are any issues, you can easily search through all of your orders to find what you need.

Order tracking automates the process without creating any extra work for you, putting less burden on your _____2_____ support team without compromising quality. By saving time and money, you have more resources to invest in other methods of improving the customer _____3_____.

2   Meet customers expectations

97% of customers expect the ability to monitor their orders throughout every step of the shipping process.

Shoppers have obviously become accustomed to having a high level of visibility into their ____4____ . Online shopping basically demands it with such a competitive e-commerce landscape. Having an e-commerce order tracking ____5____ in place is mandatory if your brand doesn't want to lose business to Amazon and other major retailers.

If you can't provide the expected level of service，shoppers will take notice，posing a risk to customer loyalty. By providing order ____6____ that gives the up-to-date information your customers want，their expectations are met and they are more likely to give you a good ____7____ ，buy from you again，or tell their friends.

3　Have more control over fulfillment

Your job is not done once the box is packed and in the carriers' hands. With order tracking，you maintain more control over the order ____8____ process and can quickly address any issues as they arise with ease. Without a system，____9____ tracking information can get missed，resulting in a backlog of emails from unhappy customers.

Customer acquisition is great but the real money is in having repeat customers who keep ____10____ more from you. The right e-commerce fulfillment strategy，which includes order tracking，can help minimize issues as well as increase the lifetime value of your customers and win more sales.

【Ex4】 Translate the following passage from English into Chinese.

Four Ways to Proactively Reduce Returns

It's clear that creating a great return policy is important for increasing sales and building customer loyalty. But with the average retailer spending 8.1% of total sales on reverse logistics，it can pay to reduce overall return volume as well.

1　Create clear product descriptions

With online shopping，what you see isn't always what you get. That's why 88% of shoppers characterize detailed product content as being extremely important to their purchasing decision.

Giving reliable info about your product upfront can also decrease returns. When what customers receive matches their expectations，they'll be less likely to return that product. Make sure that the product pages on your website are descriptive and include high-quality，accurate product photos.

2　Increase return time window

Customers expect at least 30 days to return an online purchase. But only 5% of shoppers say they return online orders more than 30 days after purchase.

Being lenient with return time limits（e.g.，a 60-day vs. 30-day policy）can actually decrease returns by creating less urgency around returns for the customer.

3 Conduct regular quality testing

If your product page seems to reflect the product accurately, and you're still getting a high rate of returned items, there may be an issue with the item itself. Assess the quality of the item, do product testing, and check in with your manufacturer to address any production or quality issues.

4 Identify trends in commonly returned items

You can also include a quick one-question survey in the returns process asking why a customer chose to return a certain product. If your returns process is easy to complete, customers will likely be happy to select a return reason from a list of preset options.

This can be particularly helpful in identifying a quality issue with a product, such as a fit issue with apparel. For example, if clothing items are being returned because they are too large, you may be able to identify a potential sizing issue with your manufacturer.

Gathering information on the return side can help you identify trends and issues with your products and make the necessary improvements to future inventory.

Text B
How to Write a Product Description in E-commerce

A product description is the marketing copy that explains what a product is and why it's worth purchasing. Its purpose is to supply customers with important information about the features and benefits of the product so they're compelled to buy.

A well-crafted product description moves buyers through your conversion funnel. If you add a bit of creativity, your product pages instantly become more compelling, leading to more conversions from casual shoppers.

To succeed in writing product descriptions, you need to answer questions customers have about your products:

- What problems does your product solve?
- What do customers gain from your product?
- What makes it better than the competition?

A product description should answer these questions in a fun and engaging way.

Online stores often make the mistake of listing product features when writing product descriptions. This likely results in lower conversions because people don't understand how the product helps them.

Let's look at how you can create perfect product descriptions that sell for you.

1 Focus on Your Ideal Buyer

Understanding how to write a product description requires putting yourself in the shoes of your audience. When you write a product description with a huge crowd of buyers in mind, your descriptions become wishy-washy and you end up addressing no one at all.

The best product descriptions address your target audience directly and personally. You ask and answer questions as if you're having a conversation with them. You choose the words your ideal buyer uses. You use the word "you".

When it comes to writing your own product descriptions, start by imagining your ideal buyer. What kind of humor do they appreciate (if any)? What words do they use? What words do they hate? What questions do they ask that you should answer?

Consider how you would speak to your ideal buyer if you were selling your product in-store, face to face. Now try and incorporate that language into your e-commerce site so you can have a similar conversation online that resonates more deeply.

2　Entice with Benefits

When we sell our own products, we get excited about individual product features and specifications. The problem is our potential buyers are not as interested in mundane features and specs. They want to know what's in it for them—how it will address their biggest pain points. How does your product make your customers feel happier, healthier, or more productive? What problems, glitches, and hassle does your product help solve?

Don't sell just a product, sell an experience.

3　Avoid "Yeah, Yeah" Phrases

When we're stuck for words and don't know what else to add to our product description, we often add something bland like "excellent product quality".

That's a "yeah, yeah" phrase. As soon as a potential buyer reads "excellent product quality" he thinks, "Yeah, yeah, of course. That's what everyone says." Have you ever heard someone describe their product quality as average, not so good, or even bad?

You become less persuasive when your potential buyer reads your product description and starts saying "yeah, yeah" to themselves. To avoid this reaction, be as specific as possible.

Product details add credibility. Product details sell your product. You can never include too many technical details in your product descriptions. Be specific.

4　Justify Using Superlatives

Superlatives sound insincere unless you clearly prove why your product is the best, the easiest, or the most advanced.

If your product is really the best in its category, provide specific proof why this is the case. Otherwise, tone your product copy down or quote a customer who says your product is the most wonderful they've ever used.

5 Appeal to Your Readers' Imagination

Scientific research has proven that if people hold a product in their hands, their desire to own it increases.

You're selling things online, so your web visitors can't hold your products. Large, crystal-clear pictures or videos can help, but there's also a copywriting trick to increase desire: let your reader imagine what it would be like to own your product.

To practice this copywriting technique, start a sentence with the word "imagine", and finish your sentence (or paragraph) by explaining how your reader will feel when owning and using your product.

6 Cut Through Rational Barriers with Mini-stories

Including mini-stories in your product descriptions lowers rational barriers against persuasion techniques. In other words, we forget we're being sold to.

When it comes to telling a story about your products, ask yourself:
* Who is making the product?
* What inspired creating the product?
* What obstacles did you need to overcome to develop the product?
* How was the product tested?

7 Seduce with Sensory Words

Adjectives are tricky words. Often they don't add meaning to your sentences, and you're better off deleting them. However, sensory adjectives are power words because they make your reader experience the copy while reading.

Dazzle your readers with vivid product descriptions. Think about words like "velvety", "smooth", "crisp", and "bright" if you're selling food products.

8 Tempt with Social Proof

When your web visitors are unsure about which product to purchase, they look for suggestions about what to buy. They're often swayed to buy a product with the highest number of positive reviews and testimonials.

Try to include an image of the customer to add credibility to a quote. It also makes your online business more approachable and relatable. You can even integrate a social media feed filled with user-generated content that shows real people using your products.

Most buyers are attracted to buying something that's popular. When it comes to your e-commerce website, highlight the products that are customer favorites.

9　Make Your Description Scannable

Is your web design encouraging web visitors to read your product descriptions?

Packaging your product descriptions with a clear, scannable design makes them easier to read and more appealing to potential customers.

Here are some areas to focus on when designing yours：

- Entice your web visitor with headlines.
- Use easy-to-scan bullet points.
- Include plenty of white space.
- Increase your font size to promote readability.
- Use high-quality product images.

10　Set Goals and KPIs

The goal of a product description is to move a shopper toward purchase. But how do you know if your descriptions are working or not?

You'll want to decide on a set of metrics to track on your product pages. Defining these metrics will help you understand what product descriptions are working best and improve on underperforming ones.

Common KPIs to monitor include：

- Conversion rate.
- Shopping cart abandonment.
- Return rate.
- Support inquiries.
- Organic search rankings.

New Words

description	[dɪˈskrɪpʃn]	n. 描述,说明
explain	[ɪkˈspleɪn]	v. 解释;说明…的理由
well-crafted	[wel krɑːftɪd]	adj. 精心设计的
creativity	[ˌkriːeɪˈtɪvəti]	n. 创造性,创造力
casual	[ˈkæʒuəl]	adj. 漫不经心的;随便的;偶然的
wishy-washy	[ˈwɪʃi wɒʃi]	adj. 软弱无力的;空洞无聊的
conversation	[ˌkɒnvəˈseɪʃn]	n. 交谈,谈话
appreciate	[əˈpriːʃieɪt]	v. 欣赏;理解,领会
resonate	[ˈrezəneɪt]	vi. 共鸣,共振
entice	[ɪnˈtaɪs]	vt. 诱惑;怂恿
mundane	[mʌnˈdeɪn]	adj. 平凡的,寻常的
spec	[spek]	n. 规格;说明书

glitch	[glɪtʃ]	n. 小过失,差错
hassle	[ˈhæsl]	n. 困难的事情;麻烦的事情
persuasive	[pəˈsweɪsɪv]	adj. 有说服力的
credibility	[ˌkredəˈbɪləti]	n. 可信度,可信性
superlative	[suˈpɜːlətɪv]	adj. 最高的;最高级的;过度的
		n. 最高级
imagination	[ɪˌmædʒɪˈneɪʃn]	n. 想象(力)
crystal-clear	[ˈkrɪstlˈklɪə]	adj. 清晰的
rational	[ˈræʃnəl]	adj. 理性的;理智的
barrier	[ˈbæriə]	n. 屏障;障碍;界限
obstacle	[ˈɒbstəkl]	n. 障碍,障碍物
seduce	[sɪˈdjuːs]	vt. 吸引,使入迷
sensory	[ˈsensəri]	adj. 感觉的,感受的,感官的
dazzle	[ˈdæzl]	v. 使目眩,眼花;使惊叹
velvety	[ˈvelvəti]	adj. 天鹅绒般柔软的
tempt	[tempt]	vt. 吸引;使…感兴趣
		vi. 有吸引力
suggestion	[səˈdʒestʃən]	n. 建议
sway	[sweɪ]	v. 摇摆
testimonial	[ˌtestɪˈməʊniəl]	adj. 表扬的
		n. 推荐信
approachable	[əˈprəʊtʃəbl]	adj. 可亲近的,可接近的
headline	[ˈhedlaɪn]	n. 标题
		vt. 给…加标题
readability	[ˌriːdəˈbɪləti]	n. 可读性

Phrases

product description	产品阐述,产品说明
conversion funnel	转化漏斗
a bit of	一点,一星半点
potential buyer	潜在买家
pain point	痛点
bullet point	商品特点描述;要点,卖点
conversion rate	转化率
shopping cart abandonment	购物车放弃
return rate	退货率
search ranking	搜索排名

Abbreviations

KPI (Key Performance Indicators)　　　　关键业绩指标

Exercises

【**Ex5**】 **Answer the following questions according to the text.**

1. What is product description? What is its purpose?

2. To succeed in writing product descriptions, what are the questions customers have about your products that you need to answer?

3. What does understanding how to write a product description require?

4. When do you become less persuasive?

5. When do superlatives sound insincere?

6. What has scientific research proven?

7. What do you ask yourself when it comes to telling a story about your products?

8. Why are sensory adjectives power words?

9. What are some areas to focus on when designing your product descriptions?

10. What do common KPIs to monitor include?

【**Ex6**】 **Translate the following terms or phrases from English into Chinese or vice versa.**

1. search ranking	1. _____
2. return rate	2. _____
3. product description	3. _____
4. conversion rate	4. _____
5. conversion funnel	5. _____
6. *n*. 可信度,可信性	6. _____
7. *n*. 交谈,谈话	7. _____
8. *adj*. 感觉的,感受的,感官的	8. _____
9. *n*. 规格;说明书	9. _____
10. *n*. 建议	10. _____

Reading Material

How to Choose Products That You Can Sell Easily

1　Product Research

If you want to sell products easily on line, you will have to carry out product research. The first thing to understand is that not all products are the same. While this may seem obvious when comparing, say, bicycles to bookshelves, it also reflects in more subtle① ways—such as how popular the product is, how well the supply chains run, how much its shipping charges will cost, and so on.

Product research simply refers to the process of choosing products with good market potential② and discovering how best to sell them.

If you don't have the right product, for the right audience, and at the right price, your listings will simply be irrelevant③ on any digital marketplace.

2 Product Criteria—What to Look Out for

At the core of every product research study is the collection and analysis of a few key metrics. While there's more to look at, you will need to put these four factors under the magnifying glass④, so to speak.

Here's what you need to observe when vetting a potential new product.

2.1 Profitability⑤

If there's one thing you shouldn't take your eye off in the e-commerce game, it's your product's actual ability to generate a profit.

By buying low and selling high, you generate a better return on investment. This means that the first thing you need to calculate when looking at a new product is the cumulative⑥ total overhead cost⑦ associated with sourcing it.

Perhaps your product cost is cheap. However, if you end up⑧ paying a significant amount in duty, shipping, payment processing fees and more, you will compromise your overall profitability, and make your business growth weak and your sustainability⑨ lower.

Try to keep your product cost price about one-third of your sales price. This brings us to...

2.2 Pricing

You might have heard of how several major companies spend ever-increasing⑩ percentages of their budgets on marketing efforts. There's a good reason why they do this.

---

① subtle ['sʌtl] *adj*. 微妙的，巧妙的。
② market potential：市场潜力。
③ irrelevant [ɪˈreləvənt] *adj*. 无关紧要的。
④ magnifying glass：放大镜。
⑤ profitability [ˌprɒfɪtəˈbɪləti] *n*. 收益性；利益率。
⑥ cumulative [ˈkjuːmjələtɪv] *adj*. 积累的，累计的。
⑦ total overhead cost：总间接费用，总管理费用。
⑧ end up：最终，到头来。
⑨ sustainability [səˌsteɪnəˈbɪləti] *n*. 持续性。
⑩ ever-increasing [ˈevə ɪnˈkriːsɪŋ] *adj*. 不断增长的。

Generating sales is extremely hard early on. Convincing[①] customers to let go of their hard-earned cash takes time and effort，even if your product is low in price. If you generate a 70% profit by sourcing a product for ＄1.50 and selling it for ＄5，you're only making a ＄3.5 profit per sale.

This means that you'll have to sell nearly 300 items before you see the cash register hit ＄1,000，which is the most common revenue goal for early e-sellers.

It goes the other way too. You could try selling a product that cost you ＄250 for ＄1250 and hit that goal in one sale. However，this is next to impossible for new sellers. At higher price points，people are extremely picky[②] and are highly unlikely to buy from someone they don't know very well，such as you.

The correct strategy should be to look at a product that makes a decent amount of money per sale but also doesn't scare off customers. Generally speaking，something at a listing price in the range of ＄100- ＄15 should work best.

2.3　Size and Weight

This one is pretty straightforward—bigger and bulkier things are more expensive to ship，and will consequently[③] be harder to sell.

On the flip side[④]，lighter products are easier to bundle with free-shipping deals and allow for more flexibility with your logistics. If you're looking to ship overseas someday，it's exponentially easier with a lightweight product.

2.4　Demand

Rather unsurprisingly[⑤]，it's quite hard to sell a product that no one asked for. Make sure that you stay clear of too-extreme niches[⑥]，and choose a product that has regular，consistent demand in the market.

While this may result in having to compete with other sellers，you certainly can't make any money without a good number of buyers on your side too.

3　Tips to Help Find Great New Products

Now that you understand the basics，let's take a look at four simple ways to discover great products to kick off your online business.

3.1　Internet Research

Most good products gain attraction organically through various channels—you'll find

---

① convince ［kən'vɪns］ *v.* 使相信，说服。
② picky ［'pɪki］ *adj.* 吹毛求疵的，好挑剔的。
③ consequently ［'kɒnsɪkwəntli］ *adv.* 因此；结果。
④ on the flip side：反过来说，另一方面。
⑤ rather unsurprisingly：不出所料。
⑥ niche ［niːʃ］ *n.* （产品的）商机，市场定位；*adj.* 针对特定客户群的（营销），细分的，专营的。

them reposted on Twitter and Instagram, highlighted on major social media marketing publications①, and even reviewed on YouTube.

You can note down how popular posts on these products are and how audiences react to their photos, videos, and features. You can also divide these by niche, allowing you to pick and choose products based on your level of familiarity②.

Pro tip: If you have the budget for it, you may want to try to train and hire a local college student or someone through a freelance③ site to gather some initial product ideas to sell. If you have them find 10-20 options with specific criteria in mind, you can further filter to find the best options and save a ton of time.

3.2　Online Marketplace Research

Sometimes, you need to go right to the source for the best information.

Websites such as Amazon, AliExpress and eBay understand this and offer detailed bestseller lists where products are ranked in order of sales figures④.

In Amazon's case, their page is updated every single hour, giving you a super-relevant snapshot of current buying trends. For eBay, here's an excellent, recently updated selection of top-selling products.

3.3　Google Trends

While this may seem like painting with broad strokes, Google Trends allows you to chart and determine how interested people are in buying certain products, or at least how interested they are in searching for them.

Let's say that you're aiming to run a store for children's clothing, and are considering branching out into footwear. You can use keywords such as "baby shoes" or "kids trainers", filtered as per your industry and location. This will help you understand how market interest in different products changes over time.

3.4　Start With What You Know

While we did say not to blindly trust⑤ your gut⑥, this one's a bit different.

Most of us are passionate⑦ about certain products already, whether it's part of a hobby⑧, an everyday skill we enjoy, or some other interest, we all have products that we're excited about and invested in.

---

① publication [ˌpʌblɪˈkeɪʃn] n. 出版物；公布，发表。
② familiarity [fəˌmɪliˈærəti] n. 熟悉度。
③ freelance [ˈfriːlɑːns] adj. 自由职业的，兼职的。
④ figure [ˈfɪɡə] n. 数字；位数。
⑤ blindly trust：盲目相信。
⑥ gut [ɡʌt] n. 直觉；adj. 本能的，直觉的。
⑦ passionate [ˈpæʃənət] adj. 热情的。
⑧ hobby [ˈhɒbi] n. 业余爱好。

By taking a serious look at products in your personal favorite niches，you benefit from：

（1）Understanding the difference between a good manufacturer and a bad one.

（2）Complete sympathy① and understanding between you and your target audience.

Excitement②！E-commerce is challenging，and being passionate about your product is a good way to stay invested in the game.

Text A 参考译文

电子商务网站设计

设计一个电子商务网站不是仅仅建立一个销售产品的网站，而是设计一种愉快的在线购物体验。

1 为信任和安全设计电子商务

首先，设计一个让顾客感到可以信任的网站非常重要。大多数顾客担心隐私以及该网站是否会通过提供安全交易保护他们的个人数据。如果感觉网站不值得信任，他们只会选择去别处购物。以下是一些传达可信度的方法：

- 包括业务概述。提供一般信息、联系信息、社交媒体链接和常见问题（FAQ）页面。
- 发布门店政策并确保它们不太难找到。提供货运和退货政策，概述退货流程和可以退货的产品，并提供能够轻松访问涵盖顾客个人和财务信息的隐私政策（这一点至关重要）。
- 用通俗易懂的语言书写，避免使用法律或内部政策术语。
- 分享产品评论。提供产品评论，以帮助顾客更多地了解产品。这将有助于缓解他们可能怀有的担忧，并提供良好的电子商务用户体验。再进一步，提供带有评论人信息的产品评论，或者提供概要评论。这一步有助于让顾客更容易充分利用他人的意见。
- 使用安全的服务器。顾客希望他们在网上购物时个人信息能够确保安全。SSL（安全套接层）证书验证网站的身份，并加密需要保持安全的信息。这是表明结账安全的重要标志。通过实施 SSL 和显示 SSL 证书徽章向顾客保证他们的数据是受到保护的。

2 电子商务用户界面设计注意事项

网站的外观和感觉是第一印象的主要驱动力。研究表明，人们将在 50 毫秒内决定他们是否喜欢一个网站。

---

① sympathy [ˈsɪmpəθi] n. 支持，赞同，同情。

② excitement [ɪkˈsaɪtmənt] n. 兴奋，刺激；令人兴奋/激动的事。

以下是 UI 设计的一些基本技巧：

- 遵循品牌标识。品牌应该在整个网站上都很明显。选择反映品牌的颜色，并设定风格，以明确销售的产品类型。确保所有渠道的品牌体验一致，无论是在线上、店内还是在移动设备上。这将有助于建立强大的品牌客户关系。
- 采用视觉层次结构。最关键的内容应显示在首屏。在某些情况下，使用较少的空白将项目放在一起比将关键内容放在首屏下面要好。
- 不要过度设计。限制字体格式，如字体、大小和颜色。当文本看起来太像图形时，它会被误认为是广告。使用高对比度文本和背景色使内容尽可能清晰。
- 坚持使用已知的符号。使用易于识别的图标或符号。不熟悉的图标只会让顾客感到困惑。
- 避免弹出窗口。弹出窗口会分散注意力。

3　无障碍电子商务网站导航的重要性

3.1　定义明确的产品类别

顶级导航应该显示网站提供的类别集。将产品分为有意义的类别和子类别。用描述产品范围的单个单词做类别标签最适合，这样顾客可以浏览它们并立即理解其所代表的内容。最好尽可能多地对网站导航进行用户测试，以获得出色的电子商务用户体验，因为它是网站成败的关键功能。

3.2　产品搜索

简单地说，如果顾客找不到产品就无法购买产品。因此，请采取以下措施构建一个搜索功能，帮助他们轻松找到要寻找的内容：

- 让搜索无处不在。将搜索框放在每个页面和熟悉的位置。搜索框应该是可见的、可快速识别的和易于使用的。放置搜索框的标准位置是页面的右上角或顶部中间，也可以放在主菜单上。
- 支持各种查询。搜索需要支持所有类型的查询，例如产品名称、类别和产品属性，以及与客户服务相关的信息。最好在输入字段中包含一个搜索查询示例，以向顾客标明各种功能的使用。
- 具有搜索自动完成功能。该使顾客更容易找到他们想要的东西，并通过在他们已经搜索的区域内提出购买建议以提升销售潜力。
- 允许对结果进行排序和筛选。让顾客根据各种标准（畅销、最高或最低价格、产品评级、最新商品等）对搜索结果进行排序，并删除不属于特定类别的商品。见图 3-1。

3.3　过滤产品

选项越多，就越难选择。通过使用过滤器帮助顾客找到合适的产品。这将帮助他们缩小选择范围，直接跳转到他们想要的产品范围。

3.4　产品快速浏览

快速浏览通过消除不必要的页面加载，减少了顾客找到合适产品所需的时间。通常，产品详细信息显示在查看页面的模态窗口中。不要试图显示所有产品的详细信息，而是包括一个指向完整产品页面的链接，以查看完整的详细信息。此外，一定要在显眼的位置放置"添加到购物车"按钮以及"保存到愿望列表"功能。见图3-2。

3.5　特别优惠

顾客总是寻找特价、折扣或最优惠的商品。显示独家优惠，以便顾客了解它们。即使价格差异不是那么大，省钱的心理感觉也会产生一种占便宜的错觉。

4　电子商务产品页面设计

设计一个产品页面，通过包含大量图像、详细产品描述以及该产品的任何其他有用和相关信息，尽可能提供类似于亲身购物的体验。让我们深入看看这意味着什么。

4.1　提供出色的产品图像

在电子商务中，顾客无法触摸、感受或试用产品。相反，一切都取决于他们在网上看到了什么。这就是为什么提供清晰展示产品各个方面的产品图像至关重要的原因。见图3-3。以下是完美产品图像的清单：

- 使用白色背景。产品图像的背景不应分散注意力或与产品本身冲突。白色背景效果最好，因为它可以让产品脱颖而出，并且几乎适用于任何风格或配色方案。
- 使用高质量的大图像。好的图像有助于销售产品。高质量的图像能够引起顾客的兴趣，并准确地展示他们要购买的东西。拥有大图像可以让顾客放大并仔细检查产品。见图3-4。
- 使用多种图像。从多个不同的角度展示产品，包括特写镜头，以提供更完整的产品感受。360°视野是一种很好的方式，顾客可以在这里移动产品，它提供近似于亲临实体店并与产品互动的体验。虚拟现实电子商务是这种体验的下一波浪潮。
- 使用视频。视频能够在短时间内传递大量信息。使用视频展示正在使用的产品，并提供尽可能多的功能信息。
- 保持一致。使用在多个页面上一致的图像，并且要与网站其他部分的外观和感觉一致。这将使一切看起来干净整洁。网站所有区域的主要产品图像都应该相同，例如产品亮点或特色项目部分。

4.2　提供适量的产品信息

向顾客提供有关产品的详细信息，以便他们做出明智的购买决定。显示可用性、不同尺寸或颜色的选项、尺寸、尺码表、使用的材料、总成本、保修等。他们对产品的剩余问题越少，购买产品的可能性就越大。见图3-5。

4.3　展示相关产品和推荐产品

展示顾客可能也喜欢的类似产品，或其他人已经购买的产品。这可以显示在产品详细信息页面或购物车中，有助于引导顾客找到满足他们需求的产品，可能会鼓励他们继续购物——这是交叉销售相关产品的一个非常好的方法。

5　购物车设计

购物车是必不可少的,因为它是顾客查看所选产品、做出最终决定并进行结账的地方。购物车的主要目标是引导顾客结账。以下是设计一个用户友好的购物车的技巧,这将鼓励顾客进一步购物。

- 使用明确的行动召唤(CTA)。购物车页面上的主要行动召唤应该是结账按钮。使用明亮的颜色、大量可点击的区域和简单的语言,使结账按钮可见、直观且易于使用。
- 提供充分的反馈。确保当一个产品被添加到购物车时,它立即得到了明确的确认。顾客会因为反馈不足而感到困惑,比如显示的确认文本不显眼。一个好办法是使用动画,因为运动会吸引人的眼球。
- 使用迷你购物车小部件。允许顾客使用迷你购物车在不离开页面的情况下将产品添加到购物车中。它还允许他们导航、发现和添加更多产品。迷你购物车小部件应始终链接到整页购物车。
- 显示产品详细信息。在购物车中显示产品名称、图像、尺寸、颜色和价格等详细信息有助于顾客记住每种产品以及比较产品。将购物车中的产品链接到完整的产品页面,以便顾客在必要时查看更多详细信息。
- 使购物车易于编辑。使顾客容易使用删除、保存或更改尺寸、颜色或数量等细节的功能。
- 避免意外的运输成本和税费。意想不到的运输成本是顾客放弃购物车的主要原因之一。应预先告知运输选项和具有精确成本计算的税费以及预期的交货日期。

6　电子商务结账设计

以下是构建设计良好的结账页面的几种方法,这将有助于成功转换:

- 提供多种付款方式。不同的顾客在付款时有不同的偏好。提供尽可能多的支付选项(视目标受众而定),以扩大客户群,并使顾客更容易完成订单。
- 把事情简单化。尽可能减少完成购买的字段和步骤数量。默认情况下,使用收货地址作为账单地址是减少字段数量的好方法。理想情况下,单独设计一个结账页面,顾客可以在其中查看购物车并输入交货和付款信息。
- 将注册设置为可选。强迫顾客在第一次购买之前创建一个账户将会赶走顾客。应该让他们在购买完成后选择注册,并在要求他们注册时强调注册的好处。这些好处包括:由于保存了收货地址或付款信息等个人信息,所以结账更快,并能获得仅限注册会员享有的独家优惠。
- 使用清晰的错误指示。没有什么比无法购买或很费劲地弄清楚原因更令人沮丧的了。不要在提交表单后显示错误,而是实时显示错误通知。将清晰、简洁的错误信息直接放在需要更正的商品上方或旁边,以便顾客注意并理解它们。
- 让人们走上正轨。当使用多页结账时,包括一个进度条,显示完成购买还剩下多少步骤。这将消除任何模棱两可之处,并确保顾客走上正确的道路。采购完成后,显示订单确认和订单状态以及发货跟踪信息。

- 提供支持。在结账过程中加入实时聊天或联系电话,这样当顾客有问题时,他们就可以快速得到答案,而不必离开网站去其他地方。

7　总结

所有在线顾客都期待无障碍的体验。在设计一个电子商务网站时,不是仅仅建立一个网站,而是创造一种在线购物体验,将被动顾客转化为付费顾客。

Unit 4

Text A

E-commerce Customer Service

Electronic commerce, or e-commerce, is a business model that lets businesses and consumers make purchases or sell things online.

1   E-commerce Customer Service

E-commerce customer service is a strategy for providing customer service to people who purchase from online businesses. Online shopping is different from in-person shopping in a lot of ways, but both kinds of customers need an easy avenue for seeking assistance. Customers who have to wait too long for answers can very easily close your tab and move on to another option.

The best e-commerce customer support experiences are fast, positive, and conclude with the successful delivery of whatever assistance needed.

2   The Importance of Investing in E-commerce Customer Service

Providing a great customer experience is one of the few ways to genuinely stand out in an already saturated online retail marketplace. Customers who don't get the service they'd prefer can simply take their business to another store.

Customer service for e-commerce is all about responsiveness. The moment your customer has an issue with your product or service, your business needs to be able to step up and help resolve it. To do that, the customer needs three things:

* They need to know where to find assistance from your business.
* The assistance needs to be fast and efficient.
* The experience needs to be positive.

3   The Benefits of Providing E-commerce Support Services

* An increase in customer acquisition. Online shopping provides a wealth of options. This can easily become overwhelming, especially if the product or service in question is complicated and requires many touchpoints in order to close a sale.

    Customer service for e-commerce allows your business to provide fast, comprehensive assistance to leads from the very beginning of the relationship. By having a system of support established from the get-go，you increase your chances of catching those customers who otherwise would have let their confusion drive them to start their shopping venture over with a new search.

- Higher customer retention. Having a fast，efficient customer support service is critical to maintaining customer loyalty. Customer service is a cornerstone to customer retention and brand loyalty.

  No matter what issues customers may have along their customer journey，offering the proper assistance ensures that the customer's experience remains positive. Because a single negative interaction—whether it involves waiting too long for an answer or resolution，encountering too many confusions during the process，or interacting with an unpleasant representative—can be enough to drive a valuable customer away forever.

- More attentive customer service. E-commerce customer service involves technology. While some business owners may be hesitant to make technology a more prevalent player in their operations，the truth is that there's a reason software tools are so popular.

  E-commerce support services tools save enormous amounts of time when handling customer service activities. And the hours saved by letting software tools organize your processes and handle repetitive tasks can be allocated to providing even more personalized，attentive care to customers.

4　The Difference Between E-commerce Customer Service and Retail Customer Service

Since the experience of online shopping has some fundamental differences to brick and mortar stores，online retailers must approach customer service slightly differently. One of the key differences involves customer context.

When a shopper enters a store，a clerk or customer service agent can begin to identify some things that will help them decide how to provide support. Is the customer in a hurry? Does the customer appear to be in a good mood? Do they look determined to buy something or are they just killing time while they wait for someone?

Having a sense of some of these bits of information will inform retailers how to best provide service. They can read body language to see what kind of mood a shopper is in，which might determine whether a customer service agent offers help or leaves the shopper alone. But online shopping doesn't give you the benefit of these types of visual clues and interpersonal relationships. E-commerce shoppers still require the same kind of assistance they'd get in a store—the difference is in how the customer service agents observe，analyze，and respond to those needs virtually.

In e-commerce customer support, context comes in the form of data, not visual observations or personal interactions. This information, gathered from whatever connected platform your customers are using to interact with your business, gives you insights into how you can provide better experiences.

5　Best Practices for Effective E-commerce Customer Service

- Offer multi channel support[①]. Different channels have different strengths and weaknesses. Measuring how customers use each channel will allow retailers to take full advantage. They might prefer direct support via chat or a chatbot, but communication (like new offerings or sales) might be better through social media.

- Personalize support and marketing. Since all activities, from browsing to buying to customer service, happen online, it's possible to track and measure customer behavior. That means when a customer reaches for support, the support agent will already have access to information about the customer, including purchase history, which will allow the agent to treat the customer like a valued individual.

- Offer self-service support. Since many customers prefer to help themselves, many online retailers benefit from offering a help center. These can include answers to frequently asked questions (FAQs), return policies[②], and more. Offering self-sufficiency as a form of customer service is a fantastic way of empowering customers to assist themselves while saving your team time.

- Use the right organizational tools. There's only so much that can be done with spreadsheets and emails. Managing your e-commerce customer support system will have to include some kind of technology tools that are designed for all of the different administrative tasks involved. Otherwise, a task as simple as retrieving an invoice could become a five-minute search if the document is lingering in someone's inbox.

- Offer a way for feedback. Letting customers offer their feedback helps to identify where customer frustrations are. You can fix solutions internally so the same issue doesn't happen again, and reach out to the customer to solve the issue—if that's still an option. Reviews are also great social proof that illustrate specific examples of when your customer service delivered as promised.

---

①　Multi-channel support is providing different methods of communication for your customers to reach you. This can include (but is not limited to) email, phone, chat, social media, knowledge base, etc. Some clients enjoy the rapid response from live chat software, others will prefer to find the answers themselves via a knowledge base.

②　Return policies are the rules a retailer creates to manage how customers return and exchange unwanted merchandise they purchased. A return policy tells customers what items can be returned and for what reasons, as well as the timeframe over which returns are accepted.

- Develop a need for speed. According to a study by Statista，12% of respondents cited lack of speed as the cause of their frustration. That means you should always be examining your current practices to see where response time is lagging，and do your best to adjust your process and eliminate those wasted minutes.

- Templates. The same issues and questions will arise again and again，which means you'll be continually supplying the same answers or resolutions. But starting from scratch for every interaction eats up valuable time. Templates for emails and call scripts allow you to standardize a response to the most common issues，while still leaving room for personalization to ensure that the communication applies directly to the customer in question.

- Have a comprehensive knowledge base. A knowledge base is like a library of information for your customers. Knowledge bases should be well organized so that they're easy to search，and the content should be clear enough for all users to follow and implement successfully，without having to reach out for help.

- Automate where it makes sense. Automation saves enormous amounts of time and effort，allowing your team to be more efficient with the tasks that really matter. Examine your process and pinpoint tasks that are eating up too much time. Very often，there are many administrative tasks that could be automated with the right software，saving your team tons of time down the road.

6　E-commerce Customer Service Automation

- Self-service widgets. These widgets live on your home page and serve as a point of entry to your help desk. It's the equivalent of having a retail support member approach you in the store and say，"I'll be over there if you need me."

- Auto responders. You can save your customer service team a lot of time by setting up autoresponders. If a customer sends a message with an inquiry about something like cancellations，refunds，or how to use your product，the automation tool identifies specific words in the message and sends an automatic response detailing the proper steps for the customer to take.

- Chatbots. Chatbots are conversational commerce tools transforming how online retailers are crafting customer experiences. These automated bots scan and interpret incoming messages，then simulate human conversation in order to assist online customers. They can be used to help direct visitors to their desired product，solve common customer issues，or gather the relevant information needed before passing them to a live representative.

7　The Most Common Customer Service Issues in E-commerce

- Checkout process is long or complicated.

- Customer service doesn't operate outside of regular business hours.
- It's difficult to track orders.
- Desired item is out of stock.
- The mobile app isn't user-friendly.
- The return process is confusing or unclear.

New Words

strategy	['strætədʒi]	n. 策略;部署
avenue	['ævənjuː]	n. 方法,途径
assistance	[ə'sɪstəns]	n. 帮助;辅助;支持
saturate	['sætʃəreɪt]	v. 使充满,使饱和
responsiveness	[rɪ'spɒnsɪvnəs]	n. 响应性
acquisition	[ˌækwɪ'zɪʃn]	n. 收购;获得;购得物
comprehensive	[ˌkɒmprɪ'hensɪv]	adj. 全面的;综合性的
loyalty	['lɔɪəlti]	n. 忠诚,忠实
cornerstone	['kɔːnəstəʊn]	n. 基石,基础
interaction	[ˌɪntər'ækʃn]	n. 互相影响;互动
unpleasant	[ʌn'pleznt]	adj. 使人不愉快的;讨厌的;不客气的
valuable	['væljuəbl]	adj. 有价值的;宝贵的
attentive	[ə'tentɪv]	adj. 周到的,殷勤的
prevalent	['prevələnt]	adj. 流行的,盛行的;普遍存在的,普遍发生的
enormous	[ɪ'nɔːməs]	adj. 巨大的;极大的
repetitive	[rɪ'petətɪv]	adj. 重复的,啰嗦的
clerk	[klɑːk]	n. 接待员,店员
agent	['eɪdʒənt]	n. 代理人;代理商;代表;经纪人
mood	[muːd]	n. 情绪;语气
platform	['plætfɔːm]	n. 平台
chatbot	[tʃætbɒt]	n. 聊天机器人
personalize	['pɜːsənəlaɪz]	vt. 个性化
activity	[æk'tɪvəti]	n. 活动,行动
browse	[braʊz]	v. (在商店里)随便看;浏览
treat	[triːt]	v. 对待,处理
self-service	['self 'sɜːvɪs]	adj. 自我服务的;(商店)自选的;(饭店)自助的
self-sufficiency	[ˌself sə'fɪʃnsi]	n. 自给自足;自立
fantastic	[fæn'tæstɪk]	adj. 极好的;极大的;奇异的
organizational	[ˌɔːgənaɪ'zeɪʃənl]	adj. 组织的

frustration	[frʌ'streɪʃn]	n. 沮丧,挫折,失败
respondent	[rɪ'spɒndənt]	n. 响应
lag	[læg]	vi. 滞后,落后
template	['templeɪt]	n. 模板;样板
call	[kɔːl]	v. 调用
script	[skrɪpt]	n. 脚本
standardize	['stændədaɪz]	vt. 使…标准化
personalization	['pɜːsənəlaɪzeɪʃn]	n. 个性化
automate	['ɔːtəmeɪt]	v. 使自动化
pinpoint	['pɪnpɔɪnt]	vt. 确定
cancellation	[ˌkænsə'leɪʃn]	n. 取消,撤销;作废
conversational	[ˌkɒnvə'seɪʃənl]	adj. 会话的,对话的
gather	['gæðə]	v. 收集,搜集

Phrases

customer service	客户服务
online retail marketplace	网上零售市场,在线零售市场
step up	行动起来;(使…)增加;(使…)加快速度
a wealth of	大量的,丰富的
brick and mortar store	实体店
body language	身体语言,肢体语言
interpersonal relationship	人际关系
multi channel support	多渠道支持
customer behavior	客户行为
purchase history	购买历史记录
return policy	退货政策
social proof	社会证明
response time	响应时间
again and again	再三地,反复地
eat up	耗尽,吃光
knowledge base	知识库
home page	主页
auto responder	自动应答器
live representative	现场代表

Exercises

【Ex1】 Answer the following questions according to the text.

1. What is e-commerce customer service?

2. What do your business need to do the moment your customer has an issue with your product or service?

3. What are the benefits of providing e-commerce support services?

4. How do you increase your chances of catching those customers who otherwise would have let their confusion drive them to start their shopping venture over with a new search?

5. What can the hours saved by letting software tools organize your processes and handle repetitive tasks be allocated to?

6. Why must online retailers approach customer service slightly differently?

7. Why is it possible to track and measure customer behavior?

8. What do templates for emails and call scripts allow you to do?

9. What are chatbots?

10. What are the most common customer service issues in e-commerce?

【Ex2】 Translate the following terms or phrases from English into Chinese or vice versa.

1. customer service   1. _____

2. brick and mortar store   2. _____

3. knowledge base   3. _____

4. customer behavior   4. _____

5. return policy   5. _____

6. *v.*(在商店里)随便看;浏览   6. _____

7. *n.*聊天机器人   7. _____

8. *n.*个性化   8. _____

9. *n.*脚本   9. _____

10. *n.*模板;样板   10. _____

【Ex3】 Fill in the blanks with the words given below.

convenient	mobile	logistics	brands	expectations
browse	gateways	engaged	personal	seamless

Five Online Consumer Behaviors and Shopping Trends

1 Convenience is a top priority

According to Linnworks' study, 76% of consumers value convenience as one of their top priorities.

One of the primary things consumers find convenient is the ability to ____1____ an online store and check out as a guest. In addition, the fewer forms consumers have to complete, the more ____2____ and better they find their overall customer buying journey (and the more likely they are to return).

2　Easy access across all devices

81% of online shoppers seek a _____3_____ transfer between devices throughout a buying journey. In fact，the expectation is now that consumers can begin a buying journey on one device，such as a desktop，and end on another，like their ___4___ device—without interruption.

This cross-device experience is also expected to include checkouts with ___5___ details already completed on whichever device customers finalize their buying journey (even if they filled in these details on a different device).

3　Access to omnichannel shopping

With access to multiple technology options，consumers are ___6___ in an "always-on" shopping experience. 70% of consumers now shop while multitasking (for example，while scrolling social media platforms). And they've come to expect that their favorite ___7___ are on the same channels where they spend the majority of their time.

This maximizes convenience by ensuring they never have to leave their favorite and trusted platforms during the buying process.

4　Effortless payment

When retailers are considering tips to keep up with consumer ___8___ and behaviors，it's essential to focus on every aspect of the customer experience.

Consumers seek convenience throughout the entire buying journey. They look to discover e-commerce online shops that have easy-to-setup payment ___9___ that also accept popular payment methods—such as "buy now，pay later".

5　Fast and reliable delivery

95% of consumers feel that fast delivery options are a must-have factor when shopping ___10___ . That's why ShipBob offers fast 2-day shipping and has a dispersed network of logistics centers to split inventory across to help reduce shipping costs，speed up delivery times，and meet customer expectations.

【Ex4】 Translate the following passage from English into Chinese.

The Benefits of a Knowledge Base

1　The quickest way to answer queries

If you're using e-commerce help desk software，you'll be able to resolve queries in the shortest time possible，but sometimes even this isn't enough. Perhaps you're in the middle of a sales rush，with orders flying in left right and center，or your support team are dealing with some particularly tricky tickets.

This is when a knowledge base can really help you out.

2　Allow your customers to help themselves

It's long been an assumption that excellent customer service requires a human touch. Perhaps it's the digital nature of e-commerce，or maybe the majority of today's consumers are simply less social. Whatever the reason, it's clear that many of your customers would prefer to use a knowledge base than deal with customer support agents.

If you give the people what they want, you'll be improving their customer experience and this will translate into business success.

3 Always provide accurate, reliable information

A knowledge base does not only make life easier for your support agents but also eliminates the chance of customers receiving incorrect, or incomplete answers to questions.

With a knowledge base, you can ensure that the information provided is always accurate and clearly articulated.

It's difficult to align your brand with customer support communications from different agents, but with a knowledge base, this aspirations becomes a reality.

4 Help to minimise support costs

The phrase 'time is money' is certainly relevant for a customer support team. If you're making more sales, you're going to get more tickets, no matter how good your products or fulfillment services are. Help desk software with an effective knowledge base is probably the only way you'll be able to manage, without hiring extra staff.

Text B

Mobile E-commerce

With the rapid development of technology, mobile e-commerce emerges as a hot trend of e-commerce. Customers are more likely to get used to shopping online, from their comfort zone. mobile e-commerce and e-commerce have interlinked relations with each other. While e-commerce serves the main function as selling and buying online, mobile e-commerce is a subcategory of e-commerce that mainly focus on purchasing via mobile devices.

1 Mobile E-commerce Basics

Mobile e-commerce (also known as m-commerce) is a business model that enables companies and individuals to deliver goods and services directly to buyers through devices such as mobile phones, smartphones, or tablets.

This type of business is growing fast in the global stage since it provides instant connection between mobile users irrespective of their geographical location and time of the day. What's more, the demand for using wireless and mobile devices is increasing at a significant rate, which means mobile e-commerce has the potential to reach various customers.

Generally speaking, mobile e-commerce is a natural progression of e-commerce.

Types of mobile e-commerce：

- Browsing for stuff online on your mobile：this type is concerned with internet shopping for groceries, daily necessaries, and electronics. Dedicated apps, optimized websites, or even social media platforms allow in-app purchases or store links.
- Purchasing app-delivery stuff：this type deals with services such as food shipping, car pick up, and others.
- Mobile banking：Mobile banking is a means of employing internet techniques to gain access to a bank's capabilities. Although several financial services organizations are currently experimenting with chatbots or messaging apps to give customer care, the transactions are completed through special apps built by apps.
- Mobile app payments：Google Pay and PayPal are the best examples of this type. It mainly focuses on making payment transactions through apps. Users will be required to register their credit or debit card and then use it whenever they want. WeChat Pay is an online payment service developed by Tencent Holdings Limited, the parent company of WeChat. It is one of the most popular digital wallets in China, allowing users to send and receive payments electronically.
- Purchasing or renting digital content（Netflix, Spotify, etc）on a mobile device：Buying or renting online services is involved in this type.

2　Differences Between Mobile E-commerce and E-commerce

2.1　Mobility

Thanks to the advanced development of mobile connectivity, security, and apps development, retailers are allowed to offer services, products, and payments right over their mobile phones. Back in the good old days, customers had to open their desktop devices to shop online. But with mobile e-commerce, things get easier as they only have to do it straight on their mobile phone. As long as there is an Internet connection and an Internet-ready device, customers are able to shop, browse, pay, bank, make a purchase, and many more things.

Today, the appearance of many mobile payment wallets such as Apple Pay or Airpay also give customers the flexibility to make transactions on the spot.

2.2　Security

Transactions at e-commerce platforms are often done by credit cards, but this type of payment may put customer financial safety at risk. In addition, the security provided by a username and password of e-commerce accounts is not safe either. In contrast, in mobile e-commerce, customers can guarantee their safety by their biometric authentication such as scans, face ID, or fingerprints. Therefore, the possibility of leaking personal information may be lessened.

2.3 Additional Data, Additional Marketing

More devices access to your business. It means you'll have more data, which is good for marketing and brand growth. It does offer some benefits as follows:

- Increase personalization: Once you receive more data, you will have a better foundation on what your customers need and you can then give them what they want. As a result, if you give them a personalized shopping experience, they are more likely to be turned into potential customers and come back to your site to make a purchase.
- More marketing touch points: mobile e-commerce allows your business to have another chance to impress customers; marketers can customize their mobile marketing to reassure that it gives consumers the best experience. The more times customers access your site, the higher possibility of getting more leads and sales are.
- Increase loyalty and customer retention: mobile e-commerce allows you to increase customer engagement by providing a new client touch point that can include exclusive benefits like mobile-only discounts, special prices for registered consumers, free shipping, and more.

2.4 Location Tracking

E-commerce shoppers are tracked by the IP address on computers which gives a loose indication of the location of buyers and it is also limited in terms of locational advertising strategies. On the other hand, mobile e-commerce apps track and identify buyer locations by GPS technology, WiFi, etc., which is a good way to create location-specific content and personalized recommendations.

2.5 Push Notifications

Using push notifications is such a good way to communicate and reach the right customer at the right time. First, when push notifications appear on the site, it reminds customers about your brand and raises brand awareness as well. Besides, businesses are able to reach many new visitors and convert them into paying customers.

3 Advantages of Mobile E-commerce

3.1 Having Better Customer Insights

As I mentioned above, mobile e-commerce with mobile apps enables retailers to collect information about their buyers. Mobile apps track customer data on their age, gender, location, and even their shopping history so it sets a firm foundation on how businesses will target their audience in a very effective way which boosts sales. Customer shopping behaviors and patterns, frequency, and personas all contribute to the effort of improving customer insight of business.

3.2 Providing Convenience

With some touch on the screen, customers get it easily with browsing, swiping, and placing orders. They can comfortably shop anywhere and anytime since they don't need to go to stores but stay at home, add products to their shopping carts, and access thousands of items from hundreds of retailers.

3.3 Improving Shopping Experience

The key element in business is to keep customers coming back constantly. Mobile e-commerce definitely knows how to enhance the customer experience by using personalization in the forms of product listings or offers. Businesses can enhance customer shopping experience by using a combination of mobile apps, analytics, and location information on a mobile e-commerce ecosystem.

3.4 Reducing ads-budget

In order to raise brand awareness as well as promote products in e-commerce, marketers have to spend a bunch of money on ad placements. In contrast, spending on ads is reduced in mobile e-commerce. Businesses can make direct connections to their customers by mobile app or push notifications.

New Words

comfort	['kʌmfət]	n. 舒适
subcategory	[sʌb'kætɪgərɪ]	n. 子类,亚类
smartphone	['smɑːrtfoʊn]	n. 智能手机
irrespective	[ɪrɪ'spektɪv]	adj. 无关的;不考虑的,不顾的
wireless	['waɪələs]	adj. 无线的
progression	[prə'greʃn]	n. 发展,进展
register	['redʒɪstə]	v. 登记;注册
mobility	[məʊ'bɪləti]	n. 移动性;流动性
connectivity	[ˌkɒnek'tɪvɪti]	n. 连通性
username	['juːzəneɪm]	n. 用户名
fingerprint	['fɪŋgəprɪnt]	n. 指纹,指印
retention	[rɪ'tenʃn]	n. 保留,保持
engagement	[ɪn'geɪdʒmənt]	n. 参与
boost	[buːst]	v. 使…增长,推动;增强,提高
convenience	[kən'viːniəns]	n. 方便
ecosystem	['iːkəʊsɪstəm]	n. 生态系统

Phrases

mobile e-commerce	移动电子商务
instant connection	即时连接
geographical location	地理位置
mobile banking	移动银行
digital content	数字内容
on the spot	立刻，当场
biometric authentication	生物识别认证
personal information	个人信息
free shipping	免运费
location tracking	位置跟踪，位置追踪
push notification	推送通知
contribute to	促成；有助于
shopping experience	购物体验
a combination of ...	…的组合
a bunch of	大量；一束；一群
ad placement	广告投放

Abbreviations

ID（IDentity）	身份标识号码
IP（Internet Protocol）	网际互联协议
GPS（Global Position System）	全球定位系统

Exercises

[Ex5] **Fill in the blanks with the information given in the text.**

1. Mobile e-commerce，also known as _____ is a business model that enables companies and individuals to deliver _____ directly to buyers through _____ devices such as mobile phones，_____, or tablets.

2. Browsing for stuff online on your mobile：this type is concerned with internet shopping for _____, _____, and _____.

3. Mobile banking is a means of _____ to gain access to _____. Although several financial services organizations are currently experimenting with chatbots or messaging apps to _____, the transactions are completed through _____.

4. Thanks to the advanced development of _____, _____, and _____, retailers are allowed to offer services，_____, and payments right over their _____.

5. Transactions at e-commerce platforms are often done by _____, but this type of payment may put _____ at risk. In addition，the security provided by _____ and

password of _____ is not safe either.

6. Once you receive more data，you will have a better foundation on _____ and you can then give them _____. As a result，if you give them _____，they are more likely to be turned into _____ and come back to your site to _____.

7. Mobile e-commerce allows you to _____ by providing a new client touch point that can include exclusive benefits like _____，special prices for _____，_____，and more.

8. E-commerce shoppers are tracked by _____ on computers which gives a loose indication of _____ and it is also limited in terms of _____.

9. Mobile e-commerce with mobile apps enables retailers to _____ about their buyers. Mobile apps track customer data on _____，gender，location，and even _____ so it sets a firm foundation on how businesses will _____ in a very effective way which boosts sales.

10. The key element in business is to _____. Mobile e-commerce definitely knows how to enhance _____ by using personalization in the forms of _____ or offers.

【Ex6】 **Translate the following terms or phrases from English into Chinese or vice versa.**

1. shopping experience   1. _____

2. mobile e-commerce   2. _____

3. push notification   3. _____

4. free shipping   4. _____

5. mobile banking   5. _____

6. *n.* 移动性；流动性   6. _____

7. *v.* 登记；注册   7. _____

8. *n.* 用户名   8. _____

9. *n.* 生态系统   9. _____

10. *n.* 方便   10. _____

Reading Material

What Is E-commerce CRM and Why Do You Need One?

1 Why Is CRM the Key to a Successful E-commerce Business?

Once you open an online business，you immediately realize that your competition is right next to the corner，waiting for a wrong step from your side. Therefore，one of the biggest tools you can use to keep up with the competition's challenges is customer retention. Apart from offering top-notch products，you need to also offer a flawless[①] customer experience.

---

① flawless [ˈflɔːləs] *adj.* 完美的，无瑕的。

In the online world, the customer life cycle is a lot faster, which means that you should put bigger efforts than in the traditional commerce. So, this is where e-commerce CRM comes into play.

2　What Is an E-commerce CRM?

First, CRM comes from customer relationship management. This software helps you to store relevant data about your current customers as well as prospect information. The greatest thing about it is that all the information is stored in one location. Therefore, CRM helps you to have an overview of your business operations and also helps you to determine potential sales opportunities. For an e-commerce business where things are developing very fast, CRM is a goldmine①. It helps all business owners to organize all the information related to customer interaction.

Some of the biggest advantages e-commerce CRM brings to businesses are as follows:

- It helps you discover and attract② new buyers.
- It gives you relevant information on the current customers and helps you to develop loyalty programs.
- You are able to understand your customer's buying particularities better.
- You will have lower customer management costs.

3　Why Do You Need Special CRM for Your E-commerce Business?

Most probably you think you can use a regular out-of-the-box③ CRM to manage your e-commerce customers. Most CRMs out there were designed to manage B2B clients. These CRMs rely on sales reps④ to log information for each customer.

CRM will be able to collect customer data by integrating with your existing systems like your e-commerce website, track customer browsing behavior and compile a customer 360 view. And when you get loads of customer queries, it will route them to agents in the most efficient manner allowing you to make the most of your workforce.

CRM helps e-commerce business owners learn about their customers' behaviors. It will give you information on why your customers are buying your products and what they expect from your side. What is more, it helps you track their purchasing history and gives you valuable insights on what marketing strategy to apply to keep them loyal to your brand.

---

① goldmine ['gəʊldmaɪn] *n*. 金矿;财源;宝库。
② attract [ə'trækt] *v*. 吸引。
③ out-of-the-box:开箱即用的。
④ sales rep:销售代表,推销员。

3.1 Tracking customer history

Wouldn't it be great to have access to the entire history of your customers' buying trends and habits? Just think that you plan to launch a new product which should be targeted to a specific type of customers. How do you know to which category of clients you should send information about this new product? E-commerce CRM helps you analyze your customers' wishes and immediately understand whether they would react[①] positively to a new product launch or not. What is more, based on your customer history, you will also be able to determine what type of products you should launch next.

What is more, based on data that e-commerce CRM stores, you will be able to determine which were the best-sold products, during which periods of the year you had the biggest sales, or which were the prices that determined the biggest purchases in the past. Thus, you are able to bring again on the market some very popular products or create new ones which meet your customers' expectations in terms of price and characteristics.

3.2 Providing efficient team management

How can a customer relationship management tool help you effectively manage your sales teams? The way your customers behaves is directly connected to how you allocate your internal resources[②]. E-commerce CRM helps you divide your customers in different groups based on certain criteria. For instance, you can have premium customers[③] who always buy the most expensive products from your website.

In addition, you can also have a medium category of clients who are loyal to your brand and buy your products on a regular basis. Would you assign the same sales team to these two categories? Of course, not! E-commerce CRM helps you to be always service-ready and smartly allocate your key account managers to different categories of customers.

3.3 Personalizing your marketing strategy

According to a recent study, customers will become loyal to a brand when they feel that the messages they receive are tailored[④] for their needs and expectations. For example, by sending emails, where you mention their name and recommending products based on their purchasing history, you will have a huge positive impact on your customers.

The best way to collect data on past purchases and details about your customers is by

---

① react [ri'ækt] v. (作出)反应。
② internal resource：内部资源。
③ premium customer：优质客户,高级客户。
④ tailor ['teilə] v. 专门制作；订做。

implementing an e-commerce CRM system with your e-commerce platform. What is more，a CRM system will also tell more about the way your customers prefer to be contacted for new offers. Why send an email to a customer who prefers to receive details on new products vis SMS?

What is more，when you start developing your marketing strategy，you need many other details about your customers. For example，you will need to know more about demographics，location，or preferred price range. CRM stores all this data. Thus，you will have access to information 24/7 and you will be able to personalize your marketing strategy to different categories of customers and improve your response rate.

3.4　Expanding businesses

Every business owner dreams to expand his business one day. But when you are overwhelmed with gathering and analyzing data about your customers，plus many other business operations，it becomes difficult to think of expansion. One of the biggest advantages that e-commerce CRM puts on the table is that it saves time. You will have access to valuable data on existing and potential customers anytime you want，at one click distance. This can be translated in an increased productivity which automatically brings increased sales.

What is more，when you invest your resources in the right direction，then business expansion will not become too complicated. E-commerce CRM helps you to keep your promises towards your clients and strengthens① your brand position on the market. And when you know exactly what your customers are waiting for from your side，then it will be very easy to decide on which area you want to expand and which steps you need to follow to succeed.

Ultimately，e-commerce CRM can become an important tool for training your employees. When you know everything about your customers and understand how and why they make their decisions，it will become easier for you to train your employees on what their potential customers expect from them. This brings clarity in your business and makes your sales teams the best on the market.

Text A 参考译文

电子商务客户服务

电子商务(electronic commerce，简称 e-commerce)是一种商业模式，让企业和消费者在线购买或销售商品。

---

① strengthen ['streŋθn] *v.* 巩固；支持；壮大；加强。

1 电子商务客户服务

电子商务客户服务是一种为从网上企业购买商品的人提供客户服务的策略。网上购物在很多方面都不同于当面购物,但这两类客户都需要一个简单的途径来寻求帮助。当客户必须等很长时间才能得到答案时,他们可能很容易地关闭你的标签,转而选择其他商家。

最好的电子商务客户支持体验是快速、积极的,并能成功提供所需的任何帮助。

2 投资电子商务客户服务的重要性

在一个已经饱和的网上零售市场上,提供良好的客户体验是真正脱颖而出的几种方式之一。当客户没有得到他们喜欢的服务时就可能直接转到另一商店。

电子商务的客户服务都是响应性的。当客户对你的产品或服务有问题时,你的企业需要能够快速行动起来,帮助解决问题。为此,客户需要三件事:

- 他们需要知道在哪里可以获得你的帮助。
- 帮助需要快速有效。
- 这种体验必须是积极的。

3 提供电子商务支持服务的好处

- 客户获取的增加。网上购物提供了丰富的选择。这很容易让人不知所措,特别是在讨论的产品或服务很复杂并且需要多次接触才能完成销售的情况下。

  电子商务客户服务让企业从一开始就为潜在客户提供快速、全面的帮助。通过从一开始就建立支持系统,你就增加了抓住那些本来因为困惑而会通过新搜索重新开始购物的客户的机会。

- 客户保留率更高。拥有快速、高效的客户支持服务对于保持客户忠诚度至关重要。客户服务是保持客户和品牌忠诚度的基石。

  无论客户在购买中遇到什么问题,提供适当的帮助都可确保良好的客户体验。因为一次消极的互动——无论是等待答案或解决方案的时间太长,在过程中遇到太多困惑,还是与客服代表令人不快的互动——都足以永远赶走一位有价值的客户。

- 更周到的客户服务。电子商务客户服务涉及技术。虽然有些企业主可能不愿让技术更普遍地参与运营,但事实是,软件工具如此受欢迎是有原因的。

  电子商务支持服务工具在处理客户服务活动时节省了大量时间。让软件工具组织你的流程和处理重复性任务所节省的时间可以用于为客户提供更个性化、更周到的服务。

4 电子商务客户服务与零售客户服务的区别

由于网上购物的体验与实体店有一些根本性的区别,因此网上零售商必须以略微不同的方式对待客户服务。其中一个关键区别涉及客户环境。

当购物者进入商店时,店员或客服代表可以开始识别某些东西,帮助他们决定如何提供支持。购物者赶时间吗?购物者看起来心情好吗?购物者看起来是下定决心要买东西还是只是消磨时间在等人？

　　了解其中一些信息将告诉零售商如何最好地提供服务。他们可以通过阅读肢体语言来了解购物者的情绪，这可能会决定客服代表是提供帮助还是让购物者独自一人逛逛。但是网上购物无法提供这些视觉线索和人际关系所带来的好处。电子商务客户仍然需要得到与在商店中购物时相同的帮助——区别在于客服代表如何观察、分析和虚拟地响应这些需求。

　　在电子商务客户支持中，情景以数据的形式出现，而不是视觉观察或个人互动。这些信息是从客户用于与你的业务互动的任何互联平台收集的，可以让你深入了解如何提供更好的体验。

5　有效电子商务客户服务的最佳实践

- 提供多渠道支持。不同的渠道有不同的优势和劣势。衡量客户如何使用每个渠道将使零售商能够充分利用这个优势。他们可能更喜欢通过聊天或聊天机器人获得直接支持，但通过社交媒体进行沟通（如新产品或销售）可能会更好。

- 个性化支持和营销。由于从浏览到购买再到客户服务的所有活动都是在网上进行的，因此可以跟踪和衡量客户的行为。这意味着，当客户寻求支持时，客服代表已经能够访问有关客户的信息，包括购买历史记录，这将使客服代表能够像对待重要人物一样对待客户。

- 提供自助服务支持。由于许多客户喜欢自助，许多在线零售商受益于提供帮助中心。其中可以包括对常见问题（FAQ）、退货政策等的解答。作为客户服务的一种形式，提供自给自足的服务是一种非常好的方式，可以让客户在自助的同时节省团队时间。

- 使用正确的组织工具。电子表格和电子邮件能做的事情就这么多了。管理电子商务客户支持系统必须包括一些针对所有不同管理任务而设计的技术工具。否则，如果文档在某人的收件箱中滞留，那么像检索发票这样简单的任务可能会变成五分钟的搜索。

- 提供反馈的途径。让客户提供反馈有助于确定客户的不满之处。你可以在内部修复解决方案，这样相同的问题就不会再次发生，并联系客户解决问题——如果这仍然是一个选项的话。评论也是很好的社会证明，可以举例说明何时按承诺提供客户服务。

- 培养对速度的需求。根据 Statista 的一项研究，12% 的受访者认为速度慢是他们感到沮丧的原因。这意味着你应该始终检查你目前的做法，找出响应时间滞后的地方，并尽最大努力调整流程，消除浪费的时间。

- 模板。同样的问题会一次又一次地出现，这意味着你会不断提供相同的答案或解决方案。但每次互动都从零开始会占用宝贵的时间。电子邮件和通话脚本模板允许你标准化地响应最常见的问题，同时仍可提供个性化服务，以确保与相关客户的直接沟通。

- 拥有全面的知识库。知识库就像是客户的信息库。知识库应该组织良好，以便易于搜索,内容应该足够清晰,以便所有客户都能遵循并成功实施,而无须寻求帮助。

- 在有意义的地方实现自动化。自动化节省了大量的时间和精力,使你的团队能够更高效地完成真正重要的任务。检查你的流程,找出占用太多时间的任务。通常,有许多管理任务可以通过正确的软件实现自动化,从而为团队节省大量时间。

6　电子商务客户服务自动化

- 自助服务小部件。这些小部件位于你的主页上,是服务台的入口。这相当于让一名零售支持成员在商店里走上前来,对你说:"如果你需要,我随叫随到。"
- 自动应答器。通过设置自动应答器,你可以为客户服务团队节省大量时间。如果客户发送信息询问取消、退款或如何使用你的产品,自动化工具会识别信息中的特定词语,并发送自动回复,详细说明客户应采取的正确步骤。
- 聊天机器人。聊天机器人是一种对话商务工具,它改变了在线零售商打造客户体验的方式。这些自动机器人扫描并解释传入的消息,然后模拟人类对话,以在线帮助客户。它们可以用来帮助客户找到他们想要的产品,解决常见的客户问题,或者在将信息传递给现场代表之前收集所需的相关信息。

7　电子商务中最常见的客户服务问题

- 结账过程漫长或复杂。
- 正常营业时间之外不提供客户服务。
- 很难追踪订单。
- 所需商品缺货。
- 移动应用程序对用户不友好。
- 退货流程混乱或不清楚。

Unit 5

Text A

Accepting Online Payments

For many small businesses，accepting payments online offers major benefits. Customers increasingly expect this facility and it can improve your cashflow significantly.

It's easy to accept cheques or invoices[①] for your online sales and to process payments in the traditional way. However，because buyers often use the Internet for a speedy service，most sales are paid for with credit and debit cards. To accept cards online，you will have to make special banking arrangements.

Online payments using cards are "card-not-present" transactions. There are higher risks of fraud with this type of payment and banks require you to operate within a well-defined set of rules and accept a higher level of commercial risk than a conventional swiped card transaction in a shop.

1 Online Payment Jargon

Debit and credit card[②] payments and their application online involve some key concepts and jargon.

1.1 Acquirers

An acquirer[③] can be a high street bank or other financial institution that offers credit and debit card accepting/processing services. It acquires the money from the customer，processes the transaction and credits your account.

1.2 Internet Merchant Accounts（IMAs）

You need to apply for a merchant service agreement if you want a bank to handle your electronic payments. For web-based online transactions you need an IMA.

---

① An invoice is a commercial document issued by a seller to the buyer，indicating the products，quantities，and agreed prices（定价）for products or services the seller has provided the buyer. An invoice indicates the buyer must pay the seller，according to the payment terms.

② A credit card is a small plastic card（塑料卡）issued to users as a system of payment. It allows its holder（持有人）to buy goods and services based on the holder's promise to pay for these goods and services.

③ An acquirer（or acquiring bank）is a member of a card association，for example MasterCard（万事达卡）and/or Visa（维萨卡），which maintains merchant relationships and receives all bankcard transactions from the merchant.

Obtaining an IMA from an acquirer may be quicker and easier if you already have "offline" card-processing facilities set up. In this case，just ask your acquirer for an additional IMA ID for use exclusively with Internet transactions. This process is normally quick，especially if the risk to your business does not change.

To help protect merchants and cardholders from fraud，the card schemes have developed a service that allows cardholders to authenticate themselves when shopping online.

1.3　Payment Service Providers（PSPs）[①]

A PSP will provide you with a "virtual" till or terminal that collects card details over the Internet and passes them to the acquiring bank. To take electronic payments over the web，you will need a PSP.

Your choice of PSP will depend on its cost and compatibility with your chosen e-commerce software solution. A fixed monthly fee starts at around ￡10，but there are some cheaper options available，starting as low as 5 pence per transaction. Usually，the higher your transaction volume the lower the rate you will be charged.

Some acquiring banks offer PSP services as part of their product and there are other less expensive options available.

2　Payment Card Industry Data Security Standard Compliance

The Payment Card Industry Data Security Standard（PCI DSS）is a worldwide security standard developed by the Payment Card Industry（PCI）[②] Security Standards Council to protect cardholder information，such as credit and debit card numbers and cardholders' personal details. It includes requirements for security management，network architecture，software design，security policies and procedures，and other protection of customer account data. The standard is applicable to any organisation that stores，transmits or processes cardholder information；be they a merchant，third-party processor or acquirer.

PCI DSS is a set of 6 principles that encompass 12 specific requirements. These

---

①　A payment service provider（PSP）offers merchants online services for accepting electronic payments by a variety of payment methods including credit card，bank-based payments such as <u>direct debit</u>（直接借记），<u>bank transfer</u>（银行转账），and real-time bank transfer based on online banking. Some PSPs provide unique services to process other next generation methods including cash payments，wallets such as PayPal，prepaid cards or <u>vouchers</u>（凭证，凭单），and even paper or e-check processing.

②　The payment card industry（PCI）denotes the debit，credit，prepaid，<u>e-purse</u>（电子钱包），ATM，and POS cards and associated businesses.

The term is sometimes more specifically used to refer to the Payment Card Industry Security Standards Council，an independent council originally formed by American Express，Discover Financial Services，JCB，MasterCard Worldwide and Visa International on Sept. 7，2006，with the goal of managing the ongoing evolution of the Payment Card Industry Data Security Standard.

requirements are equally applicable to any organisation holding personal information and are intended to reduce the organisation's risk of a data breach.

Principle 1: Build and maintain a secure network.

- install and maintain a firewall configuration to protect your cardholders' data.
- do not use vendor defaults for system passwords or other security actions.

Principle 2: Protect your cardholder data.

- protect any stored cardholder data.
- encrypt transmission of your cardholders' data across open, public networks.

Principle 3: Keep a vulnerability management plan.

- always use and regularly update your anti-virus software.
- develop and maintain secure systems and applications.

Principle 4: Implement strong access control practices.

- limit access to cardholder data to only those who need to know.
- give every person with computer access a unique ID.
- limit physical access to cardholder data.

Principle 5: Monitor and test your networks on a regular basis.

- track and monitor all access to your network resources and cardholder data.
- regularly test security systems and procedures

Principle 6: Keep an information security policy.

Always keep a policy that addresses your information security.

The PCI Security Standard Council encourages businesses that store payment data to comply with PCI DSS and become certified to help reduce financial risks from data compromises. However, it is the payment card schemes that manage the actual compliance programme. In practical terms this means the programme is managed by acquirers and you should check with your bank to seek advice on your specific compliance obligations and how your business can become certified.

Failure to be annually certified can become an issue if you have a security breach and your customers' card details are stolen, in which case penalties levied by the card schemes and costs can be heavy depending on the number of cards compromised. Even where a merchant is certified this does not protect them from potential penalties if it is deemed that their own actions through negligence, omission or accident contributed to a breach.

3　Selecting the Best Online Payment Option

You can use the following scenarios to help you choose the best option for your business.

3.1　Internet Merchant Account (IMA)

Your business already accepts debit and credit card payments for face-to-face transactions. You expect a fairly high number of online transactions, most of which will be simple and low risk. You need the greatest amount of flexibility in operating your business and cashflow is very important. If this sounds like your business, then you should:

- apply directly for an IMA and discuss your requirements with the acquiring bank.
- find the information on setting up an Internet merchant account.

3.2　Payment-processing company

Your business will not have a large number of online transactions and you do not currently accept debit or credit card transactions so do not have an IMA. You have not been trading long and cannot provide a well-documented operations history.

You value the ability to attract online sales more highly than the ability to collect sales income quickly. Your business will need some flexibility in the way in which it designs and operates its website, so you should:

- consider the facilities that a payment-processing company could offer, with the possibility of moving to a less costly option later.
- find the information on using a payment-processing company.

3.3　Online shopping mall

Your business is small, you do not currently offer debit or credit card sales and you have very limited IT skills. Your products are fairly standardised and easily understood. You do not think that your website needs any unusual features. You are prepared to pay higher transaction and fixed costs just to establish a web presence. If this applies to your business, you should:

- look at the facilities that an online shopping mall could offer.
- find the information on selling through an online shopping mall.

New Words

expect	[ɪkˈspekt]	vt. 期待,预期,盼望,指望
significantly	[sɪgˈnɪfɪkəntli]	adv. 重要地,有意义地
cheque	[tʃek]	n. 支票
traditional	[trəˈdɪʃənl]	adj. 传统的,惯例的
speedy	[ˈspiːdi]	adj. 快的,迅速的
swipe	[swaɪp]	vt. 刷(磁卡);偷盗,扒窃
jargon	[ˈdʒɑːgən]	n. 行话
acquirer	[əˈkwaɪərə]	n. 发卡行,收单银行
offline	[ˌɒfˈlaɪn]	adj. 未联机的,脱机的,离线的
exclusively	[ɪkˈskluːsɪvli]	adv. 排外地,专有地
protect	[prəˈtekt]	vt. 保护

merchant	[ˈmɜːtʃənt]	n. 商人,批发商,贸易商,店主
		adj. 商业的,商人的
cardholder	[ˈkɑːdhəʊldə]	n. 持有信用卡的人,持有正式成员证的
		人,持卡人
virtual	[ˈvɜːtʃuəl]	adj. 虚拟的,实质的
volume	[ˈvɒljuːm]	n. 量
expensive	[ɪkˈspensɪv]	adj. 花费的,昂贵的
procedure	[prəˈsiːdʒə]	n. 程序,步骤,流程,手续
transmit	[trænzˈmɪt]	vt. 传输,转送
encompass	[ɪnˈkʌmpəs]	v. 包围,环绕
requirement	[rɪˈkwaɪəmənt]	n. 需求,要求,必要条件
breach	[briːtʃ]	n. 违背,破坏,破裂,裂口
		vt. 打破,突破
password	[ˈpɑːswɜːd]	n. 密码,口令
vulnerability	[ˌvʌlnərəˈbɪləti]	n. 弱点,攻击
unique	[juˈniːk]	adj. 唯一的,独特的
regular	[ˈreɡjələ]	adj. 规则的,有秩序的,经常的
encourage	[ɪnˈkʌrɪdʒ]	v. 鼓励
compromise	[ˈkɒmprəmaɪz]	v. 危及…的安全
scheme	[skiːm]	n. 安排,配置,计划,方案
		v. 计划,设计
compliance	[kəmˈplaɪəns]	n. 依从,顺从
obligation	[ˌɒblɪˈɡeɪʃn]	n. 义务,职责
annually	[ˈænjuəli]	adv. 一年一次,每年
penalty	[ˈpenəlti]	n. 处罚,罚款
negligence	[ˈneɡlɪdʒəns]	n. 疏忽
omission	[əˈmɪʃn]	n. 冗长
accident	[ˈæksɪdənt]	n. 意外事件,事故
flexibility	[ˌfleksəˈbɪləti]	n. 灵活性,弹性,适应性
discuss	[ˌfleksəˈbɪləti]	vt. 讨论,论述
attract	[əˈtrækt]	vt. 吸引
		vi. 有吸引力,引起注意
income	[ˈɪnkʌm]	n. 收入,收益,进款,所得
skill	[skɪl]	n. 技能,技巧
establish	[ɪˈstæblɪʃ]	vt. 建立,设立,安置
presence	[ˈprezns]	n. 到场,存在

Phrases

online payment	在线支付

swiped card transaction	刷卡交易
high street	大街,主要街道
financial institution	金融机构
Internet Merchant Account（IMA）	因特网商家账号
apply for	请求,申请
acquiring bank	收单银行
monthly fee	月费
Payment Card Industry（PCI）	支付卡行业
Data Security Standard（DSS）	数据安全标准
network architecture	网络结构,网络体系
financial risk	财务风险
in practical terms	实际上
face-to-face transaction	面对面交易
online shopping mall	在线购物中心,网上购物商城

Exercises

【Ex1】 **Answer the following questions according to the text.**

1. Why are most sales paid for with credit and debit cards?

2. What does an acquirer do?

3. What have the card schemes done to help protect merchants and cardholders from fraud?

4. What is PCI DSS?

5. How many specific requirements do the PCI DSS principles have? What are they intended to do?

6. What does the PCI Security Standard Council encourage businesses that store payment data to do?

7. What manages the actual compliance programme?

8. When can failure to be annually certified become an issue?

9. What will happen if your customers' card details are stolen?

10. Which is the best online payment option offered in the passage for your business?

【Ex2】 **Translate the following terms or phrases from English into Chinese or vice versa.**

1. acquiring bank	1. _____
2. swiped card transaction	2. _____
3. online payment	3. _____
4. online shopping mall	4. _____
5. financial risk	5. _____
6. *n*. 发卡行,收单银行	6. _____

7. *n.* 支票　　　　　　　　　　　　7. _____

8. *vt.* 建立,设立,安置　　　　　　8. _____

9. *n.* 灵活性,弹性,适应性　　　　9. _____

10. *n.* 安排,配置,计划,方案　　　10. _____

【Ex3】 Fill in the blanks with the words given below.

accurate	structure	simplified	form	software
prompted	abandon	unauthorized	fail	page

Digital Wallets

A client side digital wallet requires minimal setup and is relatively easy to use. Once the ___1___ is installed, the user begins by entering all the pertinent information. The digital wallet is now setup. At the purchase/check-out ___2___ of an e-commerce site, the digital wallet software has the ability to automatically enter the user information in the online ___3___. By default, most digital wallets prompt when the software recognizes a form in which it can fill out, if you chose to automatically fill out the form, you will be ___4___ for a password. This keeps ___5___ users from viewing personal information stored on a particular computer.

Digital wallets are designed to be ___6___ when transferring data to retail checkout forms; however, if a particular e-commerce site has a peculiar checkout system, the digital wallet may ___7___ to recognize the forms fields properly. This problem has been eliminated by sites and wallet software that use ECML technology. Electronic Commerce Modeling Language is a protocol that dictates how online retailers ___8___ structure and setup their checkout forms. Participating e-commerce vendors who incorporate both digital wallet technology and ECML include: Microsoft, Discover, IBM, Omaha Steaks and Dell Computers.

Upwards of 25% of online shoppers ___9___ their order due to frustration in filling in forms. The digital wallet combats this problem by giving users the option to transfer their information securely and accurately. This ___10___ approach to completing transactions results in better usability and ultimately more utility for the customer.

【Ex4】 Translate the following passage from English into Chinese.

Digital Wallet

A digital wallet allows users to make electronic commerce transactions quickly and securely.

A digital wallet functions much like a physical wallet. The digital wallet was first conceived as a method of storing various forms of electronic money (e-cash), but with little popularity of such e-cash services, the digital wallet has evolved into a service that provides Internet users with a convenient way to store and use online shopping information.

A digital wallet has both a software and information component. The software provides security and encryption for the personal information and for the actual transaction. Typically, digital wallets are stored on the client side and are easily self-maintained and fully compatible with most e-commerce Web sites. A server-side digital wallet, also known as a thin wallet, is one that an organization creates for and about you and maintains on its servers. Server-side digital wallets are gaining popularity among major retailers due to the security, efficiency, and added utility it provides to the end-user, which increases their enjoyment of their overall purchase.

Text B

Mobile Payment

1　What Is Mobile Payment?

Mobile payment includes any transactions taking place through a mobile device. This includes things like mobile money transfers and digital wallets. You can use mobile payment technology for peer-to-peer payments as well as to pay for goods and services.

Rather than paying for your items with credit cards or cash, a mobile payment allows you to complete the transaction completely from your mobile phone. Some mobile payments use third-party apps like Venmo and PayPal, while others use a digital wallet stored on your phone. Using a mobile wallet app, you can store your banking details directly to your device.

2　Reasons to Use Mobile Payment

Mobile payment offers significant advantages over other payment methods currently available.

2.1　Secure

Security is one of the significant advantages of mobile payments, mainly when used with NFC technology. In fact, when combined with other security features already present in mobile phones, NFC offers a significant improvement over EMV.

One key aspect that makes NFC payment so attractive is tokenization. This is an encryption method that scrambles the credit card information data while being transmitted and stored. Your bank does this with a unique process and then sends it to your Apple Pay wallet for storage.

If hackers were to steal this data, all they would get is useless, meaningless gibberish. This data is also dynamic, which makes it impossible for thieves to try and decipher it.

Most mobile wallets also have layers of security to ensure that you're the one who's making a transaction. For example, Apple Pay requires that you provide your fingerprint scan using Touch ID whenever you make payments. Since it's impossible to replicate your fingerprint, thieves can't access your mobile wallet even if they steal your mobile phone.

Then there's the fact that using NFC contactless payment requires that you're physically present to make the transaction. Compared to paying over the Internet, this is a much more secure method.

2.2 Fast

Speed is the best feature of mobile payment. NFC allows you to easily tap and pay in fractions of a second. In retail stores or restaurants where there's a large volume of transactions, this is especially handy in speeding up your turnover, therefore increasing your sales.

2.3 Convenient

Using mobile payment is not just convenient for you as a business, but also for your customers.

Mobile payment doesn't require people to bring loads of cash when going out, which in itself can be a security issue. And for people who have multiple credit cards, mobile wallets provide a convenient way to consolidate them into one payment system.

Most people nowadays already have their phones at their side at all times, so mobile payment becomes an essential payment method that's available 24/7. They also don't need to buy any additional devices. As long as they have smartphones, mobile payment is built into them.

3   The Most Effective Ways to Improve Mobile Payment Experience

3.1   Provide As Many Payment Options as Possible

When it comes to e-commerce, customers usually have a very wide range of payment preferences. If your business doesn't support their preferred option of mobile payment, there's a good chance you could lose the sale altogether.

This is due to a few factors, including customers' increasing focus on privacy and security as well as a simple desire to have to sign in to as few websites as possible. Anyway, the easier you make it for your customer to pay you, the more sales you'll get.

As a result, ensuring your website is compatible with as many payment options as possible is crucial. Some of the most important payment options to include on your site are:

- Credit cards.
- Debit cards.

- PayPal.
- Apple Pay，Google Pay and Samsung Pay.
- Venmo，Stripe and other online payment platforms.

The payment landscape of China is unique and heavily dominated by mobile payment options. The top three mobile wallets are Alipay，WeChat Pay，and China UnionPay.

3.2 Don't Force Customers to Create an Account Before Paying

Encouraging your customers to create an account on your e-commerce site is indeed a great way to promote sales and collect their information. On the other hand，forcing first-time customers who may not have full trust in your brand to create an account can scare many new buyers away.

Customers prefer to only create accounts with brands they have experience with. Forcing first-time customers to create an account will not only make the customers remember another username and password，but also receive excessive marketing emails.

Allowing guest checkout is a great way to ensure your customers can make purchases as easily as possible.

3.3 Make the Checkout Design Seamless

According to Baymard，the main reason that consumers abandon a cart is due to checkout design and flow. Whether it's due to overall confusion，too many fields or long loading times，checkout design has a huge impact on conversion rates.

Since many customers make impulse buys，the more streamlined the checkout process is，the better. If possible，reduce the number of checkout steps and keep form fields to a minimum.

Checkout page design also has a significant impact on customers' likelihood to complete their purchase. Create a smooth transition from cart to checkout by using similar design elements like fonts，colors and images. Place important information where it's easily visible and guide your customer through checkout with prominent buttons and order summaries.

3.4 Provide Security and Privacy Assurances

Consumers are more concerned than ever about the privacy and security of their information. Since checkout pages handle sensitive information like credit card numbers，they're especially sensitive to perceived security violations in this area.

Improving the perceived security of your checkout page is one of the most important things you can do to drive more conversions. In addition to improving the security of your payment processing software，you can also make design choices that improve the perceived security of certain parts of a page，especially the credit card fields.

3.5 Use Clear Calls to Action（CTAs）

No matter how high your website traffic is，your revenue will stay low if your customers don't make it to the checkout page. That's why it's important to use CTAs clearly, prominently, and frequently.

CTA buttons should be large (but not too large), bright, and short. Testing is the only way to determine what button design works best for your business, but there are a few general guidelines to remember when using them:

- They should stand out from each other and from surrounding design elements.
- Text should be short and contain active verbs like "try", "get", "checkout" and "download".
- Button color matters: Orange and green are safe choices.
- Create a sense of urgency with words like "now" or "today only".
- Use plenty of white space.

New Words

transfer	[træns'fɜː]	v. 转账
peer-to-peer	[pɪə tu pɪə]	adj. 对等的,点对点的
		n. 对等网络
attractive	[ə'træktɪv]	adj. 有吸引力的;引人注目的
tokenization	[təʊ'kɪnaɪzeɪʃn]	n. 标记化;令牌化
encryption	[ɪn'krɪpʃn]	n. 编密码,加密
scramble	['skræmbl]	vt. 把…搅乱
meaningless	['miːnɪŋləs]	adj. 无意义的,无价值的
gibberish	['dʒɪbərɪʃ]	n. 无意义数据
dynamic	[daɪ'næmɪk]	adj. 动态的
decipher	[dɪ'saɪfə]	vt. 破译(密码)
contactless	['kɒntæktləs]	adj. 不接触的,无接触的
handy	['hændi]	adj. 容易做的;便利的
turnover	['tɜːnəʊvə]	n. 营业额,成交量
preference	['prefrəns]	n. 偏爱;优先权
scare	[skeə]	v. 吓跑
seamless	['siːmləs]	adj. 无缝的
likelihood	['laɪklihʊd]	n. 可能,可能性
smooth	[smuːð]	adj. 光滑的
		v. 使光滑
prominent	['prɒmɪnənt]	adj. 突出的

Phrases

mobile payment	移动支付,手机支付
digital wallet	数字钱包

peer-to-peer payment	点对点支付
consolidate … into …	把…合并到…中
payment system	支付系统
be built into …	被内置到…中
be compatible with …	与…兼容
credit card	信用卡
impact on	影响；对…有冲击
impulse buy	冲动购买
sensitive information	敏感信息

Abbreviations

NFC (Near Field Communication)	近场通信
EMV (Europay，MasterCard，Visa)	由 Europay、MasterCard 和 Visa 三家制定的智能卡标准

Exercises

【Ex5】 **Answer the following questions according to the text.**

1. What can you use mobile payment technology for?

2. What is one key aspect that makes NFC payment so attractive? What is it?

3. Why can't thieves access your mobile wallet even if they steal your mobile phone?

4. What is the best feature of mobile payment? What does NFC allow you to do?

5. Why does mobile payment become an essential payment method that's available 24/7?

6. What are some of the most important payment options to include on your site?

7. What will forcing first-time customers to create an account do?

8. What is the main reason that consumers abandon a cart according to Baymard?

9. What can you also do in addition to improving the security of your payment processing software?

10. Why is it important to use CTAs clearly，prominently，and frequently?

【Ex6】 **Translate the following terms or phrases from English into Chinese or vice versa.**

1. payment system	1. _____
2. digital wallet	2. _____
3. sensitive information	3. _____
4. peer-to-peer payment	4. _____
5. impulse buy	5. _____
6. *adj*. 不接触的,无接触的	6. _____
7. *n*. 编密码,加密	7. _____
8. *n*. 标记化;令牌化	8. _____

9. *v*. 转账   9. _____

10. *n*. 营业额,成交量   10. _____

Reading Material
Managing Risk in E-commerce

Barriers to entering e-commerce are comparatively low, but new opportunities can be accompanied by new risks.

Risk assessment① means listing all of the risks a business might face and assigning varying degrees of importance to them. Risk management means prioritising these risks and formulating policies and practices to balance and mitigate② them.

Every business can benefit from conducting a risk assessment of their e-commerce systems, although smaller businesses may not need to implement some of the more sophisticated techniques described in this guide.

This guide explains the risks that you need to be aware of or ask your e-commerce developer about. It also explains how risk assessment and management can help in recognising and quantifying the risks and how to balance them against the potential gains③.

1   Identifying Risks in E-commerce

Today's threats to e-commerce systems include:

- Physical threats—threats posed to the IT infrastructure by, for example, fire or flood.

- Data threats—threats posed to software, files, databases, etc by viruses, Trojans and so forth.

- Errors by people—e.g. employees clicking on links within messages received on social networking websites that are found to be malicious or the accidental deletion of data by an employee.

- Hoaxes④—e.g. warnings about non-existent viruses circulated by email. Although these are relatively harmless⑤ in themselves, they can spread rapidly and cause as many problems as a genuine virus by clogging up email systems.

- Technical failure—e.g. software bugs⑥.

---

① risk assessment: 风险评估。
② mitigate ['mɪtɪgeɪt] *v*. 减轻。
③ gain [geɪn] *n*. 利润,收获。
④ hoaxes [həʊksɪz] *n*. 恶作剧。
⑤ harmless ['hɑːmləs] *adj*. 无害的。
⑥ bug [bʌg] *n*. 程序缺陷。

- Infrastructure failures—e.g. server crashes.
- Credit card and payment fraud.
- Malicious attacks from inside or outside your business.
- Hacker threats should your computers become part of a larger group of infected，remote-controlled computers known as a botnet[①].

2 Typical Threats to E-commerce Systems

- Risk to corporate information and intellectual property from internal staff and trading partners. It is difficult to control how sensitive information will be handled by third parties or contract workers. Few organisations have systems in place to ensure common standards in vetting[②] staff and provide security mechanisms between trading partners.
- Hacker exploitation of errors in software application design，technical implementation or systems operation. In addition，vulnerabilities in technical security mechanisms and operating systems are now widely published for anyone to read or experiment with.
- Website defacement[③]，where the corporate image or messages on the website are changed，and virus attacks can lead to commercial embarrassment[④] and damage to the way the business is viewed by its trading partners and the public.
- Denial-of-service attacks，which use a flood of false messages to crash a business' systems，can have a devastating impact upon a business，especially if it is dependent on its e-commerce system. The growth of the Internet means that there are wider opportunities to mount such an attack，with the anonymity[⑤] afforded by the Internet meaning that there is a correspondingly lower risk of traceability[⑥]. Hackers are increasingly using botnets，a group of computers infected with malicious software and controlled remotely，to cause these attacks. They are also operating the attacks in such a manner so that servers aren't crashing but slowing down considerably.

3 Potential Impact of a Security Breach and Recent Trends

Unless swift action is taken，any problems with your e-commerce site will be immediately obvious to the world. E-commerce customers typically have little loyalty，so

---

① botnet ['bɒtnet] *n*. 僵尸网络。
② vet [vet] *v*. 审查，调查。
③ defacement [dɪ'feɪsmənt] *n*. 污损，毁损。
④ embarrassment [ɪm'bærəsmənt] *n*. 困窘，阻碍。
⑤ anonymity [ˌænə'nɪməti] *n*. 匿名。
⑥ traceability [ˌtreɪsə'bɪləti] *n*. 可追溯性。

if your website is unavailable they will simply move on to one of your competitors. In addition, technical failure can also have a significant impact on your key trading partners.

It is therefore important that you take steps to prevent problems, as this is much more cost-effective than trying to fix them once they have occurred.

3.1 Recent trends

The way malware—viruses, worms, Trojans and spyware—are being used has also changed. Infection① is usually the first step in a process aimed at stealing confidential data or opening holes in security defences for hackers to exploit.

3.2 How safe is your business from viruses?

If you answer "no" to any of the following questions, you urgently need to improve your business' anti-virus measures:

- Do you have virus defence software installed on your computer system?
- If you have virus defence software installed, do you scan all incoming email attachments? Do you regularly update your virus defence software?
- Do you and your staff know how to identify likely sources of viruses?
- Do you know who to call if your machines become infected?

4 Reduction of Threats and Vulnerabilities

You cannot completely eliminate the risks to your business so you need to plan how you will reduce the various threats and vulnerabilities.

4.1 Reduction of threats

You can reduce the threats to your e-commerce system and services by:

- Making your business less of a target. Consider what needs to be on public or shared systems and, where possible, remove sensitive business information.
- Increasing the perception of your business as secure. Ensure that all aspects of security appear to be installed and well managed.
- Ensuring that warning signs② on your website are clearly displayed to any user who attempts to access secure parts of it.
- Not providing any publicly available information regarding the security systems or operating systems in use.
- Keeping your virus defence software up to date and subscribing to a virus alert service to ensure you hear about new threats.
- Making certain that your employees are well-trained in proper email and Internet

---

① infection [ɪnˈfekʃn] n. 传染,感染。
② warning sign: 警告标志,警告信号。

usage，e.g. do not open unfamiliar attachments，click on suspicious links or forward virus warning messages.

- Configuring your email system to，by default，open attachments using a "viewer"，which prevents infection by macro viruses，which can be hidden in files.

4.2　Reduction of vulnerability

Reduced vulnerability measures are designed to reduce or remove known weaknesses in the e-commerce environment. Typical measures include：

- Installing firewalls to filter out illegitimate[①] access attempts. Such systems should be configured correctly and the rules on which they are based should reflect the needs of the business.

- Installing strong authentication processes. These guarantee the identity of users and are more secure than simple password systems. There are increasing numbers of biometric and smart-card solutions available，but you should at least consider a two-stage approach based upon something you have，e.g. a card known to the system，as well as something you know，e.g. a private personal identification number.

- Using digital certificates to provide trust between individuals，systems and trading partners. These provide secure communications by authenticating individuals，systems or organisations and protect individual transactions through the creation of digital signatures.

- Deploying virtual private networks[②]（VPNs）to provide a private channel[③] over the Internet that trading partners can use to exchange business information securely.

- Applying all available operating system and security product patches[④] to ensure that hackers are not able to exploit known vulnerabilities.

Text A 参考译文

接受在线支付

对于许多小公司来说,接受在线支付可以提供一些主要的好处。客户日益期望这种工具,并且也可以明显地增加你的现金流。

用传统方式接受在线销售的支票和发票以及处理支付是容易的。但是,因为买家通常

---

① illegitimate [ˌɪləˈdʒɪtəmət] *adj*. 非法的,不合理的。
② virtual private network：虚拟专用网络。
③ private channel：专用信道。
④ patch [pætʃ] *n*. 补丁。

为了提高速度而使用因特网,所以大部分销售都通过借记卡和信用卡支付。要在线接受这些卡,必须与银行有特别的约定。

使用卡的在线支付是"无卡"交易。这种支付有更高的欺诈风险,银行需要你在一组定义好的规则内操作,接受比商场中传统刷卡更高的交易风险。

1 在线支付的行话

借记卡和信用卡支付及其网上应用涉及一些关键概念和行话。

1.1 收单银行

收单银行是大街上的银行或其他金融机构,它们提供接受/处理借记卡和信用卡服务。收单银行从客户处获得金钱、处理这种交易并记入你的账户。

1.2 因特网商家账号(IMA)

如果要银行处理你的电子支付,需要申请商家服务协议。对于基于网站的在线交易需要 IMA。

如果已经建立了"离线"卡业务,从发卡行获得 IMA 也许比较快而且比较容易。在这种情况下,只要从收单银行请求一个因特网交易专用的 IMA ID。这个过程通常很快,尤其是当你的企业的风险没有变化时。

要使商家和持卡人避免受到欺诈,卡方案已经开发出了一种服务,使持卡人在线购物时可以鉴别自身。

1.3 支付服务提供商(PSP)

支付服务提供商给你提供一个"虚拟"的柜台或终端,让你可以通过因特网收集卡的细节并把它们传递给收单银行。要通过网络获得电子支付,需要一个 PSP。

PSP 应根据成本和与你的电子商务软件的兼容性选择。每月固定的费用大约 10 英镑,但也有一些更便宜的,低至大约每笔交易费 5 分。通常,交易量越大,负担的费用越低。

一些收单银行把 PSP 服务作为它们产品的一部分来提供,还有其他更便宜的 PSP 可供选择。

2 遵循支付卡行业数据安全标准

支付卡行业数据安全标准(PCI DSS)是由支付卡行业安全标准委员会开发的全球安全标准,以保护持卡人信息,例如借记卡和信用卡号和持卡人个人细节信息。这包括安全管理要求、网络体系结构、软件设计、安全策略和程序以及对客户账户数据的其他保护。该标准适应于存储、传输或处理持卡人信息的任何组织,可以是商家、第三方处理者或收单银行。

支付卡行业数据安全标准是包括 12 个特定要求的 6 项原则。这些要求适用于任何保存个人信息的组织,并且力图降低组织的数据被破坏的风险。

原则一:建立并维护一个安全的网络。

- 安装并维护一个防火墙配置以保护持卡人的数据。

- 不要使用经销商默认的系统密码或其他安全设置。

原则二：保护持卡人的数据。

- 保护任何存储的持卡人数据
- 对通过开放公共网络传输的持卡人数据进行加密。

原则三：制订漏洞管理计划。

- 始终使用并定期更新反病毒软件。
- 开发并维护安全系统和应用。

原则四：实现强有力的访问控制实践。

- 限制只有需要的人才可以访问持卡人的数据。
- 对每个计算机访问者给定唯一的 ID。
- 限制对持卡人数据的物理访问。

原则五：定期监控和测试网络。

- 跟踪并监控对你网络资源和持卡人信息的任何访问行为。
- 定期测试安全系统和过程。

原则六：始终拥有信息安全策略。

- 要始终拥有一个解决信息安全的策略。

PCI 安全标准委员会鼓励企业按照 PCI DSS 存储支付数据，并拥有减少因为数据破坏而产生的金融风险的资质。但是，管理实际责任程序的是支付卡方案。实际上这意味着收单银行承担管理责任，并且你应该与你的收单银行协商，寻找你要遵循的特定责任的建议，以及如何使你的公司拥有资质。

如果你有安全漏洞并且你的客户卡细节被窃，则年检可能有问题。可能按照卡方案罚款，并且依据威胁卡安全的数量提高费用。即使销售商通过年检，如果由于玩忽职守、不作为或意外事件而引起安全问题，也不能使他们免受可能的处罚。

3　选择最佳在线支付方案

你可以通过以下情景为自己的公司做出选择。

3.1　因特网商家账号（IMA）

你的公司已经接受面对面交易的借记卡和信用卡支付。你期待大量简单而低风险的在线交易。在公司运作中灵活性和现金流很重要。如果你的公司看起来就是这样的，那么你可以：

- 直接申请一个 IMA 并与收单银行讨论你的要求。
- 寻找建立 IMA 的信息。

3.2　支付处理公司

你的公司在线交易量不大并且现在还不接受借记卡或信用卡支付，那就没有 IMA。你做贸易的时间不长，也不能提供完好的运营历史文档。

你可以评估一下，看吸引在线销售的能力是否比快速得到销售收入的能力更高。你的公司在设计和运营网站方面需要某种灵活性，那么你应该：

- 考虑支付处理公司可以提供的灵活性,随后可以迁移为低成本的选择方案。
- 寻找使用支付处理公司的信息。

3.3 在线购物中心

你的公司较小,当前不使用借记卡或信用卡交易并且你的 IT 技能有限。你的产品比较标准且容易了解。你认为你的网站不需要独特的功能。你愿意支付较高的交易费和固定成本只为了有一个自己的网站存在。如果这适合你的公司,你应该:

- 考虑在线购物中心提供的工具。
- 寻找通过在线销售中心销售的信息。

Unit 6

Text A

Supply Chain Management

Supply Chain Management (SCM) is the management of a network of interconnected businesses involved in the ultimate provision of product and service packages required by end customers. Supply chain management spans all movement and storage of raw materials[①], work-in-process inventory, and finished goods from point of origin to point of consumption (supply chain).

Another definition is provided by the APICS Dictionary when it defines SCM as the "design, planning, execution, control, and monitoring of supply chain activities with the objective of creating net value, building a competitive infrastructure, leveraging worldwide logistics, synchronizing supply with demand and measuring performance globally".

1　Definitions

More common and accepted definitions of supply chain management are:
- Supply chain management is the systemic, strategic coordination of the traditional business functions and the tactics across these business functions within a particular company and across businesses within the supply chain, for the purposes of improving the long-term performance of the individual companies and the supply chain as a whole.
- A customer focused definition is given by Hines "Supply chain strategies require a total systems view of the linkages in the chain that work together efficiently to create customer satisfaction at the end point of delivery to the consumer. As a consequence costs must be lowered throughout the chain by driving out unnecessary costs and focusing attention on adding value. Throughput efficiency must be increased, bottlenecks removed and performance measurement must focus on total systems efficiency and equitable reward distribution to those in the supply chain adding value. The supply chain system must be responsive to

---

① A raw material is something that is acted upon or used by <u>human labor</u> (人力) or industry, for use as the basis to create some product or structure. Often the term is used to <u>denote</u> (表示) material that came from nature and is in an <u>unprocessed</u> (未加工的) or <u>minimally</u> (最低限度) processed state.

customer requirements".

- Global Supply Chain Forum- Supply chain management is the integration of key business processes across the supply chain for the purpose of creating value for customers and stakeholders.

- According to the Council of Supply Chain Management Professionals (CSCMP)[①], supply chain management encompasses the planning and management of all activities involved in sourcing, procurement[②], conversion, and logistics management. It also includes the crucial components of coordination and collaboration with channel partners, which can be suppliers, intermediaries[③], third-party service providers, and customers. In essence, supply chain management integrates supply and demand management within and across companies. More recently, the loosely coupled, self-organizing network of businesses that cooperate to provide product and service offerings has been called the Extended Enterprise[④].

A supply chain, as opposed to supply chain management, is a set of organizations directly linked by one or more of the upstream and downstream flows of products, services, finances, and information from a source to a customer. Managing a supply chain is "supply chain management".

Supply chain management software includes tools or modules used to execute supply chain transactions, manage supplier relationships and control associated business processes.

Supply chain event management (abbreviated as SCEM) is a consideration of all possible events and factors that can disrupt a supply chain. With SCEM possible scenarios can be created and solutions devised.

2 Problems Addressed by Supply Chain Management

Supply chain management must address the following problems:
- Distribution Network Configuration: number, location and network missions of

---

① The Council of Supply Chain Management Professionals (CSCMP) is the leading worldwide association of professionals in supply chain management. The CSCMP is a non-profit (非营利) association that provides leadership in the development, design and improvement in occupations that deal with logistics and management of supply chains.

② Procurement is the acquisition of appropriate goods and/or services at the best possible total cost of ownership (总拥有成本) to meet the needs of the purchaser in terms of quality and quantity, time, and location.

③ An intermediary is a third party that offers intermediation services between two trading parties. The intermediary acts as a conduit (渠道) for goods or services offered by a supplier to a consumer. Typically the intermediary offers some added value to the transaction that may not be possible by direct trading.

④ An Extended Enterprise is a loosely coupled, self-organizing network of firms that combine their economic output to provide products and services offerings to the market. Firms in the extended enterprise may operate independently, for example, through market mechanisms (市场机制), or cooperatively through agreements (协议) and contracts.

suppliers, production facilities, distribution centers, warehouses, cross-docks and customers.

- Distribution Strategy: questions of operating control (centralized, decentralized or shared); delivery scheme (e.g., direct shipment[①], cross docking[②], DSD (Direct Store Delivery)), mode of transportation (e.g., motor carrier), inter-modal transport (including TOFC (trailer on flatcar) and COFC (container on flatcar)); ocean freight; airfreight; replenishment strategy (e.g., pull, push or hybrid); and transportation control (e.g., owner-operated, private carrier, common carrier, contract carrier, or 3PL[③]).
- Information: Integration of processes through the supply chain to share valuable information, including demand signals, forecasts, inventory, transportation, potential collaboration, etc.
- Inventory Management: Quantity and location of inventory, including raw materials, Work-In-Progress (WIP) and finished goods.
- Cash-Flow: Arranging the payment terms and methodologies for exchanging funds across entities within the supply chain.

Supply chain execution means managing and coordinating the movement of materials, information and funds across the supply chain. The flow is bidirectional.

3 Activities/Functions

Supply chain management is a cross-function approach including managing the movement of raw materials into an organization, certain aspects of the internal processing of materials into finished goods, and the movement of finished goods out of the organization and toward the end-consumer. As organizations strive to focus on core competencies and becoming more flexible, they reduce their ownership of raw materials sources and distribution channels. These functions are increasingly being outsourced to other entities that can perform the activities better or more cost effectively. The effect is to increase the number of organizations involved in satisfying customer demand, while

---

① Direct shipment is a method of delivering goods from the supplier or the product owner to the customer directly. In most of the cases, the customer orders the goods from the product owner. This delivery scheme reduces transportation and storage costs（运输和存储成本）, but require additional planning and administration.

② Cross-docking is a practice in logistics of unloading（卸载）materials from an incoming semi-trailer truck（半拖挂车）or rail car（列车）and loading these materials directly into outbound trucks, trailers, or rail cars, with little or no storage in between. This may be done to change type of conveyance（运输工具）, to sort material intended for different destinations, or to combine material from different origins into transport vehicles (or containers（集装箱）) with the same, or similar destination.

③ A third-party logistics provider (abbreviated 3PL, or sometimes TPL) is a firm that provides a one-stop-shop service to its customers of outsourced (or "third party") logistics services for part, or all of their supply chain management functions.

reducing management control of daily logistics operations. Less control and more supply chain partners led to the creation of supply chain management concepts. The purpose of supply chain management is to improve trust and collaboration among supply chain partners, thus improving inventory visibility and the velocity of inventory movement.

Several models have been proposed for understanding the activities required to manage material movements across organizational and functional boundaries. SCOR[①] is a supply chain management model promoted by the Supply Chain Council. Another model is the SCM Model proposed by the Global Supply Chain Forum (GSCF). Supply chain activities can be grouped into strategic, tactical, and operational levels.

3.1 Strategic level

- Strategic network optimization, including the number, location, and size of warehousing, distribution centers[②], and facilities.
- Strategic partnerships[③] with suppliers, distributors, and customers, creating communication channels for critical information and operational improvements such as cross docking, direct shipping, and third-party logistics.
- Product life cycle management, so that new and existing products can be optimally integrated into the supply chain and capacity management activities.
- Information technology chain operations.
- Where-to-make and make-buy decisions.
- Aligning overall organizational strategy with supply strategy.
- It is for long term and needs resource commitment.

3.2 Tactical level

- Sourcing contracts and other purchasing decisions.
- Production decisions, including contracting, scheduling, and planning process definition.
- Inventory decisions, including quantity, location, and quality of inventory.
- Transportation strategy, including frequency, routes, and contracting.

---

① Supply Chain Operations Reference model (SCOR) is a process reference model developed by the management consulting firm (管理咨询机构) PRTM and endorsed by the Supply Chain Council (SCC) as the cross-industry de facto standard diagnostic tool for supply chain management. SCOR enables users to address, improve, and communicate supply chain management practices within and between all interested parties in the Extended Enterprise.

② A distribution center for a set of products is a warehouse or other specialized building, often with refrigeration (冷藏) or air conditioning (空调), which is stocked with products (goods) to be re-distributed to retailers, to wholesalers or directly to consumers.

③ A strategic partnership is a formal alliance (正式联盟) between two commercial enterprises, usually formalized by one or more business contracts (商业合同) but falls short of (不符合) forming a legal partnership or, agency, or corporate affiliate (加入会员) relationship.

- Benchmarking[①] of all operations against competitors and implementation of best practices throughout the enterprise.
- Milestone payments.
- Focus on customer demand.

3.3　Operational level

- Daily production and distribution planning，including all nodes in the supply chain.
- Production scheduling for each manufacturing facility in the supply chain (minute by minute).
- Demand planning and forecasting，coordinating the demand forecast of all customers and sharing the forecast with all suppliers.
- Sourcing planning，including current inventory and forecast demand，in collaboration with all suppliers.
- Inbound operations，including transportation from suppliers and receiving inventory.
- Production operations，including the consumption of materials and flow of finished goods.
- Outbound operations，including all fulfillment activities，warehousing and transportation to customers.
- Order promising，accounting for all constraints in the supply chain，including all suppliers，manufacturing facilities，distribution centers，and other customers.
- From production level to supply level accounting all transit damage cases and arrange to settlement at customer level by maintaining company loss through insurance company.

New Words

interconnect	[ˌɪntəkəˈnekt]	vt. 使互相连接
provision	[prəˈvɪʒn]	n. 供应
span	[spæn]	v. 横越，跨越
inventory	[ˈɪnvəntri]	n. 库存；财产清册，详细目录；总量
competitive	[kəmˈpetətɪv]	adj. 竞争的
infrastructure	[ˈɪnfrəstrʌktʃə]	n. 基础组织
synchronize	[ˈsɪŋkrənaɪz]	v. 同步
demand	[dɪˈmɑːnd]	n.& v. 要求，需要

---

① Benchmarking is the process of comparing one's business processes and performance metrics to industry bests and/or best practices from other industries. Dimensions（尺度，维数）typically measured are quality，time and cost. Improvements from learning mean doing things better，faster，and cheaper.

systemic	[sɪ'sti:mɪk]	adj. 系统的
strategic	[strə'ti:dʒɪk]	adj. 战略的,战略上的
coordination	[kəʊˌɔːdɪ'neɪʃn]	n. 协调,调和
tactics	['tæktɪks]	n. 战术,策略
performance	[pə'fɔːməns]	n. 履行,执行;成绩;性能
linkage	['lɪŋkɪdʒ]	n. 链接
satisfaction	[ˌsætɪs'fækʃn]	n. 满意,满足
unnecessary	[ʌn'nesəsəri]	adj. 不必要的,多余的
attention	[ə'tenʃn]	n. 注意,关心,关注
bottleneck	['bɒtlnek]	n. 瓶颈
equitable	['ekwɪtəbl]	adj. 公平的,公正的
responsive	[rɪ'spɒnsɪv]	adj. 响应的,做出响应的
forum	['fɔːrəm]	n. 论坛
crucial	['kruːʃl]	adj. 至关紧要的
collaboration	[kəˌlæbə'reɪʃn]	n. 协作
loosely	['luːsli]	adv. 宽松地,松散地
upstream	[ˌʌp'striːm]	adv. 上游地
		adj. 上游的
downstream	[ˌdaʊn'striːm]	adv. 下游地
		adj. 下游的
consideration	[kənˌsɪdə'reɪʃn]	n. 体谅,考虑
mission	['mɪʃn]	n. 任务
decentralize	[ˌdiː'sentrəlaɪz]	v. 分散
airfreight	['eəfreɪt]	vt. 空运
		n. 货物空运费
entity	['entəti]	n. 实体
bidirectional	[ˌbaɪdə'rekʃənl]	adj. 双向的
flexible	['fleksəbl]	adj. 灵活的
increasingly	[ɪn'kriːsɪŋli]	adv. 日益,愈加
satisfying	['sætɪsfaɪɪŋ]	adj. 令人满足的,令人满意的
creation	[kri'eɪʃn]	n. 创造
velocity	[və'lɒsəti]	n. 速度,速率,迅速
optimal	['ɒptɪməl]	adj. 最佳的,最理想的
commitment	[kə'mɪtmənt]	n. 委托事项,许诺,承担义务
contract	['kɒntrækt]	n. 合同,契约
frequency	['friːkwənsi]	n. 频率,发生次数
inbound	['ɪnbaʊnd]	adj. 到达的,入站的
settlement	['setlmənt]	n. 解决,结算

Phrases

in the ultimate	到最后,终于
raw material	原料
net value	净值
as a whole	总体上
as a consequence	因而,结果
drive out	消除
performance measurement	性能测定,工作状况的测定
production facility	生产设备
distribution center	配送中心
direct shipment	直接运送
cross docking	直接转运,直接换装,交叉配送
motor carrier	汽车运输
ocean freight	海运
finished good	成品
product life cycle	产品寿命周期,产品生命周期
milestone payment	分期付款
minute by minute	全时;分分秒秒

Abbreviations

SCM (Supply Chain Management)	供应链管理
CSCMP (Council of Supply Chain Management Professionals)	供应链管理专业委员会
SCEM (Supply Chain Event Management)	供应链事件管理
WIP (Work-In-Progress)	在制品
APICS (American Production and Inventory Control Society)	美国运营管理学会
GSCF (Global Supply Chain Forum)	全球供应链论坛
DSD (Direct Store Delivery)	店铺直接配送
TOFC (Trailer on Flat Car)	平车拖运
COFC (Container on Flat Car)	集装箱输送
3PL (Third Party Logistics)	第三方物流
SCOR (Supply Chain Operations Reference model)	供应链运营参考模型

Exercises

【Ex1】 **Answer the following questions according to the text.**

1. What does SCM stand for? What does it do?

2. What is supply chain management according to Global Supply Chain Forum?

3. What is a supply chain?

4. What does supply chain management software include?

5. What does SCEM stand for? What is it?

6. What problems must supply chain management address?

7. What is the purpose of supply chain management?

8. How many levels can supply chain activities be grouped into? What are they?

9. What activities are included in the tactical level?

10. What do inbound and outbound operations include respectively?

【Ex2】 **Translate the following terms or phrases from English into Chinese or vice versa.**

1. finished good

1. _____

2. milestone payment

2. _____

3. ocean freight

3. _____

4. product life cycle

4. _____

5. raw material

5. _____

6. *n*. 合同,契约

6. _____

7. *vt*. 空运 *n*. 货物空运费

7. _____

8. *n*. 基础组织

8. _____

9. *vt*. 使互相连接

9. _____

10. *n*. 库存,详细目录

10. _____

【Ex3】 **Fill in the blanks with the words given below.**

spread	stone	fashion	products	integrates
source	present	difficult	gathering	assemble

What is the Relationship between ERP, CRM and SCM?

Many SCM applications are reliant upon the kind of information that is stored inside Enterprise Resource Planning (ERP) software and, in some cases, to some Customer Relationship Management (CRM) packages. Theoretically a company could ____1____ the information it needs to feed the SCM applications from legacy systems (for most companies this means Excel spreadsheets ____2____ out all over the place), but it can be nightmarish to try to get that information flowing on a fast, reliable basis from all the areas of the company. ERP is the battering ram that ____3____ all that information in a single application, and SCM applications benefit from having a single major ____4____ to go to for up-to-date information. Most CIOs who have tried to install SCM applications say they are glad they did ERP first. They call the ERP projects "putting your information house in order". Of course, ERP is expensive and ____5____, so you may want to explore ways to feed your SCM applications the information they need without doing ERP first. These days, most ERP vendors have SCM modules, so doing an ERP project may be a way to kill two birds with one ____6____. In addition, the rise and importance of CRM systems inside companies today puts even more pressure on a company to integrate all of its enterprise wide software packages. Companies will need to decide if these ____7____ meet their needs or if they need a more specialized system.

Applications that simply automate the logistics aspects of SCM are less dependent upon ____8____ information from around the company, so they tend to be independent of the ERP decision. But chances are companies will need to have these applications communicate with ERP in some ____9____ . It's important to pay attention to the software's ability to integrate with the Internet and with ERP applications because the Internet will drive demand for integrated information. For example, if a company wants to build a private website for communicating with their customers and suppliers, the company will want to pull information from ERP and supply chain applications together to ____10____ updated information about orders, payments, manufacturing status and delivery.

【Ex-4】 **Translate the following passage from English into Chinese.**

An Enterprise Resource Planning (ERP) system is an integrated computer-based application used to manage internal and external resources, including tangible assets, financial resources, materials, and human resources. Its purpose is to facilitate the flow of information between all business functions inside the boundaries of the organization and manage the connections to outside stakeholders. Built on a centralized database and normally utilizing a common computing platform, ERP systems consolidate all business operations into a uniform and enterprise-wide system environment.

An ERP system can either reside on a centralized server or be distributed across modular hardware and software units that provide "services" and communicate on a local area network. The distributed design allows a business to assemble modules from different vendors without the need for the placement of multiple copies of complex and expensive computer systems.

Text B
E-marketplaces, Online Auctions and Exchanges

An e-marketplace is a virtual online market where organisations register as buyers or sellers to conduct business-to-business e-commerce over the Internet.

There are many types of e-marketplace based on a range of business models. They can be operated by an independent third party, or be run by some form of industry consortium that has been set up to serve a particular sector or marketplace.

Services offered by e-marketplaces include electronic catalogues for online purchasing of goods and services, business directory listings and online auctions.

This passage will describe the main components of an e-marketplace, list the main benefits that can be delivered and discuss the issues to consider prior to participating in an e-marketplace.

1　Types of E-marketplace

There are many different types of e-marketplace based on a range of business models. They can be broadly divided into categories based on the way in which they are operated.

1.1　Independent e-marketplace

An independent e-marketplace is usually a business-to-business online platform operated by a third party which is open to buyers or sellers in a particular industry. By registering on an independent e-marketplace, you can access classified ads or requests for quotations or bids in your industry sector. There will typically be some form of payment required to participate.

1.2　Buyer-oriented e-marketplace

A buyer-oriented e-marketplace is normally run by a consortium of buyers in order to establish an efficient purchasing environment. If you are looking to purchase, participating in this sort of e-marketplace can help you lower your administrative costs and achieve the best price from suppliers. As a supplier you can use a buyer-oriented e-marketplace to advertise your catalogue to a pool of relevant customers who are looking to buy.

1.3　Supplier-oriented e-marketplace

Also known as a supplier directory, this marketplace is set up and operated by a number of suppliers who are seeking to establish an efficient sales channel via the Internet to a large number of buyers. They are usually searchable by the product or service being offered.

Supplier directories benefit buyers by providing information about suppliers for markets and regions they may not be familiar with. Sellers can use these types of marketplace to increase their visibility to potential buyers and to get leads.

1.4　Vertical and horizontal e-marketplaces

Vertical e-marketplaces provide online access to businesses vertically up and down every segment of a particular industry sector such as automotive, chemical, construction or textiles. Buying or selling using a vertical e-marketplace for your industry sector can increase your operating efficiency and help to decrease supply chain costs, inventories and procurement cycle time.

A horizontal e-marketplace connects buyers and sellers across different industries or regions. You can use a horizontal e-marketplace to purchase indirect products such as office equipment or stationery.

2　Online Auctions

Online auctions are computerised versions of traditional auctions where prices are set by buyers bidding against each other. What makes online auctions so powerful is that, with Internet technology, vast numbers of businesses or individuals can bid- allowing sellers to get the best price. Conversely, the speed, simplicity and variety of auctions mean that shrewd buyers can cut the time and cost of procurement.

The two main types of auction are:

- forward auctions—where lots are sold to the highest bidder.
- reverse auctions—where suppliers compete on price and the lowest bid for a tender wins the business.

2.1　Forward auctions

Selling using a forward auction can be a cost-effective way for your business to acquire new customers, test new products or establish pricing points. Excess inventory can be disposed of quickly and sales costs are reduced because of the minimal amount spent on marketing. You can price your goods according to demand and stock levels.

Some businesses trade solely online using forward auctions on websites such as eBay.

Forward auctions can also bring benefits when buying for your business. You may be able to source non-critical supplies, e.g. stationery and office furniture, or acquire specialist, second-hand equipment at a more competitive rate. By setting up automated searches and bid alerts you can reduce the time spent on procurement.

2.2　Reverse auctions

If you are a supplier to larger companies, you may be asked to compete for their business in a reverse auction. Businesses that supply their goods through reverse auctions benefit by being able to compete for business globally. They can also make savings by gaining access to customers who are ready to buy, without having to launch a sales campaign. Reverse auctions are a good way to offload stock or build market share; however, they are normally by invitation only.

It is unusual for smaller businesses to make purchases using reverse auctions. However, buying for your business using a reverse auction can reduce time and administrative costs and you may attract a larger pool of suppliers. Reverse auctions can also help buyers manage more complex procurement contracts and you may see a reduction in your overall costs—some large companies have reported cost reductions of 10 per cent or more.

2.3　Best practice in auctions

If you are considering entering an online auction, make sure you check:

* accreditation—some auctions have qualifying criteria.
* fee structures—there may be a registration fee.
* how payment is managed—sometimes this is between the parties, sometimes through the auction site itself.
* supplier reputation—monitor feedback from previous bidders.
* the bidding system—how the bidding works and how to withdraw bids during the auction period.
* what's on offer—if the description is vague, contact the seller for more information.
* costs—make sure you factor in all the costs including taxes, packing and shipping charges.

It is worth spending some time browsing what is on offer so you can get a feel for the pricing of items you are interested in. Narrow your search down by specifying a category or using the advanced search criteria. When bidding, set yourself a maximum price you are willing to pay for an item and stick to it.

3　Catalogues and Directory Listings

Many e-marketplaces provide information about products and services offered by their supplier members. This is commonly through the use of catalogues or directories.

3.1　Catalogues

There are various different types of catalogue—some list general product information while others contain a significant amount of detail. Some are intended to be very informative. Others are used primarily for promotional purposes.

The prices published in catalogues tend to be fixed and are often not disclosed to the customer until they register with the e-marketplace. Some e-marketplaces provide a single electronic catalogue containing all the products that are available from all supplier members. Others offer a link to several catalogues, with the option to purchase goods from each catalogue either directly from the central site or from the suppliers' sites.

The attraction to the customer is that e-marketplace catalogues enable them to search an industry sector that has a wide range of products and suppliers from a single, central point. They can also then make their purchases from a single site in a single transaction.

Some e-marketplaces also offer both the buyers and the sellers the opportunity to integrate the order process with their own in-house enterprise resource planning systems. This has the significant advantage of streamlining the overall e-purchasing activity.

3.2　Directory listings

A simpler alternative to the catalogue is a basic directory listing service. E-marketplaces offering this facility list suppliers under the appropriate product or service category and include a link to each supplier website. The customer can follow this link in order to access further information about the individual suppliers and the products or services that they offer.

If your company website is listed on a directory, make sure it is in the most relevant industry sector so customers can find you easily. This can also help improve your website's search engine rankings.

4　Online Exchanges and Trading Hubs

Online exchanges, also known as trading hubs, are websites where buyers and sellers trade goods and services online.

Online exchanges vary according to the size and number of companies using them and the type of commodity traded. There are already successful exchanges in markets as diverse as energy, textiles and logistics.

Like online auctions, online exchanges allow participants to trade straightforwardly with a wide variety of buyers and sellers. Two of the biggest factors driving the growth of exchanges are that large businesses can use them to reduce stock holdings while small businesses can bid collectively to earn volume discounts or to jointly deliver a large contract.

4.1　Types of online exchange

There are different types of online exchange, each catering for a specific aspect of trading:

- request for quotation—an invitation to suppliers to provide a quote for a specific product or service.
- request for bid—an invitation to buyers to bid for a specific product or service that you are able to provide.
- commodity exchange—an ongoing process where the price of a standardised commodity such as energy or telecoms bandwidth continuously changes as a result of changes in supply and demand.

4.2　Online exchange considerations

If you are considering entering an online exchange, make sure you check the following issues:

- Choice—are all your major suppliers involved? Does the exchange have a comprehensive list of products and services so you can compare like with like?

- Business relationships—could using an exchange undermine your status as a favoured customer?
- Administration—do you have adequate systems in place for order fulfilment? Are your internal business processes suitable for active online trading?
- Disclosure—are you comfortable with publicising information on prices and stock levels where your competitors, as well as potential customers, can view it?
- Fees—how do these compare to any savings in sales and marketing costs?

5　Benefits of E-marketplaces

The potential advantages to be gained by joining an e-marketplace will vary between industries and businesses, and indeed between buyers and sellers. Some of the potential benefits are summarised below.

5.1　General business benefits

- There are greater opportunities for suppliers and buyers to establish new trading partnerships, either within their supply chain or across supply chains.
- E-marketplaces can provide greater transparency in the purchasing process since availability, prices and stock levels are all accessible in an open environment.
- Time constraints and problems with different office hours for international trade are removed as it is possible to operate on a round-the-clock basis.

5.2　Benefits for the buyer

- Updated information on price and availability makes it easier to secure the best deal.
- E-marketplaces offer a convenient way to compare prices and products from a single source rather than spending time contacting each individual supplier.
- Established e-marketplaces provide a level of trust for the buyer as they are dealing exclusively with suppliers who are members.

5.3　Benefits for the seller

- Regular requests for quotations from both new and current customers are possible.
- It provides an additional sales channel to market and sell products.
- E-marketplaces can offer reduced marketing costs when compared with other sales channels.
- The use of international e-marketplaces can provide opportunities for overseas sales that you would not otherwise be aware of.

6　Deciding If an E-marketplace Is for You

The following issues need to be considered when assessing how appropriate it is for your business to participate in an e-marketplace.

6.1 Industry fit

What is the purpose of the e-marketplace and is it compatible with your business strategy? Ensure that you understand who buys from the e-marketplace and that your business is likely to fit the profile of the sellers and/or buyers on there.

6.2 Management of the e-marketplace

It is important to establish the ownership of the e-marketplace. Successful e-marketplaces require a sound financial backing to ensure their success and longevity. So，you need to know who shares the profits and the risks. Equally，you do not want to be involved in a marketplace if your competitor is the major owner.

6.3 Costs

What does it cost to participate in the e-marketplace? Possible charges include commissions for completed transactions，membership fees and listing fees. You should also establish if there are any costs associated with changing to another e-marketplace should your original choice not live up to expectations.

6.4 Marketing

Does the e-marketplace have a strong brand or image that will assist in marketing activities? What are the marketing plans，how aggressively will the marketplace be promoted and is it likely to attract the attention of the right types of customer for your own business?

6.5 E-marketplace design

Does the overall design and functionality of the e-marketplace make it easy for would-be purchasers to locate and buy products? Does it take account of good website design principles? You should also establish how your presence will be displayed on the site. Will your logo and brand image be clearly displayed?

6.6 Technical issues

Is the e-marketplace adequately staffed to ensure that services are maintained on a round-the-clock basis，since any down time will impact directly upon your own business? Also，establish if there are any costs associated with making your own IT systems compatible with the systems used by the e-marketplace.

7 The Implications for E-purchasing

Online auctions and exchanges have played an important role in the growth of e-purchasing within businesses of all sizes and types.

7.1 E-procurement

There are two parts to the e-purchasing cycle, the more established of which is e-procurement. This has been developed in recent years to deal with the process element of electronic purchasing.

E-procurement is the use of the Internet to operate the transactional aspects of requisitioning, authorising, ordering, receipting and payment processes for the required products or services.

A number of e-marketplaces offer transaction services that automate many aspects of the procurement cycle for both the buyer and the seller.

E-procurement covers the following areas of the buying process:
- requisition against order.
- authorisation.
- order.
- receipt.
- payment.

7.2 E-sourcing

The other element of the e-purchasing cycle is e-sourcing.

E-sourcing is the use of the Internet to make decisions and form strategies regarding how and where services or products are obtained. E-marketplaces can play an important role in this activity, since the price and availability of products from multiple suppliers can be checked from a single point.

E-sourcing covers the elements of the buying process which are at the discretion of specialist buyers, including:
- knowledge specification.
- request for quotation/e-tender/e-auction.
- evaluation and negotiation.
- agreeing contractual terms.

One of the attractions of e-marketplaces in terms of product sourcing is that not only do they provide detailed product information from existing suppliers, they also give access to many new potential partners and suppliers. Furthermore, the use of reverse auctions and online exchanges enables procurement officers to obtain better prices as they encourage competitive bidding between suppliers.

New Words

consortium	[kənˈsɔːtiəm]	n. 社团,协会,联盟
auction	[ˈɔːkʃn]	n.& vt. 拍卖
quotation	[kwəʊˈteɪʃn]	n. 价格,报价单,行情表

participate	[pɑːˈtɪsɪpeɪt]	vi. 参与,参加,分享,分担
visibility	[ˌvɪzəˈbɪləti]	n. 可见度,可见性
vertical	[ˈvɜːtɪkl]	adj. 垂直的
horizontal	[ˌhɒrɪˈzɒntl]	adj. 水平的
construction	[kənˈstrʌkʃn]	n. 建筑,建筑物
textile	[ˈtekstaɪl]	n. 纺织品
		adj. 纺织的
stationery	[ˈsteɪʃənri]	n. 文具,信纸
shrewd	[ʃruːd]	adj. 精明的
excess	[ɪkˈses]	adj. 过度的,额外的
furniture	[ˈfɜːnɪtʃə]	n. 家具,设备
offload	[ˌɒfˈləʊd]	v. 卸下,卸货
accreditation	[əˌkredɪˈteɪʃn]	n. 鉴定合格
qualify	[ˈkwɒlɪfaɪ]	v. (使)具有资格,证明合格
withdraw	[wɪðˈdrɔː]	vt. 收回,撤销
vague	[veɪg]	adj. 含糊的,不清楚的
tax	[tæks]	n. 税,税款,税金
		vt. 对…征税
commodity	[kəˈmɒdəti]	n. 日用品
participant	[pɑːˈtɪsɪpənt]	n. 参与者,共享者
straightforwardly	[ˌstreɪtˈfɔːwədlɪ]	adv. 直截了当地
undermine	[ˌʌndəˈmaɪn]	v. 破坏;逐步减少效力
favoured	[ˈfeɪvəd]	adj. 受优惠的,有特权的
adequate	[ˈædɪkwət]	adj. 适当的,足够的
disclosure	[dɪsˈkləʊʒə]	n. 公开
round-the-clock	[raʊnd ðə klɒk]	adj. 全天的,连续不停的
backing	[ˈbækɪŋ]	n. 援助;支持者,赞助者
longevity	[lɒnˈdʒevəti]	n. 长命,寿命
aggressively	[əˈgresɪvli]	adv. 侵略地,攻击地
adequately	[ˈædɪkwətli]	adv. 充分地,足够地
e-tender	[iːˈtendə]	v. 电子投标
negotiation	[nɪˌgəʊʃiˈeɪʃn]	n. 商议,谈判

Phrases

virtual online market	虚拟网络市场,虚拟在线市场
register as	表现为,显示出
buyer-oriented e-marketplace	买家主导的电子市场
procurement cycle	采购周期

bid against sb.	（与某人）争出高价，抬价竞买
forward auction	正向拍卖
pricing point	价格点
dispose of	卖掉，转让，解决
according to	依照
second-hand equipment	二手设备
compete for	为…竞争
administrative cost	管理费用
procurement contract	采购合同
overall cost	总值，全部成本
registration fee	注册费，报名费
be interested in	对…感兴趣
search criteria	搜索条件
be willing to	乐于
be intended to be	规定为，确定为
promotional purposes	推广宣传目的
request for quotation	询价
request for bid	招标
participate in	参加，参与，分享
be likely to	可能
attract sb's attention	引起某人注意
in recent years	最近几年中
at the discretion of	随…的意见，由…自己处理
competitive bidding	竞标，竞争出价

Exercises

【Ex5】 Fill in the blanks with the information given in the text.

1. An e-marketplace is a _____ where organisations register as _____ to conduct _____ over the Internet.

2. An independent e-marketplace is usually a _____ online platform operated by _____ which is open to buyers or sellers in a particular industry.

3. A buyer-oriented e-marketplace is normally run by _____ in order to establish _____.

4. Supplier directories benefit buyers by _____ about suppliers for markets and regions they _____.

5. Online auctions are _____ of traditional auctions where prices are set by _____. The two main types of auction are _____.

6. If you are considering entering an online auction，make sure you check _____,

_____, _____, _____, _____, _____, and _____.

7. The prices published in catalogues tend to _____ and are often not disclosed to the customer until _____.

8. Online exchanges，also known as _____, are websites where buyers and sellers _____. There are different types of online exchange，each catering for _____.

9. If you are considering entering an online exchange，make sure you check the following issues：_____, _____, _____, _____, _____, and _____.

10. E-procurement is the use of the Internet to operate the transactional aspects of _____, _____, _____, _____, and _____ for the required products or services.

【Ex6】 **Translate the following terms or phrases from English into Chinese or vice versa.**

1. administrative cost	1. _____
2. overall cost	2. _____
3. procurement cycle	3. _____
4. request for quotation	4. _____
5. request for bid	5. _____
6. *vt*. 收回，撤销	6. _____
7. *n*. 可见度，可见性	7. _____
8. *v*. 卸下，卸货	8. _____
9. *n*. & *vt*. 拍卖	9. _____
10. *n*. 日用品	10. _____

Reading Material

SAP Supply Chain Management

You face enormous pressure to reduce costs while increasing innovation and improving customer service and responsiveness. SAP Supply Chain Management （SAP SCM） enables collaboration，planning，execution，and coordination of the entire supply network，empowering you to adapt your supply chain processes to an ever-changing competitive environment.

SAP SCM is part of the SAP Business Suite[①]，which gives organizations the unique ability to perform their essential business processes with modular software that is designed to work with other SAP and non-SAP software. Organizations and departments in all sectors can deploy SAP Business Suite software to address specific business challenges on their own timelines and without costly upgrades.

SAP SCM can help transform a linear，sequential supply chain into a responsive

---

① suite［swiːt］*n*. 套件。

supply network—in which communities of customer-centric, demand-driven companies share knowledge, intelligently adapt to changing market conditions, and proactively respond to shorter, less predictable life cycles. SAP SCM provides broad functionality for enabling responsive supply networks and integrates seamlessly with both SAP and non-SAP software. The application:

- Delivers planning and execution functions that are integrated by design.
- Supports best practices and provides preconfigured[①] software for enabling collaborative business, accelerating implementation, and reducing costs.
- Is recognized by key industry analysts as the market-leading SCM application.

1　Planning

Real-time demand and signal-based replenishment[②] need to drive supply chains. Companies need to balance supply and demand and run their businesses based on actual-versus-forecasted demand.

With SAP SCM, you can model your existing supply chain; set goals; and forecast, optimize, and schedule time, materials, and other resources with these planning activities:

- Demand planning and forecasting.
- Safety stock planning.
- Supply network planning.
- Distribution planning.
- Strategic supply chain design.

1.1　Key Planning Benefits of SAP Supply Chain Management

SAP SCM enables you to:

- Increase demand accuracy and order fulfillment satisfaction levels.
- Reduce inventory levels and increased inventory turns across the network.
- Increase profitability and productivity.
- Integrate sales and operations planning process.

Execution:

To meet the challenges of rapidly changing market dynamics, your company needs to synchronize all logistics, transportation, and fulfillment operations in a 24/7, always-on, environment.

SAP SCM enables you to carry out supply chain planning and generate high efficiency at lowest possible cost. You can respond to demand through a responsive supply network in which distribution, transportation, and logistics are integrated into

---

①　reconfigure [ˌriːkənˈfɪɡə] v. 重新装配，改装。
②　replenishment [rɪˈplenɪʃmənt] n. 补给，补充。

real-time planning processes. Features include：
- Order fulfillment.
- Procurement.
- Transportation.
- Warehousing.
- Real-world awareness.
- Manufacturing.

1.2 Key Execution Benefits of SAP Supply Chain Management

With SAP SCM，you benefit from：
- Improved order，production，and execution tracking with RFID-enabled processes.
- Seamless integration and global visibility of different transportation process steps，and higher transparency.
- Improved warehouse efficiency and extend real-time visibility and control of warehouse operations.
- Reduced costs of goods sold throughout your company.

Collaboration：

To meet pressure to reduce costs while increasing innovation challenges，you may do business in regions and countries where costs are lower，develop and maintain relationships with global suppliers，or outsource non-strategic activities to suppliers. To do so，you must foster① collaborative relationships with suppliers，outsource manufacturers，and customers.

SAP Supply Network Collaboration，included in SAP SCM，helps you connect to and collaborate with：
- Suppliers—Give them easy and seamless access to supply chain information to facilitate your ability to synchronize supply with demand.
- Customers—Provide broad capabilities for replenishment，including min/max-based vendor managed inventory（VMI）and for exclusion of promotions and transport load building.
- Contract manufacturers—Provide easy，seamless access to supply chain information by extending visibility and collaborative processes to their manufacturing processes.

1.3 Key Collaboration Benefits of SAP Supply Chain Management

With SAP SCM，you can gain these benefits：
- Streamline collaboration with your suppliers，contract manufacturers，and

---

① replenishment [rɪˈplenɪʃmənt] *n*. 补给，补充。

customers.

- Significantly decrease procurement, sales, and inventory costs.
- Enhance supply chain visibility and increases overall speed, accuracy, and adaptability① of your supply network.
- Reduce inventory levels while managing variations in supply and demand.
- Improve communications and reduces errors and processing costs.

2　Features & Functions of SAP SCM

SAP SCM includes features and functions to support collaborative supply chain planning processes, including strategic, tactical, and operational planning as well as service parts planning.

2.1　Strategic, Tactical, and Operational Planning

With SAP SCM, you can optimize a full range of planning activities, including:

- Demand planning and forecasting—Forecast and plan anticipated demand for products or product characteristics. Use state-of-the-art② forecasting algorithms for product life-cycle planning and trade promotion planning.
- Safety stock planning—Assign optimal safety stock and target stock levels in all inventories in the supply network. Meet your desired customer service levels while maintaining a minimum amount of safety stock.
- Supply network planning—Integrate purchasing, manufacturing, distribution, and transportation plans into an overall supply picture—so you can simulate and implement comprehensive tactical planning and sourcing decisions based on a single, globally consistent model. This can involve heuristics and capacity planning, optimization, and multilevel③ supply and demand matching.
- Distribution planning—Determine the best short-term strategy to allocate available supply to meet demand and to replenish④ stocking locations. To achieve this, planners can determine which demands can be fulfilled by existing supply elements.
- Supply network collaboration—Work with partners across your supply network. Using collaboration features that improve visibility into supply and demand, you and your partners can reduce inventory buffers, increase the velocity of raw materials and finished goods through the pipeline, improve customer service, and increase revenues.

---

① adaptability [əˌdæptəˈbɪlɪti] n. 适应性。
② state-of-the-art：最先进的。
③ multilevel [mʌltiˈlevəl] n. 多级。
④ replenish [rɪˈpleniʃ] v. 补充。

2.2　Service Parts Planning

With SAP SCM，you can also handle service parts planning activities，including：

- Parts demand planning—Improve the accuracy of forecasts through better modeling of demand quantities，events，and their respective deviations[①]. You can select sophisticated forecast models and optimize model parameters to improve forecasting for slow-moving parts or for parts with irregular demand patterns. Through aggregated forecast-parameter profile maintenance，you can make data maintenance more efficient.

- Parts inventory planning—Reduce inventory levels and achieve retail service levels by providing more precise demand modeling. You can distribute inventory optimally within the multi-echelon[②] supply chain to ensure high service levels while keeping inventory levels at a minimum.

- Parts supply planning—Reduce inventory in the supply chain by improving supplier alignment，increasing automation，and developing accurate supply plans. You can also reduce operational cost through efficient purchasing practices.

- Parts distribution planning—Set up stock transfers for parts within a service parts network to reduce stock-out situations and operational costs.

- Parts monitoring—Work with suppliers and customers to exchange information and handle alerts collaboratively.

Text A 参考译文

供应链管理

供应链管理（SCM）是终端客户对最终提供产品和服务的相关管理企业的管理。供应链管理涉及原材料存储和流动、在制品及成品的全过程，从起点到客户处的终点（供应链）。

APICS 把供应链管理定义为"设计、计划、执行、控制及对供应链行为的监管，目标是创造净值，建立有竞争力的基础结构，推动全球的物流，使供应与需求同步并全球化地衡量业绩"。

1　定义

一些更常见并被接受的供应链管理的定义是：

- 供应链管理系统地和从战略上协调传统企业职责和供应链中企业和特定公司内企业职责的战术，目的在于改善单个公司和供应链长期的业绩。

- 由海恩斯提供的以客户为本的定义是：供应链策略需要整体的系统观点建立该链的有效连接以实现交货时客户的满意。因此必须通过消减不必要的成本并集中关

---

① deviation [ˌdiːviˈeiʃn] *n*. 偏差。

② echelon [ˈeʃəlɒn] *n*. 梯次。

注增加值来降低最终成本。必须增加生产率,突破瓶颈。业绩衡量也必须关注整个系统的效率,以及供应链中的增值的合理奖金分配。供应链系统必须对客户的要求做出回应。

- 全球供应链论坛的定义是:供应链管理是对供应链中关键企业的整合,目的在于为客户和股东创造价值。
- 根据供应链管理专业委员会的定义,供应链包括对涉及资源、采购、转变和物流管理的全部行为的计划和管理。与渠道伙伴的协作也是非常重要的部分,这些伙伴可以是供应商、中间人、第三方服务提供者及客户。本质上,供应链管理整合企业内及企业间的供应和需求。最近,松散的、自组织的协作提供产品和服务的企业网络被称为扩展型企业。

与供应链管理相对应,供应链是一群组织,它们直接链接了产品、服务、金融和信息的许多上下游组织,从源头到客户。管理一个供应链就是供应链管理。

供应链管理软件包括一些工具和模块,用于执行供应链业务、管理供应商关系并控制相关的业务进程。

供应链事件管理(SCEM)考虑所有可能造成破坏供应链的事件和因素。通过 SCEM,就可以对可能发生的事情设计预案。

2 供应链管理解决的问题

供应链管理必须解决下列问题:

- 分布式网络结构。供应商的数量、位置和网络任务以及生产设备、配送中心、库房、交叉转运和客户。
- 配送策略。运营控制问题(集中的、分散的或共享的);交货方案(例如直接运送、直接转运、DSD(店铺直接配送))、运输模式(例如汽车运输)、协调联运(包括平车拖运和集装箱输送)、海运、空运;补充战略(拉、推或混合)以及运输管理(例如自主管理、私人承运、公共承运、合同承运或第三方物流)。
- 信息。通过供应链整合过程以便分享有用的信息,这些信息包括需求信号、预测、库存、运输合作潜力等。
- 库存管理。库存的数量和位置,包括原材料、在制品和成品。
- 现金流。安排供应链内实体间的支付项和汇兑资金方法。

供应链执行意味着管理和协调供应链内原料、信息和资金的移动。这种流动是双向的。

3 行为/职能

供应链管理是跨职能的方法,包括把原材料运输到一个组织内、确定把原材料加工为成品的内部处理过程以及把成品运出组织并交给终端客户。因为这些组织主要关注核心竞争力并更加灵活,它们减少对原材料资源和销售渠道的所有权。这些职能会越来越多地外包给其他做得更好和更有效的业。其结果是增加了满足客户要求的组织数量,也减少了日常物流运作的管理。更少的管理和更多的供应链伙伴建立了供应链管理概念。供应链管理的目的是增加供应链伙伴之间的信任与合作,这样就可以显著改善库存并提高库存货物的周转率。

人们已经提出了几种模式,以了解在组织及其功能界线间管理材料流动的行为。SCOR是由供应链委员会提出的供应链管理模型。另一个是由全球供应链论坛(GSCF)提出的SCM模型。供应链行为可以分为战略层、战术层及运作层。

3.1　战略层

- 战略网络优化,包括数量、位置、仓库规模、配送中心及设备。
- 与供应商、配送商及客户结成战略伙伴,建立紧要信息与改进运营的沟通渠道,如直接转运、直接配送和第三方物流。
- 产品生命周期管理,以便新的和现有的产品可以优化集成到供应链中并接受管理。
- 实施信息技术链。
- 做出在何处制造及自制-外购决策。
- 使组织战略与供应战略保持一致。
- 它是长期的并需要资源保障。

3.2　战术层

- 提供合同及其他购买决策。
- 生产决策,包括签订合同、调度及制订计划。
- 库存决策,包括库存的数量、位置和质量。
- 运输策略,包括频率、路线和签订合同。
- 根据竞争对手评估全部运营,并使事业整体运行在最佳状态。
- 分期付款。
- 以客户需求为本。

3.3　运作层

- 日常生产和配送计划,包括供应链上的全部节点。
- 供应链上每个制造设备的生产调度(全时的)。
- 需求计划与预测,协调全部客户的需求预测并与所有供应商分享。
- 提供计划,包括当前库存和需求预测,与所有供应商合作。
- 入站操作,包括供应商的运输和接收货物。
- 生产操作,包括原料消耗和成品流动。
- 出站操作,包括全部实施活动、入库和运送给客户。
- 订单确认,考虑供应链中的全部制约因素,包括全部供应商、制造设备、配送中心和其他客户。
- 考虑从生产层到供应层的全部运输损失并安排在客户层面上通过保险公司解决公司的损失。

Unit 7

Text A

Logistics

Logistics is the management of the flow of the goods[①], information and other resources between the point of origin and the point of consumption in order to meet the requirements of customers. Logistics involves the integration of information, transportation, inventory, warehousing[②], material handling, and packaging, and occasionally security. Logistics is a channel of the supply chain which adds the value of time and place utility. Today the complexity of production logistics can be modeled, analyzed, visualized and optimized by plant simulation software.

1 Origins and Definition

Logistics is considered to have originated in the military's need to supply themselves with arms, ammunition and rations as they moved from their base to a forward position. In ancient Greek, Roman and Byzantine empires, military officers with the title *Logistikas* were responsible for financial and supply distribution matters.

The *Oxford English Dictionary* defines logistics as "the branch of military science having to do with procuring, maintaining and transporting materiel[③], personnel and facilities". Another dictionary definition is "the time-related positioning of resources".

2 Military Logistics

In military science, maintaining one's supply lines while disrupting those of the enemy is a crucial—some would say the most crucial—element of military strategy, since an armed force without resources and transportation is defenseless.

Militaries have a significant need for logistics solutions, and so have developed

---

① In economics and accounting, a good is a product that can be used to satisfy (满足) some desire or need. More narrowly (严密地) but commonly, a good is a tangible physical (有形的) product that can be contrasted with a service which is intangible (无形的). As such, it is capable of (能够) being delivered to a purchaser and involves the transfer of ownership from seller to customer.

② A warehouse is a commercial building for storage of goods. Warehouses are used by manufacturers, importers (进口商), exporters (出口商), wholesalers, transport businesses, customs, etc.

③ Materiel in the commercial distribution context comprises the items being moved by the services of or as the products of the business, as distinct from those involved in operating the business itself.

advanced implementations. Integrated Logistics Support（ILS）[①] is a discipline used in military industries to ensure an easily supportable system with a robust customer service（logistic）concept at the lowest cost and in line with（often high）reliability, availability, maintainability and other requirements as defined for the project.

3　Logistics Management

Logistics management is that part of the supply chain which plans, implements and controls the efficient, effective forward and reverse flow and storage of goods, services and related information between the point of origin and the point of consumption in order to meet customer and legal requirements. A professional working in the field of logistics management is called a logistician.

Logistics management is known by many names, the most common are as follows:
- Materials Management.
- Channel Management.
- Distribution（or Physical Distribution）.
- Business or Logistics Management.
- Supply Chain Management.

4　Warehouse Management Systems and Warehouse Control Systems

Although there is some functionality overlap, the differences between warehouse management systems（WMS）and warehouse control systems（WCS）can be significant. Simply put, a WMS plans a weekly activity forecast based on such factors as statistics and trends, whereas a WCS acts like a floor supervisor, working in real time to get the job done by the most effective means. For instance, a WMS can tell the system it is going to need five of stock-keeping unit（SKU）A and five of SKU B hours in advance, but by the time it acts, other considerations may have come into play or there could be a logjam on a conveyor. A WCS can prevent that problem by working in real time and adapting to the situation by making a last-minute decision based on current activity and operational status. Working synergistically, WMS and WCS can resolve these issues and maximize efficiency for companies that rely on the effective operation of their warehouse or distribution center.

5　Logistics Outsourcing

5.1　Third Party Logistics（3PL）

Third party logistics involves using external organizations to execute logistics

---

① Integrated logistics support（ILS）is an integrated approach to the management of logistic disciplines in the military, similar to commercial product support or customer service organizations. Although originally developed for military purposes, it has applied by the <u>private sector</u>（私营部门）as well.

activities that have traditionally been performed within an organization itself. According to this definition, third-party logistics includes any form of outsourcing of logistics activities previously performed in-house. If, for example, a company with its own warehousing facilities decides to employ external transportation, this would be an example of third-party logistics. Logistics is an emerging business area in many countries.

5.2 Fourth Party Logistics

The concept of fourth party logistics (4PL) provider[①] was first defined by Andersen Consulting as an integrator that assembles the resources, capabilities and technology of its own organization and other organizations to design, build, and run comprehensive supply chain solutions. Whereas a third party logistics (3PL) service provider targets a function, a 4PL targets management of the entire process. Some have described a 4PL as a general contractor who manages other 3PLs, truckers, forwarders, custom house agents, and others, essentially taking responsibility of a complete process for the customer.

6　Business Logistics

Logistics as a business concept evolved in the 1950s due to the increasing complexity of supplying businesses with materials and shipping out products in an increasingly globalized supply chain, leading to a call for experts called supply chain logisticians. Business logistics can be defined as "having the right item in the right quantity at the right time at the right place for the right price in the right condition to the right customer". The goal of logistics work is to manage the fruition of project life cycles, supply chains and resultant efficiencies.

In business, logistics may have either internal focus (inbound logistics), or external focus (outbound logistics) covering the flow and storage of materials from point of origin to point of consumption. The main functions of a qualified logistician include

---

① A fourth party logistics provider, lead logistics provider, or 4th Party Logistics provider, is a <u>consulting firm</u> (咨询公司) specialized in logistics, transportation, and supply chain management. As the 4PL industry is still in its <u>infancy</u> (幼年) and currently being created throughout the world, its definition and function still leads to a lot of <u>confusion</u> (混乱), even for professionals of the transportation industry.

第四方物流是一个供应链的集成商。它不是物流的利益方,而是通过拥有的信息技术、整合能力以及其他资源提供一套完整的供应链解决方案,以此获取一定的利润。它帮助企业实现降低成本和有效整合资源,并且依靠优秀的第三方物流供应商、技术供应商、管理咨询商以及其他增值服务商为客户提供独特的和广泛的供应链解决方案。

inventory management①，purchasing②，transportation，warehousing，consultation and the organizing and planning of these activities. Logisticians combine a professional knowledge of each of these functions to coordinate resources in an organization. There are two fundamentally different forms of logistics：one optimizes a steady flow of material through a network of transport③ links and storage nodes；the other coordinates a sequence of resources to carry out some project.

7　Production Logistics

The term production logistics is used to describe logistic processes within an industry. The purpose of production logistics is to ensure that each machine and workstation is being fed with the right product in the right quantity and quality at the right time. The concern is not the transportation itself，but to streamline and control the flow through value-adding processes and eliminate non-value-adding ones. Production logistics can be applied to existing as well as new plants. Manufacturing in an existing plant is a constantly changing process. Machines are exchanged and new ones added，which gives the opportunity to improve the production logistics system accordingly. Production logistics provides the means to achieve customer response and capital efficiency.

Production logistics is becoming more important with decreasing batch sizes. In many industries (e.g. mobile phones)，a batch size of one is the short-term aim，allowing even a single customer's demand to be fulfilled efficiently. Track and tracing，which is an essential part of production logistics—due to product safety and product reliability issues—is also gaining importance，especially in the automotive and medical industries.

New Words

consumption	[kənˈsʌmpʃn]	n . 消费，消耗
integration	[ˌɪntɪˈɡreɪʃn]	n . 综合
packaging	[ˈpækɪdʒɪŋ]	n . 包装

---

①　Inventory management is primarily about specifying the size and placement of stocked goods. Inventory management is required at different locations within a facility or within multiple locations of a supply network to protect the regular and planned course of production against the random <u>disturbance</u>（干扰）of running out of materials or goods. The scope of inventory management also concerns the fine lines between replenishment lead time，carrying costs of inventory，asset management，inventory forecasting，<u>inventory valuation</u>（存货估价），inventory visibility，future inventory price forecasting，physical inventory，available physical space for inventory，quality management，replenishment，returns and <u>defective goods</u>（次品）and demand forecasting.

②　Purchasing refers to a business or organization attempting for acquiring goods or services to <u>accomplish</u>（实现）the goals of the enterprise.

③　Transport or transportation is the movement of people and goods from one location to another. Modes of transport include air，rail，road，water，cable，<u>pipeline</u>（管道），and space. The field can <u>be divided into</u>（被分为）infrastructure，vehicles，and operations.

occasionally	[əˈkeɪʒnəli]	adv. 有时候,偶尔
plant	[plɑːnt]	n. 工厂,车间,设备
military	[ˈmɪlətri]	adj. 军事的,军用的
ammunition	[ˌæmjuˈnɪʃn]	n. 军火,弹药
ration	[ˈræʃn]	n. 定量,配给量,定量配给
		v. 配给,分发
base	[beɪs]	n. 根据地,基地,本部
ancient	[ˈeɪnʃənt]	adj. 远古的,旧的
disrupt	[dɪsˈrʌpt]	v. 使中断,使分裂,使陷于混乱
enemy	[ˈenəmi]	n. 敌人,仇敌
defenseless	[dɪˈfensləs]	adj. 无防御的,无保护的,不能自卫的
significant	[sɪgˈnɪfɪkənt]	adj. 有意义的,重大的,重要的
supportable	[səˈpɔːtəbl]	adj. 可支持的,可援助的
robust	[rəʊˈbʌst]	adj. 健壮的,耐用的,坚固的
maintainability	[menˌteɪnəˈbɪləti]	n. 可维护性
logistician	[ˌləʊdʒɪˈstɪʃən]	n. 物流师;后勤人员;军需官
statistics	[stəˈtɪstɪks]	n. 统计学,统计表
operational	[ˌɒpəˈreɪʃənl]	adj. 操作的,运作的
synergistic	[ˌsɪnəˈdʒɪstɪk]	adj. 协作的
traditionally	[trəˈdɪʃənəli]	adv. 传统上
integrator	[ˈɪntɪgreɪtə]	n. 综合体,综合者
responsibility	[rɪˌspɒnsəˈbɪləti]	n. 责任,职责
globalize	[ˈgləʊbəlaɪz]	v. 使全球化
incorporate	[ɪnˈkɔːpəreɪt]	adj. 合并的,一体化的
		vt. 合并
fruition	[fruˈɪʃn]	n. 享用,成就,实现
consultation	[ˌkɒnslˈteɪʃn]	n. 请教,咨询,磋商
fundamentally	[ˌfʌndəˈmentəli]	adv. 基础地,根本地
node	[nəʊd]	n. 节点
workstation	[ˈwɜːksteɪʃn]	n. 工作站
coordinate	[kəʊˈɔːdɪneɪt]	adj. 同等的,并列的
		vt. 调整,整理
logistic	[ləˈdʒɪstɪk]	adj. 物流的
sequence	[ˈsiːkwəns]	n. 次序,顺序,序列
manufacturing	[ˌmænjuˈfæktʃərɪŋ]	n. 制造业
		adj. 制造业的
essential	[ɪˈsenʃl]	adj. 本质的,实质的
		n. 本质,实质,要素,要点

Phrases

material handling	物料输送，原材料处理
simulation software	仿真软件
forward position	前沿阵地
be responsible for	为…负责，形成…的原因
military science	军事学
in line with	符合
reverse flow	反向流动
physical distribution	实物配送，实物分销
base on	基于
in advance	预先
come into play	开始活动；开始运转；投入使用
adapt to	适合
ship out	运出
project life cycles	项目生命周期
production logistic	生产物流
batch size	批量
short-term aim	短期目标

Abbreviations

ILS（Integrated Logistics Support）	集成物流支持
WMS（Warehouse Management System）	仓库管理系统
WCS（Warehouse Control System）	仓库控制系统
4PL（Fourth Party Logistics）	第四方物流

Exercises

【Ex1】 Answer the following questions according to the text.

1. What is logistics?

2. What does logistics involve?

3. What is integrated logistics support?

4. What are the most common names for logistics management?

5. What is the difference between a WMS and a WCS?

6. What is the difference between a 3PL service provider and a 4PL service provider?

7. How can business logistics be defined?

8. What do the main functions of a qualified logistician include?

9. What are the two fundamentally different forms of logistics?

10. What is the purpose of production logistics?

【Ex2】 Translate the following terms or phrases from English into Chinese or vice versa.

1. material handling   1. _____
2. physical distribution   2. _____
3. production logistic   3. _____
4. project life cycles   4. _____
5. reverse flow   5. _____
6. *n*. 消费, 消耗   6. _____
7. *adj*. 物流的   7. _____
8. *adj*. 操作的, 运作的   8. _____
9. *adj*. 健壮的, 耐用的, 坚固的   9. _____
10. *n*. 统计学, 统计表   10. _____

【Ex3】 Fill in the blanks with the words given below.

complicated	result	margins	track	tangible
ensure	valuable	realm	minimizes	essential

What is Basic Inventory Control?

Basic Inventory Control Online (BIC-O) is a Web based product stock tracking and inventory management system.

Why Inventory Control?

Inventory control is a process by which an organization keeps ____1____ of its product counts and ensures physical product counts match what is recorded in its books. From a financial standpoint, inventory is the most ____2____ asset of an organization engaged in buying, selling, manufacturing or otherwise handling of ____3____ goods. For many organizations, proper management of inventory is pivotal to customer satisfaction and long-term success. The following are some of the challenges faced by organizations in the ____4____ of inventory control.

Companies usually handle a large number of products. Units of products move rapidly as new orders are received, products are returned, products are drop-shipped, out of stock products are backordered or products are earmarked for a delayed shipment. The sheer volume of items makes the task of monitoring inventory ____5____.

In order to minimize cash tied up in inventory and to reduce inventory handling costs, an organization must know its current inventory count accurately at all times. This information is ____6____ in knowing when to re-order products that are out of stock or are about to go out of stock. There are significant costs associated with carrying too much inventory such as cash tied up in slow moving inventory, inventory storage and handling costs, spoilage and obsolescence. On the other hand, carrying too few units could ____7____ in stock-outs and loss of sales or production stalls. The ultimate goal is not to order too many or too few goods. The more accurate the inventory count, the better an organization is in a position to order an Economic Order Quantity (EOQ) that _____8_____ inventory costs and helps negotiate best price discounts.

Cost of goods sold is the largest expense for businesses that deal with tangible products. Inventory control must track the number of units and the monetary value of the inventory. Companies need an accurate cost of goods sold in order to calculate their profit _____9_____ per product or across products.

Companies need to safeguard their inventory against pilferage, outright theft and loss. A process needs to be in place that keeps track of inventory and helps _____10_____ the physical count matches product count recorded in company books. Sound inventory control is an excellent deterrent against pilferage.

【Ex4】 Translate the following passage from English into Chinese.

Why Basic Inventory Control?

- Basic Inventory Control keeps an accurate count of products and generates list of products that need to be reordered.
- Basic Inventory Control is a perpetual inventory control system. That is, BIC provides up to date, accurate count of units in stock. Contrast a perpetual inventory control system with a periodic inventory control system where inventory counts are usually updated periodically at month, at quarter or at year end.
- Basic Inventory Control maintains a physical and available inventory count. Physical units in stock refer to products physically present on premises. Available units in stock include physical units minus the stock that has been allocated but not yet shipped.

Text B

Knowing When a WMS or WCS Is Right for Your Company

Although there is some functionality overlap, the differences between WMS (Warehouse Management Systems) and WCS (Warehouse Control Systems) can be significant. But until they are fully comprehended, companies that rely on the day-to-day movement of product in and out of a distribution center or warehouse can find themselves at a distinct disadvantage.

"A lot of companies probably don't know the difference between a WMS and a WCS system," says Jerry List, vice president of QC Software in Cincinnati. "To put it simply, the WMS plans a weekly activity forecast, based on such factors as statistics, trends and so forth. And a WCS acts like a floor supervisor, working in real time to get the job done by the most effective means."

"For instance," continues List, "a WMS can tell the system it's going to need five of SKU[①] A and five of SKU B, hours in advance, but by the time it acts, other considerations may have come in to play and all of a sudden you have a logjam on a conveyor." A WCS can prevent that problem from happening by working in real time and adapting to the situation on the spot. "It can make a 'last-minute decision' based on current activity and operational status." says List.

Warehouse management systems began to flourish in the 1980s with the introduction of mini-computers. According to Kevin Tedford of KT Consulting in Marion, Ohio, who has worked with warehouse management systems for the past 20 years, companies knew when the time was right to implement a WMS into their distribution center operation.

"Businesses saw the need for a warehouse management system when they started hitting certain 'pain points'," explains Tedford. "This usually happened when they saw the costs of delivery rising, labor costs on the increase and a need to control inventory and keep track of what their people were doing. It was the moment they first began to realize they had no control."

According to Tedford, what the warehouse management system did was to return the control to the distribution center supervisor. "The greatest advantage was it brought back inventory control and accuracy," he says. "And brought it back to a super-high level, so much so that companies could now exceed their customers' highest expectations, performing tasks in hours that at one time may have taken days or even weeks."

"Better, Faster, Cheaper"

With the turn of the century and the increase in the need to move more products faster in a shorter amount of time—and do it with fewer workers—technology began to accelerate.

The simple act of walking up and down a warehouse aisle picking products from a paper order was replaced by high-tech pick-to-light[②] and pick-to-voice technology. The pace quickened and the products increased, and so did the need for better order verification and order fulfillment.

According to Jerry List: "Suddenly, there was a 'better, faster, cheaper' mentality

---

① A SKU is a number or string of alpha and numeric characters that uniquely identify a product. For this reason, SKUs are often called underline part numbers (零件号), product numbers, and product identifiers.
SKU 是库存进出计量的单位,可以件、盒、托盘等为单位。现在已经被引申为产品统一编号的简称,每种产品均对应有唯一的 SKU 号,定义为保持库存控制的最小可用单位。
② 光拣选传感器与控制系统配合使用,可引导装配操作员或仓储人员逐步完成预先设定顺序的一组操作。操作员通常需要从一排货位架上拣取零件或货物,以确保正确装配设备或正确地履行订单。

prevalent in the warehouse. And the old school WMS mentality was being challenged. As warehouse management systems began to take on more responsibilities，a void was created which warehouse control systems nicely filled，especially as systems became faster and real-time demands were established."

Explains Jerry Lovell，senior electrical project engineer for Lakeland，FL-based material handling systems integrator TriFactor，"Over the past 10 years，distribution centers saw an increased need for improved warehouse communications，from the WMS to the WCS to the conveyor to the customer."

Adds Lovell，"Companies are now able to see the status of their material handling system in real time，with all information up-to-date. Today they can make a hard decision right on the spot，where 10 years ago they more or less had to guess. They know right away if something is wrong，and they can react with a faster response time. I once had a company executive tell me that having a WCS system in his warehouse lets him sleep at night."

Jerry List agrees，"A warehouse control system enables you to utilize new technology，which allows greater flexibility on the plant floor，" he says，"It's an integrating tool that ties everything together. Think of equipment like conveyors and picking technology as building blocks. The WCS is the mortar between the blocks that holds everything together."

Adds List，"The perfect candidate for a WCS is the company that utilizes a lot of material handling devices and needs to put a lot of decision points in their system and be able to balance them all in an efficient manner."

List points out that another key advantage to the WCS is location. "Sometimes in the case of multiple warehouses，the warehouse management system is not physically located in the warehouse，" he says，"But even if there's a network-wide problem，the warehouse control systems，being situated in the warehouse，can keep the operation up and running."

Knowing When You Need a WCS

Not every operation needs or requires a warehouse control system，particularly those that hand-pick from paper and pallets，or those have a minimal number of product lines and/or SKUs. But according to a white paper[①] produced by List and QC Software，there are some very real telltale signs that there could be a WCS in your company's future：

- Your current system is inefficient and takes too long to get a product out of the

---

① A white paper (or whitepaper) is an authoritative（权威的）report or guide that is often oriented toward a particular issue or problem. White papers are used to educate readers and help people make decisions，and are often requested and used in politics（政治），policy（策略），business，and technical fields. In commercial use，the term has also come to refer to documents used by businesses as a marketing or sales tool.

door.

- You're growing fast and can't handle the volume, especially during peak time.
- Your conveyor system has cartons everywhere, but going nowhere.
- You're creating back orders, even though the product is in stock.
- You're shipping products to the wrong place.
- It's getting too expensive to keep modifying your WMS system.

To put the difference between WMS and WCS in simple terms, WMS is a planning system, WCS is an execution system. The WMS collects a vast amount of information, such as inventory data, customer orders and historical data, and then processes it in a non-real-time mode, mapping out a workload plan for what needs to be done on the warehouse floor on a day-to-day basis. But it's the warehouse control system that has final control over the large amount of information being placed by the WMS and reacts to "actual" events on the warehouse floor.

Think of it as a symphony orchestra. The WMS is the composer, creating a musical score that feature reeds, woodwinds and strings, together making beautiful sounds. But anyone who has ever heard the dreadful noise an orchestra makes when it is tuning up knows that it needs the conductor to pull it all together. In this case, that conductor is the warehouse control system, making sure the material handling "instruments" (conveyors, sorters, pick-to-light, etc.) perform in perfect harmony and efficiency.

According to Jerry List, a company may want to explore the possibility of adding a WCS if they have the following characteristics:

- More than $50 million in sales.
- A warehouse larger than 100,000 square feet.
- A conveyor system with multiple sortation points.
- An average of four SKUs per order.
- Greater than 1,000 orders per day.

TriFactor's Jerry Lovell agrees. He feels warehouses must keep up with the technology being offered. "WMS and WCS is an important piece of the technology puzzle," says Lovell, "There's a consistency factor knowing that technology can perform the same tasks, over and over, eliminating the possibility of human error. Technology is reliability. WMS and WCS give you the peace of mind of knowing that your system is using proven technology. If your competition has it and you don't, then you are at a definite competitive disadvantage."

New Words

overlap	[ˌəʊvəˈlæp]	v. (与…)交叠
logjam	[ˈlɒɡdʒæm]	n. 阻塞,停滞状态,僵局
conveyor	[kənˈveɪə]	n. 搬运者

flourish	[ˈflʌrɪʃ]	vi. 繁荣，茂盛，活跃
realize	[ˈriːəlaɪz]	vt. 认识到，了解
supervisor	[ˈsuːpəvaɪzə]	n. 监督人，管理人，主管人
task	[tɑːsk]	n. 任务，工作
		v. 分派任务
accelerate	[əkˈseləreɪt]	v. 加速，促进
mentality	[menˈtæləti]	n. 精神，心理
void	[vɔɪd]	n. 空隙；空间
nicely	[ˈnaɪsli]	adv. 精细地
guess	[ges]	v. & n. 猜测，推测
react	[riˈækt]	vi. 起反应，起作用
candidate	[ˈkændɪdət]	n. 候选人
pallet	[ˈpælət]	n. 草垫子；托盘；平台；运货板
telltale	[ˈtelteɪl]	n. 证据
inefficient	[ˌɪnɪˈfɪʃnt]	adj. 效率低的，效率差的
workload	[ˈwɜːkləʊd]	n. 工作量
composer	[kəmˈpəʊzə]	n. 作曲家
orchestra	[ˈɔːkɪstrə]	n. 管弦乐队
reed	[riːd]	n. 簧片
woodwind	[ˈwʊdwɪnd]	n. 木管乐器
string	[strɪŋ]	n. 弦乐器
dreadful	[ˈdredfl]	adj. 可怕的
conductor	[kənˈdʌktə]	n. 管弦乐队指挥；领导者
harmony	[ˈhɑːməni]	n. 协调，融洽
sortation	[sɔːˈteɪʃən]	n. 分类
puzzle	[ˈpʌzl]	n. 难题，谜
competition	[ˌkɒmpəˈtɪʃn]	n. 竞争者；对手；竞争，比赛
definite	[ˈdefɪnət]	adj. 明确的，一定的

Phrases

rely on	依靠，依赖
floor supervisor	领班；楼层主管
all of a sudden	突然
operational status	运行状态，运营状态
on the increase	增加
at one time	同时；曾经
the turn of the century	世纪之交
pick-to-light	光拣选

pick-to-voice	语音拣选,声导选货
old school	守旧派
take on responsibilities	承担责任
right away	马上,立刻
on the plant floor	工厂车间层面
building block	积木
white paper	白皮书
peak time	高峰期
back order	延期交货,未交货;未交货订单
symphony orchestra	交响乐团
musical score	乐谱
tune up	开始演奏;调音,定弦;调整,调节
square feet	平方英尺
keep up with	跟上
over and over	反复,再三
peace of mind	安心,内心的宁静

Abbreviations

QC(Quality Control)	质量控制
SKU (Stock Keeping Unit)	库存单元,存货单元

Exercises

[Ex5] **Answer the following questions according to the text.**

1. Do a lot of companies probably know the difference between a WMS and a WCS system according to Jerry List?

2. What do WMS and WCS do respectively according to Jerry List?

3. When did warehouse management systems begin to flourish?

4. When did businesses see the need for a warehouse management system according to Tedford?

5. What does a warehouse control system enable you to do?

6. Who is the perfect candidate for a WCS?

7. Are there any very real telltale signs that there could be a WCS in your company's future? What are they?

8. What is the difference between WMS and WCS in simple terms?

9. Who has final control over the large amount of information being placed by the WMS and reacts to "actual" events on the warehouse floor?

10. What does TriFactor's Jerry Lovell think about warehouses?

【Ex6】 Translate the following terms or phrases from English into Chinese or vice versa.

1. back order	1. _____
2. peak time	2. _____
3. white paper	3. _____
4. keep up with	4. _____
5. operational status	5. _____
6. *n.* 竞争者;对手;竞争,比赛	6. _____
7. *v.* 加速,促进	7. _____
8. *vt.* 认识到,了解	8. _____
9. *n.* 分类	9. _____
10. *n.* 工作量	10. _____

Reading Material

Transportation Management System

1   TMS

A Transportation Management System（TMS）is a software system designed to manage transportation operations.

TMS is one of the systems managing the supply chain. It belongs to a sub-group called Supply chain execution（SCE）. TMS，whether it is part of an Enterprise Level ERP System or from an integrated "Best of Breed①" Independent Software Vendor（ISV）has become a critical part of any SCE and Collaboration System in which real time exchange of information with other SCE modules has become mission critical.

In more recent times，we have seen that these systems are being offered in many different types of licensing arrangements②. These different arrangements have given shippers who otherwise would not be able to afford sophisticated software the opportunity to utilize TMS to better manage this vital function. The three primary offerings are：

- On-Premise Licensing（traditional purchased license）.
- Hosted（remote，SaaS，Cloud）.
- On-Premise Hosted Licensing（a blend③ of 1 & 2）.

Additionally，we are seeing that some software providers have either been acquired or merged with traditional supply chain management consultancies and are now offering shippers "blended" managed and software services as an outsourced process. Primary

---

① Best of Breed：最好的品种,最佳组合。
② licensing arrangement：许可协议。
③ blend [blend] *vt.* & *n.* 混和。

Tier 1 TMS providers are still independent，carrier and 3PL neutral①，and ERP neutral.

TMS usually "sits" between an ERP or legacy order processing and warehouse/ distribution module. A typical scenario would include both inbound (procurement) and outbound (shipping) orders to be evaluated by the TMS Planning Module offering the user various suggested routing solutions. These solutions are evaluated by the user for reasonableness② and are passed along to the transportation provider analysis module to select the best mode and least cost provider. Once the best provider is selected，the solution typically generates electronic load tendering and track/trace to execute the optimized shipment with the selected carrier，and later to support freight audit and payment (settlement③ process). Links back to ERP systems (after orders turned into optimal shipments)，and sometimes secondarily to WMS programs also linked to ERP are also common. Most TMS systems help shipper directly work with asset-based carriers and support disintermediation④ (including avoiding use of non-asset based brokers and other intermediaries).

Transportation Management Systems manage three key processes of transportation management.

1.1 Planning and Decision Making

TMS will define the most efficient transport schemes according to given parameters，which have a lower or higher importance according to the user policy：transport cost，shorter lead-time⑤，fewer stops possible to insure quality，flows regrouping⑥ coefficient…

1.2 Transport follow-up

TMS will allow following any physical or administrative operation regarding transportation：traceability of transport event by event (shipping from A，arrival at B，customs clearance…)，editing of reception，custom clearance⑦，invoicing and booking documents，sending of transport alerts (delay，accident⑧，non-forecast stops…)

1.3 Measurement

TMS have or need to have a Logistics KPI (Key Performance Indicators) reporting function for transport.

---

① neutral ['nju:trəl] *n*.中立者 *adj*.中立的，中性的。
② reasonableness ['ri:znəblnəs] *n*.合理，妥当。
③ settlement ['setlmənt] *n*.结算。
④ disintermediation[dɪsɪntəmi:dɪ'eɪʃən] *n*.非居间化，非中介。
⑤ lead-time ['li:dtəɪm] *n*.交付周期。
⑥ regroup [ˌri:'gru:p] *v*.重组，重编。
⑦ custom clearance：报关，清关。
⑧ accident ['æksɪdənt] *n*.意外事件，事故。

Various functions of a TMS：

- Planning and optimizing of terrestrial transport rounds.
- Transportation mode and carrier selection.
- Management of air and maritime transport.
- Real time vehicles tracking.
- Service quality control.
- Vehicle Load and Route optimization.
- Transport costs and scheme simulation.
- Shipment batching of orders.
- Cost control，KPI reporting and statistics.

2　Key Benefits

2.1　Route Planning and Optimization

- Reduce Distribution Costs & Fleet Miles—Daily routes are created using powerful algorithms and street-level routing，in conjunction with your business constraints.
- Increase Resource Utilization—Make better use of existing resources by delivering more and driving less. The answer to increasing volume is not always to put more vehicles on the road，but to make smart，efficient.
- Make Sound Business Decisions—Understand how delivery costs affect the profitability of each customer by knowing the actual cost per stop[1].
- Set Driver Standards—Creating route plans and gathering actual information allows you to set performance standards and expectations—which can result in less overtime and better driver performance.
- Decrease Routing Time—Let your routers spend less time configuring routes and more time assessing what-if scenarios to produce better，more efficient routes.
- Contingency Planning—Prepare for holiday or seasonal spikes[2] and other "what if" scenarios.
- Reports—Driver manifests[3]，maps，directions，resource utilization，customer delivery cost，actual versus projected by route and by stop，planned route summaries and many more reports to help you consistently evaluate your success.

2.2　Load Optimization

- Accurate and Quick Load Design for Multiple Route Types—Each type of route requires different loading patterns. Determine（or assign）equipment to

---

① cost per stop：每站费用。
② seasonal spike：季节性高峰。
③ manifest ['mænɪfest] *n.* 载货单。

warehouse bays with capacities, preferences or even empty bays for returned goods.

- Multiple Loading Strategies—Different delivery operations require different loading strategies. Our warehouse-friendly software allows for greater picking efficiencies by grouping SKUs. Driver-friendly software groups product by stop, minimizing the number of bays a driver must visit at each stop.
- Pre-Build Orders—Load orders to be picked, built and pre-staged throughout the day, all while continuing to have them allocated to the correct route and truck during the final loading pass.
- Load Design to Reduce Product Breakage[①]—Most breakage occurs within the first 10 minutes of a route due to poor packing. FleetLoader's leading loading algorithms allow for proper mixing and stacking to reduce breakage.
- Reports—Final load sheet, driver check-out, load validation and pick sheets provide you with all of the detailed information you need.

Text A 参考译文

物 流

物流管理货物和信息流动以及其他在起点和消费点中为满足客户需求而形成的资源流动。物流是信息、运输、库存、物料处理、包装也可能还有安全的综合。物流是供应链通道,可以增加时间和空间的利用价值。当今生产物流的复杂性可以通过工厂模拟软件建模、分析、可视化和优化。

1 起源和定义

人们认为物流起源于军事中武器、弹药的供应以及将它们从基地配送到前线。在古希腊、罗马和拜占庭帝国,头衔为 Logistikas 的军官负责资金和供应。

牛津英语词典把物流定义为"军事科学中的分支,与购置、供应和运输原料、人员和设备有关"。另一个词典的定义是"与时间相关的资源配置"。

2 军事物流

在军事科学中,保持自己的供应链而破坏敌人的供应链是军事策略中至关重要的元素——有些人会说是最重要的元素,因为没有资源和运输的武装部队是没有防备能力的。

军事对物流解决方案有重要的需求,所以开发了许多先进的执行方法。集成物流支持(ILS)是军工行业的一个学科,确保一个有强健的客户服务(物流)理念的便捷支持系统,其成本最低并符合(通常是高度符合)可靠性、有效性、可维护性以及该项目的其他需求。

---

① breakage ['breɪkɪdʒ] *n.* 破损,破损量。

3　物流管理

物流管理是供应链的一部分,供应链制订计划、执行计划并控制效率、有效的供货和退货流及货物存储、服务以及相关的信息,这些信息包括起点到满足客户订单和法律需求的消费终点。在物流管理领域工作的专业人士被称为物流师。

物流管理有许多名称,最常见的如下:

- 物料管理。
- 渠道管理。
- 配送(或物质配送)。
- 商务或物流管理。
- 供应链管理。

4　库存管理系统和库存控制系统

虽然库存管理系统(WMS)和库存控制系统(WCS)的某些功能有重叠,但它们之间的差别非常重要。简单地说,WMS 根据基于统计和趋势因素的预测制订周行动计划;而 WCS 像基层管理人员,通过最有效的方法实时工作。例如,WMS 可以提前数小时告诉系统需要5个 A 货位和5个 B 货位,但到实际操作时其他因素可能会起作用——也许传输带上可能出现堵塞。WCS 可以实时工作并根据当前活动和运行状态做出最终决策以防止这个问题的发生。通过协作,WMS 和 WCS 可以解决这些问题并依靠库房或配送中心的有效运作使公司的效率最大化。

5　物流外包

5.1　第三方物流

第三方物流(3PL)指使用外部组织完成那些传统上一直在自己组织内部进行的物流行为。根据这个定义,第三方物流包括以前内部执行的任何形式的物流行为的外包。例如,有自己库存设施的公司决定雇用外部公司进行运输,这就是第三方物流的例子。在许多国家,物流是新兴的商务领域。

5.2　第四方物流

第四方物流提供者的概念首先由安达信咨询公司定义为:它是综合集成本公司和其他组织的资源、能力和技术来设计、建立和运行综合的供应链解决方案。第三方物流服务提供者的目标在于某一功能,而第四方物流的目标在于管理整个过程。一些人把第四方物流描述为管理其他第三方物流、运输者、转运者海关代理及其他服务者的总承包商,实质上它为客户负责全部过程。

6　企业物流

企业物流的概念是在20世纪50年代提出的,其原因是日益全球化的供应链中物料供应和产品运输复杂性的提升,导致对被称为供应链物流师的专业人才的需求。企业物流可以被定义为"在适当的时间,以合格的质量和数量,在合适的地方,以合适的价格把合适的产品交给合适的用户"。物流工作的目的在于管理项目生命周期、供应链并得到有效结果。

在企业中,物流可能既关注内部(输入物流)也关注外部(输出物流),覆盖了从起点到消费终点物料的存储和流动。合格物流师的主要作用包括库存管理、采购、运输、入库、咨询以及这些活动的组织和计划。物流师结合这些功能的专业知识,协调组织的资源。物流有两种主要的基本形式:其一,对物料通过相链和存储节点的运输网络的稳定流动实施优化;其二,协调一系列资源,完成某些项目。

7 生产物流

术语生产物流用来描述一个行业内的物流过程。其目的是确保对每部机器和工作站的送料:在适当的时间、以合格的质量和数量、把合适的产品交给合适的用户。其焦点不是运输自身,而是增值过程流程的改进和控制,还涉及消除非增值过程。生产物流既可用于现有的工厂,也可用于新的工厂。现有工厂的制造是经常变化的过程。机器的调换和新增给改进生产物流提供了机会。生产物流提供了实现客户响应速度和资金效益的方法。

生产物流对减少批次日益重要。在许多行业(例如移动电话)中,批次是一个短期目标,使得即使单个客户的需求也可以有效地满足。路径和追踪(实际上是生产物流的一个重要部分)——由于产品安全性和可靠性问题——也越来越重要,尤其是在汽车和医疗行业。

Unit 8

Text A

Applications and Cases of Artificial Intelligence in E-commerce

Many e-commerce businesses are already using AI to better understand their customers, generate new leads and provide an enhanced customer experience.

1 Applications

1.1 Chatbots

E-commerce websites are using chatbots to improve the customer support service. Chatbots are providing 24/7 customer support to buyers. When visiting any recognized e-commerce website, you will be prompted with a chat box asking what you want or how you can be helped. You can tell your requirements in the chat box and you will be served with highly filtered results. Chatbots are built using artificial intelligence and are able to communicate with humans. They can also collect your past data and provide you with a very personalized user experience.

1.2 Image Search

Have you ever come across a situation where you like some product or item but don't what it is called or what it is? Artificial intelligence service eases this task for you. The concept of image search is implemented in e-commerce websites with the application of artificial intelligence. Artificial intelligence has made it possible to understand images. Buyers can make a search on the basis of images. Mobile apps of e-commerce websites can find the product by just pointing the camera towards the product. This eliminates the need for keyword searches.

1.3 Handling Customer Data

E-commerce has to deal with a lot of data every day. This data can be anything like daily sales, the total number of items sold, the number of orders received in an area,etc. It has to take care of customer data as well. Handling that amount of data is not possible for a human. Artificial intelligence can not only collect this data in a more structured form but also generate proper insights out of this data.

1.4 Recommendation Systems

Have you ever experienced how e-commerce websites like Amazon are constantly showing products similar to the one you just checked? Well, this is the application of artificial intelligence in e-commerce. AI and machine learning algorithms can predict the behaviour of the buyer from his past searches, likings, frequently bought products. By predicting the behaviour of the user, e-commerce websites are able to recommend the products that user is highly interested in. This improves the user experience as the user no longer has to spend hours searching the product. It also helps the e-commerce websites to improve their sales.

1.5 Inventory Management

The inventory management is one of the most important areas in any business. You have to keep yourself updated on how much inventory you are holding and how much more is needed. There are thousands of product categories over the e-commerce websites. Keeping an eye on the inventory of all the products daily is not possible for a human. This is where artificial intelligence comes into the picture. Artificial intelligence applications have helped e-commerce in managing the inventory. Moreover, the inventory management system will get better over the time. AI systems build a correlation between the current demand and the future demand.

1.6 Cyber security

Artificial intelligence has also improved the cyber security of the e-commerce websites. It can prevent or detect any fraudulent activities. E-commerce has to deal with a lot of transactions on a daily basis. Cyber criminals and hackers can hack the user's account to gain unauthenticated access. This can lead to the exposure of private data and online fraud. The reputation of the business will also get a big blow. To prevent this, machine learning algorithms are developed that can mitigate the chances of fraud activities over the website.

1.7 Better Decision Making

E-commerce can make better decisions with the application of artificial intelligence. Data analysts have to handle a lot of data every day. This data is too huge for them to handle. Moreover, analyzing the data also becomes a difficult task. Artificial intelligence has fastened the decision-making process of e-commerce. AI algorithms can easily identify the complex patterns in the data by predicting user behaviour and their purchasing pattern.

1.8 After Sales Service

Selling the product is not enough. Businesses have to aid the customer in the complete buying cycle. After sales service is an integral part of e-commerce. Artificial intelligence applications can automate the feedback form，replacements and handling any other ambiguity in the product. By solving the buyer's issues，the brand value of the website gets improved.

1.9　CRM

In the past，Customer Relationship Management（CRM）relied on people to collect a huge amount of data in order to collect the data and serve the clients. But today，artificial intelligence can predict which customers are most likely to make a purchase and how we can better engage with them. Artificial intelligence applications can help to identify the trends and plan the actions according to the latest trends. With the help of machine learning algorithms，advanced CRM can learn and improve over time.

1.10　Sales Improvement

Artificial intelligence applications can generate and predict the accurate forecast of the e-commerce business. The study of historical data，data analytics，and latest trends can help in optimizing the resource allocation，build a healthy pipeline and analyze the team performance. The managers can analyze the trends and can improve the sales by making strategies well before time.

2　Cases

2.1　Amazon

Alexa is one of Amazon's most popular and most famous AI product. It helps drive the algorithms that are essential to Amazon's targeted marketing strategy. AI allows Amazon to predict what products will be the most demanded to provide customized recommendations based on customer searches. And it is said Amazon's recommendation engine[①] drives 35 percent of total sales.

2.2　JD.com

Beijing-based JD.com has partnered up with Siasun Robot & Automation Co Ltd. to use automation technology，such as robots，to improve warehouse operations. The key idea is to improve the speed and efficiency of product sorting and delivery in warehouses，cutting down the costs and increasing revenue. JD.com aims to use artificial intelligence to reduce the number of employees from approximately 120,000 to 80,000 over a decade to increase efficiency by reducing manual work and therefore increase the

---

① A recommendation engine is a type of data filtering tool using machine learning algorithms to recommend the most relevant items to a particular user or customer. It operates on the principle of finding patterns in consumer behavior data，which can be collected implicitly or explicitly.

profit margin.

2.3 Alibaba

As for Alibaba, probably what comes to our mind first are AI assistants—Tmall Genie and Ali Assistant. Basically, Alibaba wants to enhance its competitive edge by using AI. Its customer service chatbot processes 95 percent of customer inquiries, both written and spoken ones, and it is very powerful now. What is more, Alibaba says that AI algorithms help to drive internal and customer service operations including smart product and search recommendations. Alibaba also uses AI to help map the most efficient delivery routes. Works quite well! And Alibaba claims that smart logistics has resulted in a 10 percent reduction in vehicle use and a 30% reduction in travel distances.

2.4 eBay

eBay sees AI as a way to maintain consumer interest and a competitive edge. The eBay Shopbot helps users easily find products that they are interested. Besides, customers can communicate with the bot via text, voice or using pictures taken with their phone. Right now, machine learning is an integral component of eBay's business strategy.

2.5 ASOS

Fashion retailer ASOS continues investing in AI and voice recognition[①] systems to influence buyer behaviors. In addition, it has already heavily invested in image recognition[②] technology by introducing a visual search capability which allows ASOS app to match users' photos with similar clothing sold online.

2.6 Rakuten

Rakuten, Japan's largest e-commerce company, continues to invest in AI to better predict customer behaviors as it is critical to the e-commerce success. Right now, with their Rakuten Institute of Technology, they are able to analyze their 200 million products to forecast sales with a high degree of accuracy. Now they are also capable of segmenting buyers more accurately using real-time data. In Rakuten Fits Me app, they use image-recognition technology with the objectives to improve customer satisfaction and sales productivity.

3 Conclusion

Artificial intelligence is going to have a huge impact on the e-commerce industry. AI

---

① Voice recognition is a technique in computing technology by which specialized software and systems are created to identify, distinguish and authenticate the voice of an individual speaker.

② Image recognition, in the context of machine vision, is the ability of software to identify objects, places, people, writing and actions in images. Computers can use machine vision technologies in combination with a camera and artificial intelligence software to achieve image recognition.

ensures that online shoppers get a simpler, faster, more personalized, more comfortable, and more seamless shopping experience than ever before.

New Words

enhance	[ɪnˈhɑːns]	v. 提高,增强;改进
collect	[kəˈlekt]	v. 收集
concept	[ˈkɒnsept]	n. 概念;观念
keyword	[ˈkiːwɜːd]	n. 关键字,关键词
insight	[ˈɪnsaɪt]	n. 见解;洞察力
constantly	[ˈkɒnstəntli]	adv. 不断地,时常地
cyber	[ˈsaɪbə]	adj. 计算机(网络)的,信息技术的
detect	[dɪˈtekt]	v. 发现;检测
fraudulent	[ˈfrɔːdjələnt]	adj. 欺骗的,不诚实的
account	[əˈkaʊnt]	n. 账号
exposure	[ɪkˈspəʊʒə]	n. 接触;泄露,暴露
fraud	[frɔːd]	n. 欺诈,骗子;伪劣品,冒牌货
mitigate	[ˈmɪtɪɡeɪt]	vt. 使缓和,使减轻;使平息
		vi. 减轻,缓和下来
huge	[hjuːdʒ]	adj. 巨大的
handle	[ˈhændl]	v. 处理;应付
integral	[ˈɪntɪɡrəl]	adj. 基本的;必需的;完整的
replacement	[rɪˈpleɪsmənt]	n. 替换,更换;替代品,替换物
engage	[ɪnˈɡeɪdʒ]	v. (使)参与;吸引;引起(注意、兴趣)
trend	[trend]	n. 趋势,倾向
accurate	[ˈækjərət]	adj. 精确的;精准的
forecast	[ˈfɔːkɑːst]	n. 预报
		v. 预测
pipeline	[ˈpaɪplaɪn]	n. 管道,渠道
case	[keɪs]	n. 案例,事例
influence	[ˈɪnfluəns]	v. 影响;支配

Phrases

customer support service	客户支持服务
chat box	聊天框
image search	图像搜索
deal with	处理,应付
machine learning	机器学习
inventory management	库存管理,存货管理

unauthenticated access	未经身份验证的访问
private data	私人数据
decision-making process	决策程序,决策过程
user behaviour	用户行为
purchasing pattern	购买模式
after sales service	售后服务
brand value	品牌价值
data analytic	数据分析
customized recommendation	定制推荐
manual work	手工作业
profit margin	利润率
competitive edge	竞争优势
delivery route	交货路线,送货路线
voice recognition system	语音识别系统
image recognition	图像识别

Abbreviations

AI（Artificial Intelligence）	人工智能
CRM（Customer Relationship Management）	客户关系管理

Exercises

[Ex1] **Answer the following questions according to the text.**

1. What are many e-commerce businesses already using AI to do?

2. What are e-commerce websites are using chatbots to do?

3. What are e-commerce websites able to by predicting the behaviour of the user?

4. What is one of the most important areas in any business? What do you have to do?

5. What did CRM do?

6. What can the study of historical data，data analytics，and latest trends do?

7. What is Alexa? What does it do?

8. What does JD.com aim to do?

9. What does Alibaba claim?

10. What do they do in Rakuten Fits Me app?

[Ex2] **Translate the following terms or phrases from English into Chinese or vice versa.**

1. after sales service   1. _____

2. customized recommendation   2. _____

3. image search   3. _____

4. machine learning   4. _____

5. profit margin   5. _____

6. *n.* 账号   6. _____

7. *adj.* 精确的;精准的   7. _____

8. *n.* 见解;洞察力   8. _____

9. *n.* 关键字,关键词   9. _____

10. *adj.* 欺骗的,不诚实的 10. _____

【Ex3】 Fill in the blanks with the words given below.

heatmap	promote	shopping	search	patterns
automate	previous	conversion	offer	recommend

Product Recommendation—Types and Tips to Seize More Sales

1 Homepage Recommendations

Unlock the full potential of your homepage by incorporating personalized product recommendations. By applying this feature, e-tailers have witnessed a mindboggling increase in ___1___ rate by as high as 248%.

You should, within your homepage, track clicks, mouse movements, and scrolls. This will enable you to create a ___2___ of where each visitor fixates their attention. Place your recommendations strategically by analyzing where most of the interactions happen.

2 Category Recommendations

Instead of recommending products from the entire vastness of your store, it is a better idea to ___3___ best-selling products from the categories your customers in the past ordered from. This will help them discover the products they might have missed while shopping from your brand in the past.

Category page recommendations create algorithms to be able to ___4___ categories precisely, suiting the shoppers using the data on their previous browsing sessions and/or purchases.

The fantastic news is that this type of recommendation type does not only work for ___5___ shoppers. For those visiting your site for the first time and those you don't have any data on, recommend your best-selling products or ___6___ sales o new arrivals.

3 Product Page Recommendation

Capture consumers' shopping ___7___, behavior, purchase history, and wishlist to present recommendations that vary from shopper to shopper. These collected insights can further be used to identify and create critical personas or social groups and ___8___ the process of providing the customers with intelligent and relevant recommendations that can increase the average order value.

And the most obvious way to use these personalized product recommendations is on the product page itself. As your website visitors navigate deeper into the pool of the product pages, you can simultaneously unlock their real interests with the data collected on how they browse and ___9___ . Subsequently, remodel the recommendations—dynamically adapting to the products they are looking at.

4   Shopping Cart Recommendations

Some online stores display a one-step checkout process, which makes their intention of seeking conversion above anything else, clear. This is the right approach as long as you know this is another opportunity to increase the average ___10___ cart through cross-selling.

Try and inject up-selling and cross-selling techniques as the shopping cart is a great touchpoint for the same purpose based on the shopper's browsing activity and purchase history.

【Ex4】 Translate the following passage from English into Chinese.

Use Cases for E-commerce Machine Learning

1   Personalization

Today consumers don't want to get treated as one of many customers. They prefer a highly personalized customer experience. It's that kind of personalization that keeps a customer loyal to your brand. If you can't provide it, they'll find a competitor who can.

Your site can show each user product recommendations based on their known preferences. Such a recommendation engine is an excellent way to deliver personalized customer experiences. It's also the tech utilized by hugely successful brands like Amazon and Netflix.

2   Site Search

Anyone who's used Google lately can tell you that online search has come a long way. Far too often, though, site searches on e-commerce stores don't measure up. Unless you know precisely what to type, it can be extremely hard to find the products you want.

There's no excuse for that in the age of big data and machine learning. Intelligent algorithms—leveraged correctly—make smart searches very easy.

3   Managing supply and demand

E-commerce is about supply and demand. As an online retailer, you must ensure you have the right stock in the correct amounts to satisfy consumer's needs.

Those needs change over time. As such, the more proactive your inventory and supply chain management, the better. That's why demand forecasting is so crucial to online stores. Being able to predict fluctuating customer needs keeps you ahead of the competition. Machine learning helps you make those real-time, accurate predictions.

4   Fraud detection

In this age of cybersecurity awareness, you may think e-commerce fraud is a thing of the past. Unfortunately, you'd be mistaken. The value lost by online retailers to fraud continues to grow steadily.

Fraud detection and fraud protection, then, are essential processes for all online stores. Machine learning technology can beef up these processes and make them more efficient.

5 Improved customer service

All e-commerce businesses understand the importance of customer service. Where machine learning comes in is when it comes to improving the responses of chatbots. An AI-enabled bot can use the interactions it has to learn and tweak its future replies. The more a chatbot gets used, the more human it seems, and the better the information it provides.

Text B

Recommendation Systems in E-commerce

Recommendation systems have gained great importance in recent years, and appear very promising for e-commerce, especially in connection with big data. By working with large amounts of data and using sophisticated algorithms, you can increase the conversions of online stores with modern recommendation systems. You are no doubt familiar with the classic notifications "customers who bought this item also bought..." or "the following products may interest you..." in online shopping. These tips, corresponding to the individual preferences of the user, result from considerable computing power and complicated algorithms. In e-commerce, recommendation systems are already incorporated.

1 What Are Recommendation Systems?

A recommendation system (also known as "recommendation engine", or "recommendation platform") is, according to the definition, an information filtering system that attempts to predict the "rating" or "preference" that a user might give to an item or product. It analyzes past behavior and previous orders, and automatically searches for similar and interesting products for the user.

Recommendation systems are applied in various fields. You will recognize recommendations from web stores, streaming services, and online publications—wherever large amounts of objects are, whether they are books, clothes, or movies—but only a small amount has any relevance to the user. Considering the amount of data and possible search paths, recommendations help by selecting a small amount in advance from the confusing selection and presenting it to the user.

Advantages of recommendation systems:

These systems should make searching a lot easier for the user. Instead of clicking through lots of offers and pages to find the right product, this pre-selection aims to exclude irrelevant and uninteresting offers so that the ones displayed are the ones most suited to the user.

Operators also hope for a positive effect, such as an increase in visitor numbers in the content sector or an increase in sales in e-commerce. In online stores, suitable suggestions should ideally lead to bigger shopping carts, which can significantly increase margins.

2　How Do Recommendation Systems Work?

Recommendation services are always based on sets of data. Depending on the nature of this data set, a distinction is made between different types of systems. These are typically content-based and collaborative systems. Furthermore, there are also context-sensitive recommendation services, as well as those that include the chronological sequence or demographic user data in the analysis.

2.1　Content-based recommendation systems

Content-based recommendation systems suggest objects or content similar to what the user has already searched for, viewed, bought, or rated highly. The systems must be able to establish a similarity between objects. This is done through content analysis. For music streaming services, for example, the system analyzes a piece of music (e.g. the structure of the music) to find pieces that have a similar bass track.

2.2　Collaborative recommendation systems

When it comes to collaborative methods, the suggestions are based on users with similar rating behavior. If they showed a lot of interest in a particular object in the past, the system continues to suggest it. Information or knowledge about the object itself is not necessary at this point. Amazon, for example, uses this method extensively.

2.3　Different prediction methods

Recommendation services use different learning methods. In general, either the memory-based or the model-based method is used. The memory-based method uses all stored evaluation data and calculates the similarity between users or objects. The result is the base, which enables user-object combinations to be predicted. Model-based recommendation services, on the other hand, work with the principles of machine learning. Based on the data, the system can create a mathematical model that can be used to predict the user's interest in a particular product.

3　Examples of Well-Known Recommendation Systems

In e-commerce, product recommendations are basically based on classic cross-selling: users are shown matching or supplementary products. Amazon is well ahead regarding product recommendations. The market leader has a huge pool of user-generated data available. Early on, the e-commerce giant recognized the fact that with the right product recommendations, the customer's shopping carts would fill up more quickly. In the meantime, you can find up to five different types of product recommendations at different points in the purchasing process(Figure 8-1):

- Customers who viewed this item also viewed.
- Customers who bought this item also bought.
- Frequently bought together.
- What do customers buy after viewing this item?
- Your recently viewed items and featured recommendations.

Figure 8-1　Different Product Suggestions in Amazon's Online Store

Amazingly, Amazon has released its deep-learning software DSSTNE as open source. The software is the basis for recommendations on Amazon. Basically, there's a trend towards more in-depth recommendation systems in e-commerce. In addition to the possibility of displaying "Popular items", more and more companies rely on highly personalized recommendations. As a rule, several recommendation strategies are brought together: purchasing interests, popular items, and other factors, such as product availability and price changes, are automatically included.

4　Software for Recommendation Systems in E-commerce

In e-commerce, recommendation systems are a particularly important topic. This is because online stores have the possibility to increase their conversion rate through suitable recommendations and generate more sales. Many shop systems have integrated standard features for product recommendations. This allows a solid analysis and calculation, but the best way is to use a special software solution.

Various providers offer companies SaaS（Software as a Service）solutions. Most providers promise software solutions, which are individually tailored and capable of self-learning, as recommendation services based on their own personalization technology (model-based method). The great advantage of SaaS solutions is that they significantly reduce the time and effort required for implementation. Store owners don't have to invest in hardware or software. Most cloud-based solutions also feature a large range of functions. The software solutions take on three important steps: database tracking, feature engineering, and data processing and analyzing at the end.

4.1 Tracking databases

In order to be able to analyze data, you have to collect it first. This can be done through classic tracking methods for most software solutions. Tracking includes relevant data on the location, shopping cart, date and time, behavior, and usually the completely traceable customer journey. The program collects all this information and keeps it in a database.

4.2 Feature Engineering

When it comes to feature engineering, the goal is to filter out features (i.e. characteristics, properties) from the database. These features can be of a different nature, such as the time of the visit and its duration, the distances between actions, and many more. However, few features are of any relevance to the predictions later on. The challenge that the system faces is to precisely identify these important features. For this purpose, the system needs to find the characteristics that have a significant influence on the purchasing behavior, and ultimately, the purchase decision. The individual composition of the features varies according to the store, so an intelligent analysis is required.

4.3 Processing and analyzing data

Based on the features defined for the online store i.e. the relevant characteristics and properties, the system can now calculate predictions for product recommendations. Creating these prognosis models requires a huge amount of computing power, and sometimes takes several hours. The system saves the models, which then serve as a basis for calculating recommendations. Every store visitor receives up-to-date tips and recommendations tailored to them.

5 Conclusion

Personalization is becoming increasingly important in online marketing. This is not only due to the fact that companies feel under pressure from their competition and have to constantly strive to stand out from the crowd, but also because of users' changed perceptions. Today users are able to identify advertisements more quickly and ignore them. If you are，however，able to attract attention by providing customized and relevant information，and by addressing users directly，the chance of conversion is much higher. The same is true for recommendation systems，which are becoming more sensitive and accurate. Finding the right strategy and reaching potential customers can have a positive impact on sales and the success of a company in e-commerce.

New Words

considerable	[kənˈsɪdərəbl]	adj. 相当大的，相当多的
rate	[reɪt]	v. 评估，评价
publication	[ˌpʌblɪˈkeɪʃn]	n. 出版；出版物
pre-selection	[pˈriːsɪlˈekʃn]	n. 预筛，预选
margin	[ˈmɑːdʒɪn]	n. 利润，盈余
collaborative	[kəˈlæbərətɪv]	adj. 合作的，协作的
context-sensitive	[ˈkɒnteksˈsensətɪv]	adj. 与内容相关的，上下文相关的
chronological	[ˌkrɒnəˈlɒdʒɪkl]	adj. 按时间排序的
extensively	[ɪkˈstensɪvli]	adv. 广泛地
combination	[ˌkɒmbɪˈneɪʃn]	n. 结合(体)；联合(体)
cross-selling	[krɒs-ˈselɪŋ]	n. 交叉销售
supplementary	[ˌsʌplɪˈmentri]	adj. 增补的，追加的
user-generated	[ˌjuːzər-dʒenəreɪtɪd]	adj. 用户创造的(内容)，用户产生的
availability	[əˌveɪləˈbɪləti]	n. 可用性；有效性
solid	[ˈsɒlɪd]	adj. 可靠的；可信赖的
self-learning	[ˈselfˈlɜːnɪŋ]	n. 自学习(能力)
traceable	[ˈtreɪsəbl]	adj. 可追踪的
duration	[djuˈreɪʃn]	n. 持续时间；期间
strive	[straɪv]	vi. 努力奋斗，力求，力争
ignore	[ɪgˈnɔː]	v. 忽视；佯装未见

Phrases

recommendation system	推荐系统
sophisticated algorithm	复杂算法
individual preference	个人偏好
recommendation engine	推荐引擎
recommendation platform	推荐平台
information filtering system	信息过滤系统
data set	数据集
content-based collaborative system	基于内容的协作系统

search for	搜索;查找
content analysis	内容分析
at this point	此时此刻
prediction method	预测方法
memory-based method	基于记忆的方法
model-based method	基于模型的方法
mathematical model	数学模型
fill up	(使)充满;填充
cloud-based solution	基于云的解决方案
database tracking	数据库跟踪
feature engineering	特征工程
calculate prediction	计算预测
prognosis model	预后模型
computing power	计算能力
stand out from	脱颖而出

Abbreviations

SaaS (Software as a Service)	软件即服务

Exercises

【Ex5】 **Answer the following questions according to the text.**

1. What has happened to recommendation systems in recent years?

2. What is a recommendation system according to the definition?

3. What should these systems do?

4. What do content-based recommendation systems do?

5. What can the system do based on the data?

6. What are the five different types of product recommendations you can find at different points in the purchasing process?

7. Why are recommendation systems a particularly important topic in e-commerce?

8. What is the great advantage of SaaS solutions?

9. What is the goal when it comes to feature engineering?

10. Why is personalization becoming increasingly important in online marketing?

【Ex6】 **Translate the following terms or phrases from English into Chinese or vice versa.**

1. data set   1. _____

2. individual preference   2. _____

3. mathematical model   3. _____

4. prediction method   4. _____

5. recommendation platform   5. _____

6. *adj*. 与内容相关的   6. _____

7. *n*. 交叉销售   7. _____

8. *adj*. 用户创造的,用户产生的   8. _____

9. *n*. 可用性;有效性   9. _____

10. *adj*. 可追踪的   10. _____

Reading Material

E-commerce Chatbots

Chatbots are a form of conversational① AI designed to simplify human interaction with computers. Chatbots are programmed to simulate human conversation and exhibit② intelligent behavior that is equivalent to that of a human.

In the e-commerce world, retail companies and telecommunication providers use chatbots as an additional interaction channel with their customers. Chatbots are becoming the most popular way to digitally communicate with customers around the world. They are enabling retailers to have better shopping experiences. The chatbots are designed to lead customers through a linear③ process flow to complete requests or transactions. They are part of a wider transition to automate business processes and systems that support customer service in the e-commerce industry. They streamline④ a vast matrix of complex interactions and drive business forward.

1 The Benefits of Chatbots

In the e-commerce world, chatbots are recreating the experience users have with businesses and replacing it with an experience they have with friends. Since they are built with AI and driven by a predefined set of rules⑤, they learn and adapt themselves to complex business problems and offer quick solutions to user inquiries—just as humans would. There are many benefits of using chatbots for your e-commerce business. The following are only some of them.

1.1 24×7 Support

Most customers expect businesses to be available 24 hours a day, 7 days a week. While having a customer service team around-the-clock⑥ is an expensive option, with

---

① conversational [ˌkɒnvəˈseɪʃənl] *adj*. 会话的,谈话的,对话的。

② exhibit [ɪɡˈzɪbɪt] *v*. 表现。

③ linear [ˈlɪniə] *adj*. 线性的。

④ streamline [ˈstriːmlaɪn] *vt*. 使简单化。

⑤ set of rule:规则集。

⑥ around-the-clock [əˌraʊnd ðəˈklɒk] *adj*. 连续不断的。

chatbots you can eliminate that cost and still ensure your customers are catered to immediately by chatbots—irrespective of what time of the day it is. Offering 24-hour support is a great way to ensure customer satisfaction[①].

1.2　Personalization

Chatbots can also be used to collect data about your visitors and use it to make better product suggestions and recommendations. Understanding customer inquiries, their needs and preferences can allow you to personalize product pages and build customer loyalty and affinity[②]. What's more, chatbots can also notify customers when items are out of stock[③], and suggest appropriate alternate products[④] based on their preferences while informing them about their expected delivery date and time. Retail giant H&M's chatbot asks customers some questions about their style and offers products accordingly. When it comes to e-commerce, personalization is everything, and chatbots are a great way to forge a stronger and more relevant connection.

1.3　Reduced Costs

Having chatbots do most (or probably all) of your customer service activities can help you save a substantial amount of money on your customer service team. Efficient customer assistance by chatbots requires less human support, allowing you to drive your focus on more critical aspects of your e-commerce site, such as page layout or checkout. You can also dramatically reduce human error and enable efficient customer service with minimal resource costs.

1.4　Product Guidance

Very often, e-commerce visitors get lost in the maze[⑤] of millions of products. Chatbots can help such customers find the exact product they are looking for in a huge catalog and directly jump to the checkout page, or obtain information on current sales. By providing answers or advice to specific customer inquiries, chatbots can guide clients and enable them to make purchases on the fly. For example, eBay's ShopBot guides customers through their products, asks questions to understand their needs, and offers recommendations like a real sales associate.

1.5　Cart Recovery

Contrary to[⑥] popular belief, an abandoned cart can also be a great source of

---

① satisfaction [ˌsætɪsˈfækʃn] n. 满足,称心。
② affinity [əˈfɪnəti] n. 密切关系。
③ out of stock: (商店等中)无现货的。
④ alternate product: 替代产品。
⑤ maze [meɪz] n. 迷宫。
⑥ contrary to: 与…相反。

revenue. Chatbots can remind users of items in their abandoned shopping cart and ask them if they are willing to proceed towards checkout or if they would like to clean their cart. On most occasions，such reminders push customers to revisit their cart and enable them to purchase some if not all of the items in their cart.

2　E-commerce Chatbot Best Practices

E-commerce customers are always on the lookout for high-value experiences that make their shopping journey exciting and personal. One way to achieve this is by allowing consumers to engage in one-to-one conversations with chatbots and have their questions answered quickly and easily. If you're planning on building your own chatbot and offering a customer experience like never before，here are some tips.

2.1　Be Transparent

Although chatbots can hold conversations just as fluently as humans，never let customers assume they are speaking to a human and not a bot. Automated responses can help gather basic information from customers.

2.2　Protect Customer Privacy

Every customer appreciates his/her privacy，therefore，never let the chatbot get too intrusive①. Allow it to communicate only when asked to. Also，since customers might share a lot of personal and private information with the chatbot，safeguard and protect that data and value their privacy under all circumstances②.

2.3　Deeply Integrate AI

Since chatbots are expected to have answers to all possible customer inquiries，make sure yours is equipped and trained appropriately. Deeply integrating AI into your chatbot can enable it to locate and provide accurate information to customers.

2.4　Prioritize③ Responsiveness

Since chatbots are built to provide instant customer service，make sure they are extremely responsive and relevant. Do not make customers wait. When customers speak to chatbots，the chatbots should be able to understand their issues and offer immediate suggestions or solutions. Ensure the chatbots provide easy options and concise④ information that is sufficient for customers to take an action.

2.5　Know When to Refer to a Human

To error is human，and it holds the same for chatbots as well. If a customer comes

---

① intrusive [ɪnˈtruːsɪv] *adj*. 打扰的；侵入的。
② circumstance [ˈsɜːkəmstəns] *n*. 条件；环境；情况。
③ prioritize [praɪˈɒrətaɪz] *vt*. 优先处理。
④ concise [kənˈsaɪs] 简明的，简洁的。

up with an inquiry or question to which the chatbot has no answer，instead of offering the same response over and over again，referring the customer to a human customer service agent will be the ideal course of action.

3　Stay Ahead of Competition with E-commerce Chatbots

The e-commerce industry is a very competitive one；with millions of other merchants selling exactly the same products as you do，staying ahead of the curve is extremely important. Although chatbots will never be able to replace humans，they are still an incredible① asset to your e-commerce strategy. If you're looking to serve your customers in efficient ways—guide them through your e-commerce website，personalize their experiences，and offer 24×7 support—it's time you build your own chatbot and support your buyers efficiently and personally.

Text A 参考译文
人工智能在电子商务中的应用及案例

许多电子商务企业已经在使用人工智能以更好地了解他们的客户，产生新的潜在客户，并提供更好的客户体验。

1　应用

1.1　聊天机器人

电子商务网站正在使用聊天机器人改善客户支持服务。聊天机器人为买家提供全天候的客户支持。当访问任何公认的电子商务网站时，你都会收到一个聊天框提示，询问你想要什么或如何能帮助你。你可以在聊天框中说出你的要求，你会得到高度过滤的结果。聊天机器人使用人工智能构建，能够与人类交流。它们还可以收集你过去的数据，为你提供非常个性化的用户体验。

1.2　图像搜索

你有没有遇到过这样的情况——你喜欢某种产品或物品，但不知道它叫什么或是什么？人工智能服务为你简化了这项任务。图像搜索的概念是通过在电子商务网站中使用人工智能技术实现的。人工智能使理解图像成为可能。买家可以根据图片进行搜索。电子商务网站的移动应用程序只需将相机指向产品即可找到产品，这样就不需要进行关键字搜索。

1.3　处理客户数据

电子商务每天都要处理大量数据。这些数据可以是每日销售额、售出商品总数、某个

---

① incredible［ɪnˈkredəbl］*adj.* 惊人的；难以置信的。

地区收到的订单数量等。它还必须处理客户数据。人类不可能处理这么多的数据。人工智能不仅能够以更结构化的形式收集这些数据，还可以从这些数据中产生合适的见解。

1.4　推荐系统

你有没有体验过像亚马逊这样的电子商务网站是如何不断展示与你刚刚查看的产品类似的产品的？这就是人工智能在电子商务中的应用。人工智能和机器学习算法可以根据买家过去的搜索、喜好和经常购买的产品预测买家的行为。通过预测用户的行为，电子商务网站能够推荐用户非常感兴趣的产品。这将改善用户体验，因为用户不再需要花费数小时搜寻产品。这也有助于电子商务网站提高销售额。

1.5　库存管理

库存管理是任何企业中最重要的领域之一。你必须随时了解你持有多少库存以及还需要多少库存。电子商务网站上有数千种产品类别。对一个人来说，每天关注所有产品的库存是不可能的。这就是人工智能的用武之地。人工智能应用程序帮助电子商务管理库存。此外，随着时间的推移，库存管理系统将变得更好。人工智能系统在当前需求和未来需求之间建立关联。

1.6　网络安全

人工智能还提高了电子商务网站的网络安全性。它可以防止或检测任何欺诈活动。电子商务每天都必须处理大量的交易。网络犯罪分子和黑客可以侵入用户的账户以获得未经验证的访问权限。这可能会导致私人数据曝光和网络欺诈，这家企业的声誉也将受到重创。为了防止这种情况，开发了机器学习算法，这可以减少网站上欺诈活动的机会。

1.7　更好的决策

通过使用人工智能，电子商务可以做出更好的决策。数据分析师每天都要处理大量数据。这些数据的规模太大，他们无法处理。此外，分析数据也成为一项困难的任务。人工智能加快了电子商务的决策过程。人工智能算法可以通过预测用户行为及其购买模式，轻松识别数据中的复杂模式。

1.8　售后服务

仅仅销售产品是不够的，企业必须在整个购买周期中帮助客户。售后服务是电子商务不可或缺的一部分。人工智能应用程序可以自动反馈表单，替换和处理产品中的任何其他歧义。通过解决买家的问题，网站的品牌价值得到提升。

1.9　客户关系管理

过去，客户关系管理（CRM）依靠人们收集的大量数据为客户服务。但如今，人工智能可以预测哪些客户最有可能购买，以及企业如何更好地与客户互动。人工智能应用程序可以帮助企业识别趋势，并根据最新趋势制订行动计划。在机器学习算法的帮助下，高级CRM可以随着时间的推移进行学习和改进。

1.10　销售改进

人工智能应用程序可以生成并做出电子商务业务的准确预测。对历史数据、数据分析和最新趋势的研究有助于优化资源配置，建立健康的渠道，并分析团队绩效。销售经理可以分析趋势，通过提前制定策略提高销售额。

2　案例

2.1　亚马逊

Alexa 是亚马逊最受欢迎和最著名的人工智能产品之一。它有助于驱动对亚马逊有针对性的营销战略至关重要的算法。人工智能允许亚马逊预测哪些产品将是客户最需要的，以根据客户搜索提供定制推荐。据说亚马逊的推荐引擎促成的交易占总销售额的 35%。

2.2　京东

总部位于北京的京东已与 Siasun Robot&Automation 公司合作，利用机器人等自动化技术改善仓库运营。其核心思想是提高仓库产品分拣和交付的速度和效率，降低成本，增加收入。京东的目标是利用人工智能在 10 年内将员工数量从大约 12 万人减少到 8 万人，通过减少体力劳动提高效率，从而提高利润率。

2.3　阿里巴巴

说到阿里巴巴，我们首先想到的可能是人工智能助手——天猫精灵和阿里助手。基本上，阿里巴巴希望通过使用人工智能增强其竞争优势。它的客户服务聊天机器人处理了 95% 的客户查询，包括文字和口头查询，而且现在它非常强大。此外，阿里巴巴表示，人工智能算法有助于推动内部和客户服务运营，包括智能产品和搜索推荐。阿里巴巴还使用人工智能绘制最高效的配送路线，效果很好。阿里巴巴声称，智能物流使车辆使用量减少了 10%，运送距离减少了 30%。

2.4　易趣

易趣将人工智能视为维护消费者利益和竞争优势的一种方式。eBay Shopbot 帮助用户轻松找到他们感兴趣的产品。此外，客户还可以通过文本、语音或使用手机拍摄的照片与机器人沟通。目前，机器学习是 eBay 商业战略不可或缺的组成部分。

2.5　ASOS

时装零售商 ASOS 继续投资人工智能和语音识别系统，以影响买家行为。此外，该公司已经在图像识别技术上投入巨资，引入了一种视觉搜索功能，允许 ASOS 应用程序将用户的照片与在线销售的类似服装进行匹配。

2.6　乐天

日本最大的电子商务企业——乐天继续投资人工智能，以更好地预测客户行为，因为它对电子商务的成功至关重要。现在，凭借乐天技术研究院（Rakuten Institute of

Technology),它们能够分析 2 亿件产品,以高度准确地预测销售额。现在,乐天还能够使用实时数据更准确地划分买家。在乐天 Fits Me 应用程序中使用了图像识别技术,旨在提高客户满意度和销售效率。

3　结论

人工智能将对电子商务行业产生巨大影响。人工智能确保网上购物者获得比以往任何时候都更简单、更快捷、更个性化、更舒适、更无缝的购物体验。

Unit 9

Text A

Securing Your E-commerce Systems

As the use of the Internet continues to grow, websites are assuming greater importance as the public face of business. Furthermore, the revenues generated by e-commerce systems mean that organisations are becoming increasingly reliant on them as core elements of their business.

With this high level of dependency upon the services provided by e-commerce systems, it is essential that they are protected from the threats posed by hackers, viruses, fraud and denial-of-service attacks.

Every business should take steps to secure their e-commerce systems, although smaller businesses may choose to work with third-party specialists to implement some of the more sophisticated security controls.

This passage looks at the security threats posed to e-commerce systems and the damage they can potentially cause to your business. It provides advice on how best to address these threats, by identifying the risks that they pose and implementing the appropriate level of security controls to counter them.

1   E-commerce Security Issues

E-commerce systems are based upon Internet use, which provides open and easy communications on a global basis. However, because the Internet is unregulated, unmanaged and uncontrolled, it poses a wide range of risks and threats to the systems operating on it.

The use of the Internet means that your internal IT and e-commerce systems are potentially accessible by anyone, irrespective of their location.

1.1   Threats from Hackers and the Risks to Business

Some of the more common threats that hackers pose to e-commerce systems include:
- carrying out Denial-of-Service (DoS[①]) attacks that stop access to authorised users

---

①   A Denial of Service (DoS) attack is an incident in which a user or organization is deprived of the services of a resource they would normally expect to have.

拒绝服务攻击的目的是阻止合法用户对正常网络资源的访问，它是用超出被攻击目标处理能力的海量数据包消耗可用系统、带宽资源，致使网络服务瘫痪的一种攻击手段。

of a website, so that the site is forced to offer a reduced level of service or, in some cases, ceases operation completely.

- gaining access to sensitive data, such as price lists, catalogues and valuable intellectual property, and altering, destroying or copying it.
- altering your website, thereby damaging your image or directing your customers to another site.
- gaining access to financial information about your business or your customers, with a view to perpetrating fraud.
- using viruses to corrupt your business data.

1.2　Impact of a Security Incident on the Business

If your website is hacked into, it can have a significant impact upon a business running an e-commerce service. The potential business implications of a security incident include the following:

- direct financial loss as a consequence of fraud or litigation.
- subsequent loss as a result of unwelcome publicity.
- criminal charges if you are found to be in breach of the Data Protection or Computer Misuse Acts, or other regulation on e-commerce.
- loss of market share if customer confidence is affected by a DoS attack.

The image presented by your business, together with the brands under which you trade, are valuable assets. It is important to recognise that the use of e-commerce creates new ways for both image and brands to be attacked.

2　Identifying E-commerce Threats and Vulnerabilities

It is important that you understand the risks facing your e-commerce system, and the potential impact of any security incident.

2.1　What are the Threats?

Threats to e-commerce systems can be either malicious or accidental. The procedures and controls you put in place to protect your site should help minimise both.

Malicious threats could include:

- hackers attempting to penetrate a system to read or alter sensitive data.
- burglars stealing a server or laptop that has unprotected sensitive data on its disk.
- imposters posing as legitimate users and even creating a website similar to yours.
- authorised users downloading a webpage or receiving an email with hidden active content that attacks your systems or sends sensitive information to unauthorised people.

You should consider potential threats to sensitive information from three angles:

- Where (or who) are the potential sources of threats?

- What level of expertise is the hacker likely to possess? How much effort are they likely to expend in attempting to breach your security?
- What facilities and tools are available to them?

The real threat may not be the most obvious one. Attacks from authorised users (such as a disaffected employee or partner) are far more common than attacks by hackers.

2.2 E-commerce Systems Risk Assessment

A risk assessment can be carried out to provide an organisation with a clear understanding of the risks facing its e-commerce system and associated business processes, and the potential impact if a security incident arises.

A key part of a risk assessment is defining the business' information access requirements. This will cover the rules of access for different groups of users. For example, different rules may apply for employees, consultants, managed service providers, suppliers, customers, auditors and government agencies.

Any analysis should also take account of how electronic transactions are verified. How do you know that an order has actually come from a known customer? Where contracts are exchanged electronically, who can sign them and how can it be proved which is the signed version?

3 Common E-commerce Security Controls

You should introduce sufficient security controls to reduce risk to e-commerce systems. However these controls should not be so restrictive that they damage the employees' performance.

Some of the common security controls are listed below.

3.1 User Authentication

There are several techniques that can identify and verify someone seeking to access an e-commerce system. These include:

- A user name and password combination, where the password can vary in length and include numbers and characters. Remember to include a system that prompts employees to change their passwords at regular intervals.
- "Two-factor" authentication requiring something the user has (eg an authentication token) and something the user knows (eg a personal identification number).
- A digital certificate that enables authentication through the use of an individual's unique signing key.
- A person's unique physical attribute, referred to as a biometric. This can range from a fingerprint or iris scan, through to retina or facial-feature recognition.

3.2　Access control

This restricts different classes of users to subsets of information and ensures that they can only access data and services for which they have been authorised. These include using：

- network restrictions to prevent access to other computer systems and networks.
- application controls to ensure individuals are limited in the data or service they can access.
- restrictions on what can be copied from the system and stored on pen drives，memory sticks or CDs/DVDs[①].
- limits on the sending and receiving of certain types of email attachments.

Changes to access privileges must be controlled to prevent users retaining them if they transfer between departments or leave the business.

3.3　Data encryption

Encryption scrambles data，and is used to protect information that is being held on a computer，copied onto CDs or DVDs or transmitted over a network. It uses technologies such as Virtual Private Networks (VPNs) and secure socket layers.

3.4　Firewall

This is a hardware or software security device that filters information passing between internal and external networks. It controls access to the Internet by internal users，and prevent outside parties from gaining access to systems and information on the internal network.

A firewall can be applied at the network level to provide protection for multiple workstations or internal networks，or at the personal level where it is installed on an individual PC.

3.5　Intrusion detection

These products monitor system and network activity to spot any attempt being made to gain access. If a detection system suspects an attack，it can generate an alarm，such as an email alert，based upon the type of activity it has identified.

Despite the sophistication of these controls，they are only as good as the people who use them. A continual awareness programme is a vital component of any security policy.

---

① A type of compact disc able to store large amounts of data，especially high-resolution audio-visual material.

4　Risks from Viruses，Trojans，Worms and Botnets

Viruses，Trojan horses[①]，worms[②] and botnets[③] are all computer programs that can infect computers.

Viruses and worms spread across computers and networks by making copies of themselves，usually without the knowledge of the computer user.

A Trojan horse is a program that appears to be legitimate but actually contains another program or block of undesired malicious，destructive code，disguised and hidden in a block of desirable code. Trojans can be used to infect a computer with a virus.

A back-door Trojan is a program that allows a remote user or hacker to bypass the normal access controls of a computer and gain unauthorised control over it. Typically，a virus is used to place the back-door Trojan onto a computer，and once the computer is online，the person who sent the Trojan can run programs on the infected computer，access personal files，and modify and upload files.

A botnet is a group of infected，remotely-controlled computers. The hacker sends out a virus，Trojan or worm to ordinary computers. The virus，Trojan or worm gains access to the computer，usually through some malicious application that they are carrying. This in turn allows the hacker to gain full control of the now-infected computers. These computers can then be used to launch denial-of-service attacks，distribute spam emails and commit click fraud，identity theft and thefts of log-in details and credit card numbers.

Risks can also come from popular social networking sites. Be aware of messages containing links to current events，entertainment，or other high traffic content. It has been reported that these links take the user to phishing websites where personal user details can be stolen or worms，Trojans or viruses can strike.

Botnets are very difficult to prevent by the use of software tools alone，it is important that users follow best practice guidance with regards to emails and website usage. It is important that you ensure that all software and anti-virus tools are up to

---

①　A Trojan horse，or Trojan，is <u>malware</u>(恶意软件) that appears to perform a desirable function for the user prior to run or install but instead facilitates unauthorized access of the user's computer system.

木马程序是指潜伏在计算机中,受外部用户控制以窃取本机信息或者控制权的程序。

②　A computer worm is a self-replicating malware computer program. It uses a computer network to send copies of itself to other nodes (computers on the network) and it may do so without any user intervention.

蠕虫病毒是自包含的程序,能传播自身功能的副本或它的某些部分到其他的计算机系统中(通常是经过网络连接),与一般病毒不同,蠕虫不需要将其自身附着到宿主程序。

③　A botnet is a number of Internet computers that，although their owners are unaware of it，have been set up to forward transmissions (including spam or viruses) to other computers on the Internet.

botnet 也被称作僵尸网络,是许多台被恶意代码感染、控制的与互联网相连接的计算机。感染的计算机能够被黑客远程控制,用来发送垃圾邮件、传播计算机病毒、发动拒绝服务攻击。

date, to prevent malicious code from exploiting security holes in software and making your system vulnerable.

5 Risks to E-commerce Systems

While some viruses are merely irritants, others can have extremely harmful effects. Some of the threats that they pose to e-commerce systems include:

- corrupting or deleting data on the hard disk of your server.
- stealing confidential data by enabling hackers to record user keystrokes.
- enabling hackers to hijack your system and use it for their own purposes, which may include adding it to a larger group of botnets.
- using your computer for malicious purposes, such as carrying out a denial-of-service attack on another website, alone or as part of a botnet.
- harming customer and trading partner relationships by forwarding viruses to them from your own system.

6 How Do Viruses Spread?

Viruses are able to infect computers through a number of different routes. These include:

- CDs and other forms of removable media containing infected documents.
- emails containing infected attachments.
- Internet worms that exploit holes in your system's operating system when you are connected to the Internet.

7 Spyware

Spyware is software that is placed on your computer when you visit certain websites. It is used to secretly gather information about your usage and sends it back to advertisers or other interested parties. In addition to tracking your system use, it can also slow down or crash your computer.

8 Preventing Problems from Viruses, Trojans, Worms and Botnets

Anti-virus software should be used to protect against viruses. It can detect viruses, prevent access to infected files and quarantine any infected files.

There are different types of anti-virus software:

- Virus scanners- must be updated regularly, usually by connecting to the supplier's website, in order to recognise new viruses.
- Heuristics software- detects viruses by applying general rules about what viruses look like. While it does not require frequent updates, this software can be prone to giving false alarms.

The threat of virus infection can be minimised by：

- using a virus checker on your Internet connection to trap viruses both entering and leaving the business' IT systems.
- running virus checkers on servers to trap any viruses that have managed to evade the above check.
- running individual virus checkers on users' PCs to ensure that they have not downloaded a virus directly，or inadvertently introduced one via a CD or other forms of removable media.

New Words

reliant	[rɪˈlaɪənt]	adj. 信赖的，依靠的
threat	[θret]	n. 威胁
pose	[pəʊz]	v. 形成，引起，造成
hacker	[ˈhækə]	n. 黑客
virus	[ˈvaɪrəs]	n. 病毒
specialist	[ˈspeʃəlɪst]	n. 专家
potentially	[pəˈtenʃəli]	adv. 潜在地
appropriate	[əˈprəʊpriət]	adj. 适当的
counter	[ˈkaʊntə]	v. 抵制，抵消
unregulated	[ˌʌnˈregjʊleɪtɪd]	adj. 无控制的，无调节的
authorise	[ˈɒθəraɪz]	vt. 批准
destroy	[dɪˈstrɔɪ]	vt. 破坏，毁坏，消灭
perpetrate	[ˈpɜːpətreɪt]	v. 犯(罪)，做(错事)，干(坏事)
corrupt	[kəˈrʌpt]	vt. 破坏，损坏
impact	[ˈɪmpækt]	n. 碰撞，冲击，影响，效果
implication	[ˌɪmplɪˈkeɪʃn]	n. 含意，暗示；牵连
incident	[ˈɪnsɪdənt]	n. 事件
litigation	[ˌlɪtɪˈgeɪʃn]	n. 诉讼，起诉
subsequent	[ˈsʌbsɪkwənt]	adj. 后来的，并发的
regulation	[ˌregjuˈleɪʃn]	n. 规则，规章
confidence	[ˈkɒnfɪdəns]	n. 信心
asset	[ˈæset]	n. 资产
recognise	[ˈrekəgnaɪz]	v. 承认，识别，认可
accidental	[ˌæksɪˈdentl]	adj. 意外的
burglar	[ˈbɜːglə]	n. 窃贼
unprotected	[ˌʌnprəˈtektɪd]	adj. 无保护的，无防卫的
disaffected	[ˌdɪsəˈfektɪd]	adj. 不满的，不忠的
assessment	[əˈsesmənt]	n. 评估，估价

consultant	[kənˈsʌltənt]	n.顾问,商议者,咨询者
restrictive	[rɪˈstrɪktɪv]	adj.限制性的
character	[ˈkærəktə]	n.字符
biometric	[ˌbaɪəʊˈmetrɪk]	n.生物特征
iris	[ˈaɪrɪs]	n.虹膜
retina	[ˈretɪnə]	n.视网膜
subset	[ˈsʌbset]	n.子集
ensure	[ɪnˈʃʊə]	v.确保,确保,保证
attachment	[əˈtætʃmənt]	n.附件
privilege	[ˈprɪvəlɪdʒ]	n.特权
firewall	[ˈfaɪəwɔːl]	n.防火墙
intrusion	[ɪnˈtruːʒn]	n.闯入,侵扰
suspect	[səˈspekt]	v.怀疑,猜想
alarm	[əˈlɑːm]	n.警报
		vt.警告
sophistication	[səˌfɪstɪˈkeɪʃn]	n.复杂巧妙,高水平
awareness	[əˈweənəs]	n.知道,察觉
component	[kəmˈpəʊnənt]	n.成分
		adj.组成的,构成的
Trojan	[ˈtrəʊdʒən]	n.特洛伊木马
worm	[wɜːm]	n.蠕虫
botnet	[ˈbɒtnet]	n.僵尸网络
infect	[ɪnˈfekt]	vt.传染,感染
undesired	[ˈʌndɪˈzaɪəd]	adj.不受欢迎的
destructive	[dɪˈstrʌktɪv]	adj.破坏(性)的
disguise	[dɪsˈgaɪz]	v.假装,伪装,掩饰
		n.伪装
desirable	[dɪˈzaɪərəbl]	adj.期望的,合意的,令人想要的
bypass	[ˈbaɪpɑːs]	vt.绕过,迂回
		n.旁路
ordinary	[ˈɔːdnri]	adj.平常的,普通的,平凡的
entertainment	[ˌentəˈteɪnmənt]	n.娱乐
vulnerable	[ˈvʌlnərəbl]	adj.易受攻击的
irritant	[ˈɪrɪtənt]	n.令人烦恼的事物,造成麻烦的事物
harmful	[ˈhɑːmfl]	adj.有害的
confidential	[ˌkɒnfɪˈdenʃl]	adj.秘密的,机密的
keystroke	[ˈkiːstrəʊk]	n.键击,按键
hijack	[ˈhaɪdʒæk]	vt.劫持

harm	[hɑːm]	vt. & n. 伤害,损害
removable	[rɪˈmuːvəbl]	adj. 可移动的
spyware	[ˈspaɪweə]	n. 间谍软件
advertiser	[ˈædvətaɪzə]	n. 登广告者,广告客户
heuristic	[hjuˈrɪstɪk]	adj. 启发式的
checker	[ˈtʃekə]	n. 检测程序
inadvertently	[ˌɪnədˈvɜːtəntli]	adv. 不注意地,无意地

Phrases

protect from	保护
take steps	采取措施
cease operation	停止运行
price list	价格表
intellectual property	知识产权
with a view to	为了…,以…为目的
market share	市场份额,市场占有率
potential impact	潜在影响
government agency	政府机构
take account of	考虑
at regular intervals	每隔一定间隔
personal identification number	个人身份号码
facial-feature recognition	面部特征识别
memory stick	存储条,存储棒
network level	网络层
Trojan horse	特洛伊木马
back-door Trojan	后门特洛伊木马
send out	放出
spam email	垃圾电子邮件
be aware of	知道
security hole	安全漏洞
hard disk	硬盘
be prone to …	有…的倾向,易于
false alarm	假警报

Abbreviations

DoS(Denial-of-Service)	拒绝服务
VPN(Virtual Private Network)	虚拟专用网
CD(Compact Disc)	光盘

DVD（Digital Video Disc）　　　　数字视频光盘

PC（Personal Computer）　　　　　个人计算机

Exercises

【Ex1】 **Answer the following questions according to the text.**

1. What does this passage talk about?

2. Why does the Internet pose a wide range of risks and threats to the systems operating on it?

3. What are the more common threats that hackers pose to e-commerce systems mentioned in the passage?

4. Why do people carry out risk assessment?

5. What are some of the common security controls mentioned in the passage?

6. What is a Trojan horse?

7. What do some of the threats that viruses pose to e-commerce systems include?

8. How do viruses spread?

9. What is spyware?

10. How many types of anti-virus software are listed in the passage? What are they?

【Ex2】 **Translate the following terms or phrases from English into Chinese or vice versa.**

1. intellectual property	1. _____
2. security hole	2. _____
3. spam email	3. _____
4. virtual private network	4. _____
5. facial-feature recognition	5. _____
6. *n.* 僵尸网络	6. _____
7. *n.* 检测程序	7. _____
8. *n.* 字符	8. _____
9. *vt.* 劫持	9. _____
10. *vt.* 传染，感染	10. _____

【Ex3】 **Fill in the blanks with the words given below.**

Developed	security	passing	encryption	supports
downloaded	based	handled	integral	standard

Secure Sockets Layer

The Secure Sockets Layer（SSL）is a commonly-used protocol for managing the ___1___ of a message transmission on the Internet. SSL has recently been succeeded by Transport Layer Security（TLS），which is ___2___ on SSL. SSL uses a program layer located between the Internet's Hypertext Transfer Protocol (HTTP) and Transport Control Protocol (TCP) layers. SSL is included as part of both the Microsoft and Netscape browsers and most Web server products. ____3____ by Netscape, SSL also gained the support of Microsoft and other Internet client/server developers as well and became the de facto ____4____ until evolving into Transport Layer Security. The "sockets" part of the term refers to the sockets method of ____5____ data back and forth between a client and a server program in a network or between program layers in the same computer. SSL uses the public-and-private key ____6____ system from RSA, which also includes the use of a digital certificate.

TLS and SSL are an ____7____ part of most Web browsers (clients) and Web servers. If a Web site is on a server that ____8____ SSL, SSL can be enabled and specific Web pages can be identified as requiring SSL access. Any Web server can be enabled by using Netscape's SSLRef program library which can be ____9____ for noncommercial use or licensed for commercial use.

TLS and SSL are not interoperable. However, a message sent with TLS can be ____10____ by a client that handles SSL but not TLS.

【Ex4】 Translate the following passage from English to Chinese.

What Is a Key?

In computer cryptography, a key is a long sequence of bits used by encryption / decryption algorithms. For example, the following represents a hypothetical 40-bit key:

00001010 01101001 10011110 00011100 01010101

A given encryption algorithm takes the original message, and a key, and alters the original message mathematically based on the key's bits to create a new encrypted message. Likewise, a decryption algorithm takes an encrypted message and restores it to its original form using one or more keys.

Some cryptographic algorithms use a single key for both encryption and decryption. Such a key must be kept secret; otherwise, anyone who had knowledge of the key used to send a message could supply that key to the decryption algorithm to read that message.

Other algorithms use one key for encryption and a second, different key for decryption. In this case the encryption key can remain public, because without knowledge of the decryption key, messages cannot be read.

In general, keys provide the necessary protection to encrypt and decrypt network communications on the Internet.

Text B

Common Risks with E-commerce and How to Avoid Them

E-commerce businesses are unique in many ways. Their focus is all about selling online，so it is absolutely critical that their site is secure，and their data protected in every possible way. Any downtime can be disastrous and costly for an e-commerce store. Today online shopper will quickly move on to a competitor if they feel that the e-commerce store is not secure or if the Customer Experience（CX）is poor.

E-commerce vendors have much to protect，but knowing the risks makes it easier to shore up the defences. So let's start by outlining the top 10 e-commerce risks and look at some actionable tips to help you solve them.

1 Data Privacy and Online Security

Hackers are becoming more and more sophisticated every day. It's easier for malicious actors to find their way into your systems，obtaining employee credentials through phishing，or by deploying malware and ransomware in fraudulent links in emails.

Solution

The best way to avoid a data breach is to prevent it. Establish and enforce a strong data privacy and online security policy，train your staff，and incentivize them to become data security champions. Implement protocols like Two-Factor Authentication（2FA）to add an extra layer of accountability.

2 Unauthorized Access

Unauthorized access accounts for a significant amount of data loss. Fortunately，there is a lot you can do to prevent unauthorized access，and these strategies should be a part of your overarching data security posture.

Solution

Here are a few things you can to do prevent unauthorized access：

- Restrict access. Employees should only be able to access files they need. For example，your content creators do not need access to your back-end code.
- Implement 2FA. 2FA gives you an added layer of accountability and prevents people from using login credentials that do not belong to them.
- Use a single-sign-on solution. Single sign-on enables you to restrict and monitor access to company files.
- Implement role-based access. Most file systems can be configured to restrict access by role or by credentials. Look for a single-sign-on solution that offers these features.
- Change passwords regularly. Enforce password updates across your network to mitigate unauthorized access.
- Revoke credentials when employees quit or are let go. Be diligent in managing credentials and revoke immediately when an employee moves on.

3 Exploitation of Vulnerabilities

Malicious actors are always standing by to take advantage of any vulnerabilities in your network. Unpatched software, legacy systems, and lax endpoint protection leave you open to attack.

Solution

Keep software, SaaS, and plugins up to date. Remove and uninstall incompatible plugins and themes immediately. Enable firewalls and virus protection. Look into more comprehensive solutions based on your data protection needs.

Larger organizations might consider a periodic security audit or penetration testing to understand their vulnerabilities.

4 Human Error

We've all deleted a file or "lost" a folder at one point or another. Human error is still the most common cause of data loss and most of the time, it's just an innocent mistake.

Solution

Deploy a backup and recovery solution. Online backups allow you to restore and recover quickly after an error, minimizing downtime and helping you get back to work faster.

5 Platform Downtime

Even the world's most reputable platforms, like Shopify, BigCommerce, and QuickBooks Online, need to schedule downtime to update servers, security, and maintain their code. However, lengthy or frequent downtime will impact your productivity and reputation.

Solution

Do your homework and choose wisely. Look at what others are saying about the company, both through reviews and on user forums. Check comparison sites so you understand the pros and cons of each platform. Choose a company with a good reputation and high uptime.

This also extends to any third-party apps or SaaS you choose. Dependencies between apps could cause your site to lose functionality if an app were to fail.

6 Bad CSV Files

CSV files are a great way to upload high volumes of data quickly, but they don't always work. The problem is you often won't know where the error lies. If you're on a timeline, this can be a major problem, impacting sales and causing a great deal of stress.

Solution

Installing a backup and recovery solution won't fix your bad CSV files, but it will help you get back to a pre-error state until you find the issue.

7　Non-Compliance

The regulatory framework for data privacy and protection is stringent—and comes with massive financial penalties for non-compliance. The risks are manifold here, as outlined in HIPAA, the GDPR, PCI, and other regional and international data privacy legislation.

Essentially, these policies state that if you do business online, you must adhere to their mandates. If you are selling internationally, make sure your business follows the Organization for Economic Cooperation and Development's e-commerce policies.

Solution

- Be sure you understand your obligations under all applicable data privacy laws.
- Do not assume that the GDPR does not apply to you.
- Update your websites and online properties to ensure you are using current versions.
- Fully vet and qualify all vendors as the question of who controls data and where it is stored may become an issue if there is a breach or complaint.
- Ensure all third-party SaaS is compliant with international data privacy and security laws.

8　Incompatible Software or Plugins

We all rely on third-party SaaS to make our lives easier, but not all apps are created equal. If it's incompatible with your platform, theme, or other apps on your system, you might be in for an unwelcome surprise when suddenly nothing works or looks as it should.

Additionally, new app companies go out of business at an alarming rate. The app might still work but if there is no support or updates, your e-commerce store might be vulnerable.

Solution

Use software plugins and add-ons from reputable vendors. Do your research before you deploy. Update and audit regularly to ensure there are no issues.

9　Poor CX

CX is everything these days. If your site is slow to load, if visitors can't find what they're looking for, your site is difficult to navigate or understand, or if your content (images, descriptions, blogs, etc.) is low-quality, most of them won't hesitate to click away—and they probably won't return.

Solution

- Invest time and effort into improving your website and store design.
- Make sure your e-commerce store is responsive—meaning it is mobile friendly and looks and performs the same on any device.
- Put your most popular products up front and create landing pages for all your ads.

Basically，the idea is to make it as easy as possible for your customers to do business with you. Good CX translates to loyalty，which means more sales.

10 Loss of Premises Due to Disaster

Disasters happen，and they come in many guises. Fire，flooding，building collapse，electrical grid failure，power surges，internet failure—and the list goes on. Having the right protections in place will help you get back up and running so your e-commerce business can carry on.

Solution

Design and implement a Disaster Recovery Plan（DRP）that covers every possible scenario.

Every company operates differently，so it's critical to look at your business model and determine what makes sense for you. You can find DRP templates on the web to get you started，but these are just a jumping-off point. An effective DRP is a dynamic document that you'll update as needed throughout your business life cycle.

One significant aspect of any comprehensive DRP is cloud backup and recovery software. With your e-commerce store and all its data secured in the cloud，you can be confident that none of your vital data is lost，no matter what happens.

New Words

risk	[rɪsk]	n. 风险,危险;隐患
		v. 冒风险
absolutely	[ˈæbsəluːtli]	adv. 绝对地;确实地
downtime	[ˈdaʊntaɪm]	n. 停机时间,停工期
disastrous	[dɪˈzɑːstrəs]	adj. 灾难性的;极糟糕的
defence	[dɪˈfens]	n. 防御
actionable	[ˈækʃənəbl]	adj. 可操作的,可行动的
malicious	[məˈlɪʃəs]	adj. 恶意的,有敌意的
actor	[ˈæktə]	n. 行动者,行为者
phishing	[ˈfɪʃɪŋ]	n. 网络仿冒,网络钓鱼
malware	[ˈmælweə]	n. 恶意软件,流氓软件
ransomware	[rænsəmweə]	n. 勒索软件

enforce	[ɪnˈfɔːs]	v. 强制执行；强迫
incentivize	[ɪnˈsentɪvaɪz]	vt. 以物质刺激鼓励
accountability	[əˌkaʊntəˈbɪləti]	n. 责任，有义务
posture	[ˈpɒstʃə]	n. 态度；立场
restrict	[rɪˈstrɪkt]	vt. 限制，约束
credential	[krəˈdenʃl]	n. 凭证，凭据
single-sign-on	[ˈsɪŋgl saɪn ɒn]	n. 单点登录
revoke	[rɪˈvəʊk]	vt. 撤销，取消；废除
diligent	[ˈdɪlɪdʒənt]	adj. 认真的；勤奋的
lax	[læks]	adj. 松弛的；松懈的；不严格的
plugin	[ˈplʌgɪn]	n. 插件
periodic	[ˌpɪəriˈɒdɪk]	adj. 周期的；定期的
folder	[ˈfəʊldə]	n. 文件夹
deploy	[dɪˈplɔɪ]	v. 部署，调集
reputable	[ˈrepjətəbl]	adj. 值得尊敬的，声誉好的
uptime	[ˈʌptaɪm]	n. (计算机等的)正常运行时间
dependency	[dɪˈpendənsi]	n. 依赖，依靠
timeline	[ˈtaɪmlaɪn]	n. 时间轴，时间表
fix	[fɪks]	v. 修复，修理
non-compliance	[ˌnɒnkəmˈplaɪəns]	n. 不兼容
regulatory	[ˈregjələtəri]	adj. 监管的
manifold	[ˈmænɪfəʊld]	adj. 多种多样的；多方面的
legislation	[ˌledʒɪsˈleɪʃn]	n. 立法，制定法律
vet	[vet]	vt. 审查
blog	[blɒg]	n. 博客；网络日志
		v. 写博客
hesitate	[ˈhezɪteɪt]	v. 犹豫；顾虑
scenario	[səˈnɑːriəʊ]	n. 设想；可能发生的情况
confident	[ˈkɒnfɪdənt]	adj. 坚信的，自信的；肯定的

Phrases

shore up	支撑，支持；加强
data breach	数据泄露，资料外泄
unauthorized access	未授权的访问，越权访问
back-end code	后端代码
role-based access	基于角色的访问
be configured to	配置为
unpatched software	未修补的软件

legacy system	遗留系统，老旧系统
endpoint protection	端点保护
security audit	安全监察，安全审计
penetration testing	渗透测试
online backup	在线备份
user forum	用户论坛
data privacy	数据隐私
adhere to	遵循
Organization for Economic Cooperation and Development	经济合作与发展组织
landing page	登录页面
electrical grid failure	电网故障
power surge	电涌
jumping-off point	起点，出发点

Abbreviations

CX（Customer Experience）	客户体验
2FA（Two-Factor Authentication）	双因素认证
CSV（Comma Separated Value）	逗号分隔值
HIPAA（Health Insurance Portability and Accountability Act）	健康保险携带和责任法案
GDPR（General Data Protection Regulation）	通用数据保护条例
PCI（Payment Card Industry）	支付卡行业
DRP（Disaster Recovery Plan）	灾难恢复计划

Exercises

【Ex5】 **Fill in the blanks with the information given in the text.**

1. The best way to avoid a data breach is _____. Establish and enforce a strong data privacy and _____ policy，train your staff，and incentivize them to become _____.

2. Here are a few things you can to do prevent unauthorized access：
   - _____.
   - Implement _____.
   - _____.
   - Implement _____.
   - _____.
   - Revoke credentials when employees quit or are let go.

3. Malicious actors are always standing by to take advantage of _____ in your network. Unpatched software，_____，and _____ leave you _____.

4. Online backups allow you to _____ and _____ quickly after an error，minimizing _____ and helping you _____.

5. Do your homework and _____. Look at what others are saying about the company，both through _____ and on _____. Check comparison sites so you understand _____ of each platform.

6. CSV files are a great way to _____ quickly，but they don't always work. The problem is you often won't know _____.

7. If you are selling internationally，make sure your business follows _____.

8. We all rely on _____ to make our lives easier，but not all apps are created equal. If it's incompatible with _____, theme, or _____ on your system，you might be in for _____ when suddenly nothing works or looks as it should.

9. If your site is _____, if visitors can't find _____, your site is difficult to _____, or if your content（images, descriptions, blogs, etc.）is low-quality，most of them won't hesitate to _____—and they probably won't return.

10. Every company operates differently，so it's critical to look at _____ and determine _____ for you. One significant aspect of any comprehensive DRP is _____ software.

【Ex6】 Translate the following terms or phrases from English into Chinese and vice versa：

1. data privacy   1. _____
2. security audit   2. _____
3. unauthorized access   3. _____
4. data breach   4. _____
5. online backup   5. _____
6. *n*. 防御   6. _____
7. *v*. 部署，调集   7. _____
8. *adj*. 恶意的，有敌意的   8. _____
9. *n*. 恶意软件，流氓软件   9. _____
10. *vt*. 限制，约束   10. _____

Reading Material

Key Legal Issues Concerning E-commerce

E-commerce remains a strong segment of economy. Online enterprises are attractive to entrepreneurs for several reasons. Without the need for a brick-and-mortar store，they're a more accessible form of startup. You don't even have to build a website，product or distribution system from scratch[①]；with third-party vendor arrangements

---

①   from scratch：从头做起，从零开始。

through Amazon, for example, the infrastructure is already in place.

Despite their relative ease of entry and low cost to get off the ground, however, online businesses still face numerous legal considerations①. The following are only some of the key legal considerations.

1　Warranties and Liability②

Whenever products are bought and sold, liability issues are lingering in the background. Product liability is a complex area of law. Defective product claims can impact not only sellers, but manufacturers and distributors, too. For this reason, it's important to establish a clear understanding for who is accountable③—particularly if you rely on third parties to supply or fill orders. Whether you are providing goods or services, warranties and return policies should also be spelled out in detail including any limitations or exclusions④.

2　Privacy and Data Protection

Consumer privacy concerns have come to the forefront in recent years. Conducting business transactions online requires processing and storing a wealth of personal data: names, addresses, social security numbers, phone numbers, birth dates, credit card numbers and even online activity. Keeping that data safe and secure must be a top priority⑤ for any online business. That means, among other things:

- Establishing a privacy policy and placing it prominently on the website or app.
- Utilizing only the most trusted and secure platforms to process payments.
- Obtaining users' consent to collect and store information (i.e., via "cookies").

3　Contractual⑥ Arrangements

Many of the same contractual considerations that affect brick-and-mortar businesses also come into play for e-commerce enterprises. The ongoing operations of your online business might rely on contractual arrangements with multiple parties, including:

- Website hosting services.
- Payment platforms.
- Third-party vendors (suppliers, distributors, etc.).
- Employees or independent contractors.

---

① consideration [kənˌsɪdəˈreɪʃn] *n*. 仔细考虑。
② liability [ˌlaɪəˈbɪləti] *n*. 责任。
③ accountable [əˈkaʊntəbl] *adj*. 有责任的；应作解释的。
④ exclusion [ɪkˈskluːʒn] *n*. 排除。
⑤ priority [praɪˈɒrəti] *n*. 优先，优先权；重点。
⑥ contractual [kənˈtræktʃuəl] *adj*. 合同的，契约的。

- Software licensors①.

On the front end，getting an e-commerce business off the ground may also involve contracting with web designers，app developers，SEO consultants and other professionals.

As with any business，establishing solid contracts is essential for protecting your interests and avoiding costly legal disputes②.

4 Intellectual Property

Intellectual property③(IP) is an area of law that protects ideas. With respect to the Internet there are generally four areas of intellectual property. They are copyright，trademarks，domain names④，and patents⑤.

If you are setting up a simple website that provides information about your business then one of your primary considerations is protecting your company's intellectual property.

4.1 Copyright

Copyright is the right to make a copy and applies to pictures and written materials on your website. People who create original works automatically have copyright protection over their work. It can also relate to computer codes used to create computer programs.

Copyright considerations：

- Do you have the right to use all the materials (including text and images) on your website?
- Have you obtained permission⑥ for the use of any copyright material (including information found on the Web)?
- Do you have an agreement with your web developer with respect to copyright? Your web developer may have copyright over the material on your website (information and images). If you want to own the copyright to the work contained on your website，you will need to have a written agreement that transfers the copyrights to you.

4.2 Trademarks⑦

A trademark can be any word，phrase，symbol，design，or a combination of these

---

① software licensor：软件许可方，软件授权方。
② legal dispute：法律纠纷。
③ intellectual property：知识产权。
④ domain name：域名。
⑤ patent ['pætnt] *n*.专利权 *v*.得到专利权 *adj*.有专利的。
⑥ permission [pə'mɪʃn] *n*.准许；许可证。
⑦ trademark ['treɪdmɑːk] *n*.(注册)商标。

things that identifies your goods or services. It's how customers recognize you in the marketplace and distinguish you from your competitors. If you have a unique name for your business or product you should seek advice from an experienced trademark lawyer①.

Once a trademark has been granted，the owner receives three key benefits：

- A notice of claim to any other businesses thinking of using the same symbol or word as its trademark.
- A legal presumption② of ownership③，which can help fend off would-be users.
- The exclusive right④ to use the claimed trademark.

4.3　Domain names

A domain name（a term often used interchangeably⑤ with "URL"）is a reader-friendly representation of a collection of Internet Protocol（IP）addresses.

Domain names should be carefully selected so that you do not violate⑥ the trademark of another business. Consult a lawyer if you think you might be infringing on another company's trademark. Your domain name should not include the name of another company or product.

4.4　Patent

A patent is an exclusive right granted for an invention—a product or process that provides a new way of doing something，or that offers a new technical solution to a problem. A patent provides patent owners with protection for their inventions. Protection is granted for a limited period，generally 20 years.

Patents provide incentives to individuals by recognizing their creativity and offering the possibility of material reward for their marketable inventions. These incentives encourage innovation，which in turn enhances the quality of human life.

5　Jurisdiction⑦

Your business is subject to the laws of any jurisdiction in which you seek to sell your products or services.

The rules for forming a contract can vary from one jurisdiction to another，and there may be special rules for online contracts. It is important to consider those requirements when deciding where to do business online and with whom.

---

① lawyer ['lɔːjə] *n*. 律师。
② presumption [prɪ'zʌmpʃn] *n*. 推定。
③ ownership ['əʊnəʃɪp] *n*. 所有权。
④ exclusive right：专有权。
⑤ interchangeably [ˌɪntə'tʃeɪndʒəbli] *adv*. 可交换地，可交替地。
⑥ violate ['vaɪəleɪt] *v*. 侵犯。
⑦ jurisdiction [ˌdʒʊərɪs'dɪkʃn] *n*. 司法权；管辖权；管辖范围。

Jurisdiction considerations：

- Does your website define the geographical area of your sales territory?
- Are you aware of the laws in the jurisdiction(s) where you would like to sell? For example，in some jurisdictions where a credit card is used，the purchaser can deny the agreement because the credit card is not physically present at the time of the sale. This can result in more "chargebacks". A chargeback occurs when the customer asks the credit card company to reverse the charges.
- Are you aware of the rules for forming contracts online in the jurisdiction you would like to sell?
- Have you obtained appropriate accounting，tax and legal advice?

6　Taxation

It is important that you know what taxes apply to various products and services you may be selling.

Taxation considerations：

Have you obtained tax advice on which taxes apply to the product or service you are selling to ensure that you are meeting your legal obligations[①]?

7　Internet Advertising and Marketing

Advertising is the technique and practice brands use to bring products and services to the public's notice for the purpose of getting them to respond to what a brand has to offer—whether product，service，cause，or idea.

Advertising helps sustain[②] brands. It's focused on getting a message out to a specific customer type or audience in order to get them to take a certain action. Types of advertising include video，display，paid search，paid social，print，email，radio，TV，and outdoor.

Advertising laws require that advertising be truthful[③]，fair and accurate.

8　Other issues

This is by no means an exhaustive[④] discussion of the legal considerations impacting e-commerce businesses. Countless issues can arise at any point during the life cycle of an online business. Securing knowledgeable，proactive legal counsel is essential for the success of any business，including those that operate amid the still-developing legal landscape of e-commerce.

---

① legal obligation：法律义务。
② sustain [səˈsteɪn] vt. 维持；支撑，支持。
③ truthful [ˈtruːθfl] adj. 真实的，诚实的。
④ exhaustive [ɪgˈzɔːstɪv] adj. 详尽的，彻底的。

Text A 参考译文

保护你的电子商务系统

随着因特网使用的日益增加,网站越来越成为企业向公众展现自己形象的重要地方,而且通过电子商务系统产生的利润意味着这些组织日益依靠网站,把它们看作企业的核心元素。

使用电子商务系统提供的可信度高的服务,它们就不会受到黑客、病毒、欺骗和拒绝服务工具的威胁,这一点很关键。

尽管一些较小的公司会选择与第三方专家一起实施一些复杂的安全控制,但是每个公司都应该采取措施保护它们的电子商务系统的安全。

本文讨论对电子商务系统的安全威胁及可能对你的企业带来的损害。提出了通过识别这些威胁可能引起的危险并实行适当的安全等级控制排除它们的最佳建议。

1 电子商务安全问题

电子商务系统基于因特网应用,因特网提供开放的和易用的全球通信。但是,因为因特网无规则、无管理和无控制,对于运行在其上的系统会带来许多风险和威胁。

使用因特网意味着你内部的 IT 和电子商务系统可能被任何人访问而不管其位于何处。

1.1 黑客威胁与商务风险

黑客对电子商务系统造成的一些较常见的威胁包括:

- 进行拒绝访问攻击,阻止了网站合法用户的访问,这样该网站被迫降低服务水平,或者在某些情况下完全终止运行。
- 获得敏感数据,如价目表、目录及有价值的知识产权,并改变、破坏或复制它。
- 改变你的网站,从而破坏你的形象或把你的客户转向另一网站。
- 访问你公司或你客户的财务信息,以偷梁换柱。
- 利用病毒破坏你的业务数据。

1.2 安全事故对企业的影响

如果你的网站被攻入,可能对你的电子商务服务产生重要影响。安全事故的潜在影响包括:

- 由于欺骗和诉讼引起的直接经济损失。
- 由于公布了令人讨厌的内容引发的后续损失。
- 如果你违背了数据保护或计算机滥用条例或其他的电子商务准则将面临刑事指控。
- 如果客户的信心受到拒绝服务攻击的影响,企业可能会丢失市场份额。

你的企业形象和品牌都是重要的资产。认识到这一点很重要:使用电子商务会给企业形象和品牌带来新的被攻击的途径。

2　识别电子商务威胁和弱点

了解电子商务系统面临的风险和任何安全事故的潜在影响是重要的。

2.1　有哪些威胁?

对电子商务系统的威胁既有恶意的也有无意的。对网站进行适当的保护和控制可以使这些威胁最小化。

恶意威胁可能包括:

- 黑客试图进入系统,阅读或改写敏感信息。
- 窃贼偷窃磁盘上有未受保护的敏感数据的服务器或笔记本计算机。
- 骗子冒充合法用户,甚至建立一个与你类似的网站。
- 授权的用户下载带有隐含活动内容的页面或接收这样的邮件,这些活动内容可以攻击你的系统或把敏感信息发送给未经授权的人。

可以从以下三个角度考虑对敏感信息带来的潜在威胁:

- 哪里(或谁)是潜在威胁源?
- 黑客具有的技术水平可能有多高?他们要攻破你的安全系统有多费劲?
- 他们拥有哪些工具和手段?

真正的危险也许不是最明显的。来自合法用户(如心怀不满的雇员或合伙人)的攻击远比黑客的多得多。

2.2　电子商务系统的风险评估

风险评估可以使组织清楚地了解其电子商务系统和相关商务过程所面临的风险,以及出现安全问题后所面临的潜在影响。

风险评估的关键部分是定义业务信息访问需求。这将包括不同用户群体的访问准则。例如,适用于雇员、顾问、管理服务提供者、供应商、客户、审核员和政府机构的准则不同。

任何分析都应考虑电子交易如何核实。如何知道订单的确来自某个已知客户?合同在哪里进行电子形式的交换?谁可以签署合同?怎样证实签署的版本?

3　普通电子商务安全控制

应该充分采用安全控制减少电子商务系统的风险。但是,这些控制不能太过分,限制并影响雇员的工作。

普通电子商务安全控制如下所列。

3.1　用户认证

有几种技术可以辨认和验证电子商务系统访问者的身份。它们包括:

- 用户名与口令结合,口令的长度可变并包括数字和字符。记住要有一个系统提示雇员定期改变其口令。
- 双因素认证要求用户具有某些东西(如一个认证令牌)和用户知道的东西(如身份证号码)。

- 能够用个人唯一的数字钥匙证明其身份的数字证书。
- 一个人独有的身体特征,被称为生物特征。其范围包括从指纹或虹膜扫描到视网膜或面部特征识别。

3.2 访问控制

限制不同等级的用户可以访问不同的信息子集并确保他们只能访问数据和接受授权的服务。这包括:

- 网络限制,用来阻止访问其他计算机系统和网络。
- 应用控制,用来确保个人只能访问他们可以访问的数据或服务。
- 既限制他们从系统复制信息也限制在笔式驱动器、存储卡和 CD/DVD 上存储信息。
- 限制发送和接收特定类型的电子邮件附件。

必须控制访问权限的改变,以便防止用户在部门之间调换工作或离开公司时保留原来的权限。

3.3 数据加密

加密改变数据并用于保护信息,这些信息可以存储在计算机上,复制到 CD 或 DVD 上,或者通过网络传输。它使用虚拟专用网络(VPN)和安全套接字层这样的技术。

3.4 防火墙

这是硬件或软件安全设备,可以过滤通过内部和外部网络中的信息。它控制内部用户对因特网的访问,也防止外部团体对内部网络上的信息和系统的访问。

防火墙可以应用在网络层面,提供对多个工作站或内部网络的保护;也可以将其安装在个人 PC 上,实现在个人层面的应用。

3.5 入侵检测

这些产品监控系统和网络行为以便发现任何访问企图。如果检测系统怀疑有攻击行为,它可以报警(如电子邮件报警),这取决于它检测到的行为的类型。

尽管这些控制很先进,但也要看使用者的水平。一个持续运行的检测程序是任何一个安全策略中的重要部分。

4 来自计算机病毒、木马程序、蠕虫和僵尸网络的风险

计算机病毒、木马程序、蠕虫和僵尸网络都是可以感染计算机的程序。

计算机病毒和蠕虫程序通过复制自身在网络和计算机中传播,通常计算机用户并不知晓。

木马程序以合法程序的面貌出现,但实际上包含了另一程序或者恶意的、破坏性的代码,伪装并隐藏在用户所需的代码块中。木马可以和病毒一起感染计算机。

后门木马程序让远程用户或黑客绕过计算机的正常访问控制并通过它获得未经授权的访问。通常,一个病毒把后门木马程序放到计算机中,而且一旦计算机在线,发送木马的人可以在被感染的计算机上运行程序、访问个人文件并修改和上传文件。

僵尸网络是一组被感染并被远程控制的计算机。黑客给一个普通的计算机发送一个计算机病毒、木马程序或蠕虫。通常计算机病毒、木马程序、蠕虫可以通过它们所携带的某些恶意程序访问计算机。反过来,这使黑客获得对现已感染的计算机的完全控制权,可以用这些计算机发起拒绝服务攻击、发布垃圾邮件并进行点击欺骗、窃取身份和偷窃登录细节及信用卡号。

风险也可以来自流行的社交网站。应注意包含时事、娱乐或其他高流量内容链接的消息。有报告说这些链接把用户引到钓鱼网站,在那里用户的个人详细信息可能被偷窃,或者被蠕虫、木马或病毒捕获。

仅仅通过软件工具防止僵尸网络是非常困难的,重要的是用户要遵循电子邮件和网站使用的最佳实践指导。重要的是要确保所有的软件和防病毒程序及时升级,以防止利用软件中的安全漏洞进入的恶意代码并使系统变得易受攻击。

5 电子商务系统的风险

有些病毒只是令人烦恼,其他一些可能非常有害。它们对电子商务系统的威胁包括:
- 破坏并删除服务器硬盘上的数据。
- 通过记录用户的击键偷窃机密数据。
- 劫持你的系统并为黑客所用,可能包括将它加入到一个更大的僵尸网络组中。
- 恶意使用你的计算机,例如独自或作为僵尸网络的一部分执行对其他网站的拒绝服务攻击。
- 通过从你自己的系统把病毒转发给客户和贸易伙伴而损害你与之的关系。

6 病毒是如何传播的?

病毒可以通过多种路径感染计算机。包括:
- 含有感染文档的 CD 和其他形式的可移动介质。
- 含有感染附件的电子邮件。
- 当你连接到因特网时,因特网蠕虫可以利用你的操作系统的漏洞。

7 间谍软件

间谍软件是当你访问某些网站时被放置到你计算机上的软件。它秘密地收集你的使用信息并把它发送给广告商或其他有关人员。间谍软件除了跟踪系统的使用外,也可以使计算机变慢或崩溃。

8 防止计算机病毒、木马程序、蠕虫和僵尸网络的问题

应该用防病毒软件对抗病毒。它可以检测病毒、阻止访问被感染的文件并隔离任何被感染的文件。

有几种不同类型的防病毒软件:
- 病毒扫描——必须定期更新,通常通过连接到供应商的网站,以便识别新的病毒。
- 启发式软件——通过应用病毒特征的通用规则检测病毒。尽管这种软件不需要频

繁更新,但它容易假报警。

可以通过以下方法最小化感染病毒的威胁:

- 当连接到因特网时使用病毒检测程序,以防止病毒进出公司的 IT 系统。
- 在服务器上运行病毒检测程序,以防止任何病毒逃脱以上检查。
- 在用户的 PC 上运行个人的病毒检测程序,以保证他们不会直接下载病毒,或者无意间通过 CD 或其他形式的可移动介质引入病毒。

Unit 10

Text A

Cross-Border E-commerce

1　What Is Cross-Border E-commerce?

Cross-border e-commerce refers to selling products to customers beyond your nation's geographical boundaries. It may happen between a business and a consumer (B2C) or between two businesses (B2B).

2　Benefits of Cross-Border E-commerce

2.1　Expanded Market Reach

Cross-border e-commerce benefits both sellers and brands in that there is access to new markets. No matter how healthy your sales volume is at the moment, cross-border selling can skyrocket it higher by opening your online storefront to more untapped markets.

In addition, you get to conquer new territories by extending access to your products to millions of potential customers who haven't had the chance to buy your products.

2.2　Increased Sales and Revenue

Perhaps the most popular reason many business owners adopt cross-border e-commerce is that it opens them up to increased sales and higher revenue. By taking your business global, you are positioning it to reach a much larger base of customers. The more people know about your brand, the higher the demand for your products.

Every country you add to your list potentially represents a new pathway to business growth and increased revenue. Cross-border e-commerce could be the shot of life your company needs to take its revenue to new heights.

2.3　Demand All Year-Round

By penetrating markets in different climates and seasons, you can enjoy consistent demand throughout the year. Businesses that sell in the same country often get confined in the same season, climate, occasions, and more.

However, when you sell to an international market, you get to take advantage of peaks in demand for your product all year round. Your business benefits from the seasonal surges that occur at different times of the year in different countries and their weather conditions.

2.4 Brand Visibility

Another top advantage of cross-border e-commerce is brand awareness. Merchants who sell to customers in other countries get brand awareness in the international market.

By selling products that meet the needs and requirements of customers beyond your country, you're increasing your brand visibility and recognition, which helps create a global brand.

2.5 Competitive Advantage

Many companies engage in cross-border e-commerce to gain a competitive advantage over their rivals. You're probably aware that if you don't fill a gap in the market, your competitors will. If there's an opportunity for your products to penetrate international markets and you don't quickly seize it, someone else will.

The benefit of this type of selling is that you gain the first-mover advantage, which allows you to build strong brand awareness with potential customers before your competitors do. It's vital to keep one step ahead of the competition, and cross-border e-commerce allows you to do just that.

3 Tips for Building a Cross-Border E-commerce Strategy

3.1 Research Local Demand

Before getting into the international e-commerce market, it is necessary for e-commerce businesses to know the buying trends of the foreign market. Customers have different values and purchasing habits on the internet. It is necessary for them to know goods that sell and goods that don't sell for their cross-border customers.

Offering a unique product does not guarantee an easy purchase from customers. A deep-dive local demand research helps cross-border e-commerce businesses to prepare for the local competition in their target country. The competitor data, coupled with insights on buying trends and customer purchasing habits help them build a rapport with their cross-border customers.

3.2 Analyze Your International Competitors

To build a strong market approach, it is crucial for e-commerce businesses to analyze their international competitors who run cross-border e-commerce activities. They should optimize their market entry based on research conducted on pricing, communication channels and keyword terminology of their cross-border target market.

3.3 Spot the Potential Markets

Instead of attempting to sell everywhere at once, it is effective to analyze which product will fit which market. For this, the e-commerce business needs to check the target country's commercial guidelines, culture, business climate and competition in those markets.

3.4 Determine and Follow Target Country's Rules and Regulations

Once an e-commerce business does local demand research and spots the potential markets, it should determine the rules and regulations of that market. Each country holds a set of guidelines for trade and commerce that e-commerce businesses should follow mandatorily.

Every country has varying modes of communication and different legal restrictions on products and taxation policies. For instance, it is illegal to ship plant materials, soils and plants to Australia. Egypt legally prohibits the shipment of smoked salmon.

Irrespective of services, taxes and charges, e-commerce businesses should stay transparent with their customers. This builds trust for the brand in the minds of foreign customers.

3.5 Ensure That Website Speaks the Customers' Language

Language determines how much e-commerce businesses can connect with their customers. Speaking the local language helps businesses get closer to their customers, gain their trust and increase sales. Majority of logistics experts cite that customers do not prefer getting services in foreign languages.

An e-commerce business can translate their website to a local language to gain more trust from its buyers. The option to switch languages is one of the major reasons for many online marketplaces to have a global reach. Today, online tools and platforms have made it easier for them to integrate all languages native to countries they intend to sell in.

3.6 Offer local payment options to customers

Local payment options are another key component apart from language to win the customers' hearts. People often exit online shopping websites when they see foreign currencies in their shopping cart.

Beyond building transparency and trustworthiness with customers, local currency payment options reduce the fear of fraudulent services. Cross-border e-commerce businesses can find payment gateways for their target countries and integrate them with their website. This reduces the shopping cart abandonment and maximizes sales.

3.7 Set Up Local Return Options

Many international e-commerce businesses do not provide local return options as the return costs are higher than product prices. They can provide options for cross-border customers to return their purchases to a local logistics center. These local return options are a good solution for businesses and help them easily attract customers with multiple choices.

3.8 Localize Product Data

E-commerce businesses can tailor their product data in a number of ways based on their cross-border target market. They can design product feeds suitable for Facebook, Instagram and other channels.

Beyond meeting the requirements of the new channel, the product must be relevant for the target customer. For instance, posting product sizes that suit France customers to the US audience won't make any sense. Also, e-commerce businesses should identify key holidays in their cross-border target market to boost their sales.

3.9 Testing the New Cross-Border Market

Before entering the new cross-border market for online business, it is important for e-commerce companies to test their products. Rather than testing all products at a time, they should consider testing a few products at a time. This helps them exit the market with minimal losses in case their product testing is unsuccessful.

Cross-border market testing helps businesses to obtain a deeper knowledge of their target market and optimize their product listings. It helps them find out and adjust the key information like pricing, language, communication channels etc. This ensures that their entry strategy is agile enough for further e-commerce business operations.

New Words

geographical	[ˌdʒiːəˈgræfɪkl]	adj. 地理的
boundary	[ˈbaʊndri]	n. 边界；界限；分界线
reach	[riːtʃ]	v. 达到；到达；抵达；碰到，触及
		n. 波及范围；影响范围
skyrocket	[ˈskaɪrɒkɪt]	vi. 突升，猛涨
untapped	[ˌʌnˈtæpt]	adj. 未开发的，未利用的
conquer	[ˈkɒŋkə]	v. 占领；攻克
territory	[ˈterətɔːri]	n. 领域，管区，地盘；领土；版图
adopt	[əˈdɒpt]	v. 采用
position	[pəˈzɪʃn]	vt. 定位
penetrate	[ˈpenətreɪt]	v. 渗透，进入
confine	[kənˈfaɪn]	vt. 限制；限定
occasion	[əˈkeɪʒn]	n. 场合
surge	[sɜːdʒ]	n. 汹涌；激增
		v. 汹涌；激增；飞涨
rival	[ˈraɪvl]	n. 对手；竞争者

		adj. 竞争的
competitor	[kəmˈpetɪtə]	*n*. 竞争者
rapport	[ræˈpɔː]	*n*. 友好关系;融洽,和谐
spot	[spɒt]	*v*. 注意到
mandatorily	[mændəˈtərili]	*adv*. 强制地,命令地
restriction	[rɪˈstrɪkʃn]	*n*. 限制;管制
transparent	[trænsˈpærənt]	*adj*. 透明的;易懂的
trustworthiness	[ˈtrʌstwɜːðɪnəs]	*n*. 可信赖,确实性
maximize	[ˈmæksɪmaɪz]	*vt*. 最大化
localize	[ˈləʊkəlaɪz]	*vt*. 使本地化,使局部化
minimal	[ˈmɪnɪməl]	*adj*. 最小的,极少的
unsuccessful	[ˌʌnsəkˈsesfl]	*adj*. 不成功的,失败的
adjust	[əˈdʒʌst]	*v*. 调整,调节
operation	[ˌɒpəˈreɪʃn]	*n*. 活动;运行

Phrases

cross-border e-commerce	跨境电子商务
potential customer	潜在顾客
international market	国际市场
take advantage of	利用
all year round	全年,一年到头
brand awareness	品牌意识;品牌知名度,品牌认知度
brand visibility	品牌知名度
global brand	全球品牌
competitive advantage	竞争优势
fill a gap	填补空白,弥补缺陷,弥合差距
first-mover advantage	先发优势
purchasing habit	购买习惯
foreign market	国外市场
coupled with	加上,外加
target market	目标市场
commercial guideline	商业指南
business climate	商业氛围
taxation policy	税收政策
local language	当地语言,本土语言
local payment	本地支付
local logistics center	当地物流中心
target customer	目标客户

product listing   产品清单

Exercises

【Ex1】 **Answer the following questions according to the text.**

1. What does cross-border e-commerce refer to?

2. How do you get to conquer new territories?

3. How can you enjoy consistent demand throughout the year?

4. How are you increasing your brand visibility and recognition?

5. What is it necessary for e-commerce businesses before getting into the international e-commerce market?

6. What does a deep-dive local demand research do?

7. What should an e-commerce business do once it does local demand research and spots the potential markets?

8. What does language determine? What does speaking the local language do?

9. When do people often exit online shopping websites?

10. What is it important before entering the new cross-border market for online business?

【Ex2】 **Translate the following terms or phrases from English into Chinese or vice versa.**

1. brand visibility   1. _____

2. local logistics center   2. _____

3. target market   3. _____

4. competitive advantage   4. _____

5. local payment   5. _____

6. *vt*. 使本地化，使局部化   6. _____

7. *v*. 调整，调节   7. _____

8. *v*. 采用   8. _____

9. *v*. 渗透，进入   9. _____

10. *vt*. 定位   10. _____

【Ex3】 **Fill in the blanks with the words given below.**

concerned	increasing	conflict	determine	channels
promotions	collecting	purchase	insights	strategies

Five Ways Big Data Is Changing E-commerce

1 **Personalization**

    With more data collected from customers through various touch points such as loyalty programs, visitor browsing patterns, and past ____1____ behavior, companies can process this information to carry out customer segmentation and thus push out personalized content and ____2____.

2　Dynamic pricing/offers

A relatively accurate profile can be created for every customer after ____3____ and processing data. This customer profile will thus offer ____4____ as to what price would re-engage the customer and persuade him to make another purchase. Note that this has been proved to be the most effective for customer retention ____5____. This would also help expedite the process of deciding whether a $10 off or 20% discount would work the best on any particular customer.

3　Customer service

68% of online visitors leave because of poor customer service, so improving this aspect is critical in ____6____ sales. Big data can help in coordinating the various communication channels, including phone calls, emails, or live chat features. Understanding which issues customers are ____7____ with, or identifying time periods where customer support is most needed can also help companies best allocate resources more efficiently. Any customer ____8____ can thus be resolved more effectively within a shorter period of time.

4　Supply chain management

Any e-commerce company knows that transparent visibility and careful management of its supply chain process are important. Big data allows retailers to ____9____ patterns which can be useful to forecast any potential hiccups and disruptions to the process, and thus quickly act on preventative measures. For instance, any changes in warehousing or shipping updates can be captured real-time and communicated to the retailer immediately.

5　Predictive Analytics

Big data allows you to derive a more in-depth picture of the different ____10____ in your business, including sales, and inventory. Knowing how to forecast gives you the added flexibility in deciding the next steps of your business operations.

【Ex4】 **Translate the following passage from English into Chinese.**

Cross-Border E-commerce

1　What is cross-border e-commerce?

As the name suggests, cross-border e-commerce is the process of selling products or services to an international audience, using an online or e-commerce store or platform.

While cross-border e-commerce is specific to online sales, there is also another process called cross-border commerce, which refers to selling overseas to an international audience via any sales channel, online or offline.

2　Why should you consider cross-border e-commerce?

The biggest benefit of using cross-border e-commerce is that you can expand your business internationally to receive exposure from global markets and audiences. This will also help you grow your brand's popularity.

With a bigger audience, the number of customers and potential customers your business has will begin to grow. This will improve your revenue.

In some cases, products that are lower in demand within a domestic market will be more popular across borders. For this reason, cross-border e-commerce can improve your chances of selling slow-moving or dead stock.

3 What are the challenges of cross-border e-commerce?

3.1 Payment fraud

The most common mode of payment used during cross-border e-commerce transactions is credit cards. In order to prevent credit card fraud, most online sellers enable address verification systems, which authorize credit cards used by buyers. While this does reduce the chances of payment frauds, it, however, doesn't accept customers from countries where address verification systems does not operate.

3.2 Shipping complications

While shipping within the country, most taxes and laws are the same, so the entire process is relatively straightforward. However, when shipping across borders, it becomes more challenging, as new taxes, laws, and import and export rules are added to the picture.

3.3 Language and currency differences

In order for an e-commerce seller to support international users, their website should be able to support international languages as well as currencies.

Text B

Benefits of Applying Big Data in E-commerce

More e-commerce executives agree on the following: big data holds the key to the amazing future of the e-commerce industry. Big data enables e-commerce companies to improve decision making, gain a competitive advantage, enhance their performance, products and operational processes. It also allows customer behavior analysis and prompts the discovery of actionable insights.

1 Understand Your Customers Better

The big data technologies provide colossal means to analyze customer behavior, needs and experiences. Companies can use data analysis to identify and predict which offerings will better suit customer needs in the future. A better understanding of customer needs and expectations will also increase customer satisfaction and retention, and as a result, it will help more e-commerce businesses grow.

Big data allows you to inform your marketing strategy by analyzing search results and trends. You can see which results are trending and craft your SEO and marketing efforts accordingly. Additionally, this will help you better understand customer behavior as you can analyze which search results are popular among your customers.

2 Reduce Cost for Your Team

Operational cost cutting is another benefit big data brings to e-commerce corporations. Big data resources allow advancements in every aspect of business strategy and planning, from customer experiences to marketing and supply chains. These advancements bring key changes in budgeting as they reduce operational costs.

3 Make More Strategic Business Decisions

With the help of big data, e-commerce companies can make more strategic and clever managing decisions. In fact, about 50% of the structured data collected from the Internet of Things (IoT) is already used in decision making. The very same analytical tools that help marketers better understand their customers can be used to improve corporate decision-making.

E-commerce executives can leverage big data and real-time analytics to make more informed and strategic decisions. For example, when e-commerce executives know which customers have the highest long-term value, they can spend more money acquiring, targeting, and later retaining these customers.

4 Improve Operational Processes

Lastly, big data resources have the potential to improve operational processes and efficiency. Operational processes can largely benefit from algorithms analyzing customer behavior and their shopping data. Big data enables the implementation of predictive analytics as well. For instance, companies can use predictive analytics to calculate the average checkout wait time. Later, this data can be used to improve customer experiences and, as a result, get a better checkout wait time.

Big data algorithms also assist e-commerce companies in analyzing market trends and supply chains. This factor is especially helpful in identifying the optimum inventory levels warehouses need to maintain for more effective operations.

Amazon is a great example of how big data can transform operational processes. The company uses big data to monitor customer behavior, shipping details, and personal information. Then, Amazon uses big data and IoT to link with manufacturers and track inventory to make sure all orders are shipped quickly.

Special algorithms select an Amazon's fulfillment center (warehouse) closest to the customer and figure out the fastest route to deliver goods. This process allows operational processes optimization and cost cutting by 10-40%.

5 Give Users an Enhanced Shopping Experience

Big data unlocks access to enhanced shopping experiences. Big data and analytics allow e-commerce professionals to better understand their customers and tailor product offerings concerning each customer's needs, pain points, and expectations. This leaves companies thriving as their customers feel more satisfied with their shopping experiences.

Amazon's use of big data is a great example of how strategic use of algorithms can improve customer shopping experiences. By allowing algorithms to figure out the best way to deliver items, Amazon doesn't only optimize their logistics but also enhance the shopping process for its customers. In this case, big data allows Amazon to deliver products faster with a minimum chance of misplaced packages.

Delivery drones are another big data-enabled technology that is predicted to become mainstream in the nearest future. Amazon is currently testing different drones to figure out a way to enhance customer experiences with faster delivery.

Alternatively, e-commerce companies can use big data algorithms to analyze Net Promoter Score (NPS) surveys and customer reviews. Later, this feedback can be analyzed to tailor better shopping experiences.

6 Implement Stronger, Better Targeted Personalization

Personalization and targeted advertising are likely the biggest trends in e-commerce marketing. Marketers who understand the importance of timely, relevant, and personalized experiences have already employed big data technology to deliver more targeted ads.

Big data enables big personalization. By monitoring user information, like browsing requests and preferences, e-commerce professionals can shape marketing campaigns around each customers' needs. This way, corporations can deliver more personalized experiences and focus on per-customer profitability.

7 Predict What Customers Will Buy and When

Many e-commerce executives successfully implement big data tools to enable predictive lead scoring. Lead scoring includes analyzing the behavior of prospective customers to determine whether the prospects are valid. And if they are, ranking them based on their value.

Big data enables automation of predictive lead scoring algorithms. This is certainly helpful for e-commerce businesses as they can predict which prospects are more likely to convert into paying customers.

8 Provide Elevated Customer Service Practices

Big data technologies have the potential to revolutionize customer service. With big data, corporations can analyze the report data through email letters, social media campaigns, and online self-service tools. All of the collected data can be analyzed to identify possible customer service drawbacks.

9 Offer More Secure Online Payment Processes

Big data analytics enable greater security of online payment processes. Since big data algorithms are effective in analyzing huge sets of information, companies use these capabilities to detect banking frauds and ensure safe payment on their websites.

For example, PayPal is using big data resources to enable machine learning algorithms. These algorithms analyze billions of transactions to identify potentially fraudulent transactions. Additionally, big data can be used to view which payment methods are working best and which are the most popular among customers.

10 Optimize Product Pricing

Data-backed price management proves to be extremely effective in e-commerce. In fact, research shows that data-driven price management initiatives facilitate considerable results in the short-term perspective, including a 2%-7% growth in business margins and a 200%-350% average growth in ROI over a one year period.

So, how does big data enable e-commerce companies to optimize product pricing? The answer is by analyzing large quantities of data, including previous purchases, cookies, clickstream as well as enterprise resource planning systems. Thorough analysis helps to set prices dynamically concerning the real-time data.

Besides, big data and automation tools can provide live analytics showing your team how discounting will impact your profitability or how likely your audience is to respond to particular discounts.

The immense power of data analytics plays a central role in facilitating the growth of the e-commerce sector.

- Big data allows e-commerce businesses to understand customers better through customer behavior analysis.
- Big data resources enable optimization logistics, supply chain management, and operational process. This contributes to better performance and significant cost reductions.
- Data analysis is paramount for strategic and well-informed decision making.
- With big data analytics, e-commerce companies can bring enhanced shopping experiences to their customers through faster shipment, more personalized

offerings，and better customer service.
- Predictive analysis can be used to create more tailored product offerings.
- E-commerce companies can offer more secure payment options and detect potential frauds with the help of big data.
- Big data resources help to shape product pricing and discounts as they provide real-time analytics.

New Words

colossal	[kəˈlɒsl]	adj. 巨大的
suit	[suːt]	vt. 适合于
		vi. 合适,相称
inform	[ɪnˈfɔːm]	v. 了解;通知
craft	[krɑːft]	v. 精心制作
		n. 手艺,技巧
marketer	[ˈmɑːkɪtə]	n. 市场营销人员
corporate	[ˈkɔːpərət]	adj. 公司的;法人的
leverage	[ˈliːvərɪdʒ]	v. 利用;发挥杠杆作用
		n. 杠杆作用;优势
fulfillment	[fʊlˈfɪlmənt]	n. 完成;实现;实施;履行
drone	[drəʊn]	n. 无人机
mainstream	[ˈmeɪnstriːm]	n. 主流;主要倾向,主要趋势
shape	[ʃeɪp]	v. 塑造;决定…的形成
profitability	[ˌprɒfɪtəˈbɪləti]	n. 获利(状况),盈利(情况);收益性
rank	[ræŋk]	v. 分等级;排列
elevate	[ˈelɪveɪt]	v. 提升;提高
revolutionize	[ˌrevəˈluːʃənaɪz]	vt. 彻底改革
short-term	[ˌʃɔːt-ˈtɜːm]	adj. 短期的
clickstream	[klɪkstriːm]	n. 网站浏览记录;点击流
paramount	[ˈpærəmaʊnt]	adj. 最重要的,主要的

Phrases

big data	大数据
customer behavior analysis	客户行为分析
supply chain	供应链
real-time analytic	实时分析
strategic decision	战略决策
long-term value	长期价值
operational process	运营过程;操作过程

checkout wait time	结账等待时间
market trend	市场趋势
optimum inventory level	最佳库存水平
track inventory	跟踪库存
figure out	找出
big data-enabled technology	大数据支持技术
customer review	客户评论
targeted advertising	目标广告
convert into	转化为
online self-service tool	在线自助服务工具
data-backed price management	数据支持的价格管理
data-driven price management initiatives	数据驱动的价格管理计划
enterprise resource planning system	企业资源规划系统
real-time data	实时数据
automation tool	自动化工具
live analytic	实时分析

Abbreviations

SEO (Search Engine Optimization)	搜索引擎优化
IoT (Internet of Things)	物联网
NPS (Net Promoter Score)	净推荐值,净促进者得分,口碑
ROI (Return On Investment)	投资利润,投资回报率

Exercises

【Ex5】 **Answer the following questions according to the text.**

1. What do more e-commerce executives agree on?

2. What do the big data technologies do?

3. What do big data resources do?

4. What can perational processes largely benefit from?

5. What do big data and analytics allow e-commerce professionals to do?

6. What are likely the biggest trends in e-commerce marketing?

7. What does lead scoring include?

8. What can corporations do with big data?

9. What are big data algorithms effective in? What do companies use these capabilities to do?

10. How does big data enable e-commerce companies to optimize product pricing?

【Ex6】 **Translate the following terms or phrases from English into Chinese or vice versa.**

1. supply chain   1. _____

2. track inventory　　　　　　2. _____

3. real-time data　　　　　　　3. _____

4. enterprise resource planning system　4. _____

5. big data　　　　　　　　　　5. _____

6. *n*. 完成;实现;实施;履行　　6. _____

7. *n*. 主流;主要倾向,主要趋势　7. _____

8. *n*. 获利(状况),盈利(情况)　8. _____

9. *v*. 分等级;排列　　　　　　9. _____

10. *n*. 网站浏览记录;点击流　10. _____

Reading Material

Livestream Shopping①

1　What Is Livestream Shopping?

Livestream② shopping combines livestreaming with the ability to buy products directly via the livestream. It is an emerging trend that offers consumers a more engaging experience than simply clicking and filling a virtual shopping cart③. Similar to shopping in person, potential shoppers can interact with the host via comments. This way they can ask questions about the product and request to see the product from a different angle.

2　What Are the Benefits of Livestream Shopping?

2.1　Provide a digitalized brick-and-mortar experience

If there is one thing that e-commerce has been missing, it is the brick-and-mortar vibe of shopping. In the offline world, visiting a store is not simply about making a purchase, it's an experience that involves human interaction and a touch point with a different world. You enter a space where you are surrounded by novelties④ and interesting products, you look around, ask the shopping assistant about the items you like, see how products work, touch them. This is something you simply cannot do online. Or at least it used to be.

Live streaming e-commerce allows you to deliver the best of both worlds. Your customers can enjoy the comfort of their home, and at the same time virtually be at the shop and ask the host questions in real-time. The host, on the other hand, can show

---

① livestream shopping:直播购物,直播带货。
② livestream [ˈlaɪvstriːm] *n*. 直播。
③ virtual shopping cart:虚拟购物车。
④ novelty [ˈnɒvlti] *adj*. 新奇的;风格独特的。

them how the products work, give them close-ups①, and make a demonstration② of their qualities.

The digital experience can even be better than visiting a shop. Well, yes, there is still no way to touch a product online. But you can have your favorite celebrity or influencer③ as a shopping assistant and that doesn't happen every day.

Live shopping can be entertaining and fun for the customer while bringing profits to the store.

2.2 Quickly generate enormous sales

The best thing about live shopping events is that they can help you quickly generate enormous sales. If you do your marketing campaign well, people will know about it and will be looking forward to it. Once they are watching and they are having fun, they can invite other people to join. All you have to do is to provide an exciting experience they'd want to share with others.

That's why it's so important to choose the right host for the event, it has to be someone who can fascinate④ people and make them want to buy what you're selling.

For example, one of the most popular livestream influencers in China, Li Jiaqi, once managed to sell 15,000 lipsticks in five minutes, yeah, you read it correctly. He's become popular by trying on lipsticks to show how they really look on the lips, rather than just demonstrate it on his hand skin. In just a few years, his liveselling videos made him a millionaire.

2.3 Inspire impulse buying

Livestream shopping is not just a shopping event, it's a show. What's more, it is a show the customer is involved in. People get excited because they feel like a part of something, it gives them a sense of belonging⑤. And they want to make this feeling last and turn it into a story to share with their friends. This setting alone is enough to make them want to purchase something.

But livestream shopping also inspires the fear of missing out, one of the driving forces of impulse buying⑥.

People will want to buy the product while the e-commerce live event lasts not only because it might be discounted, but because they see other people buying it right now, before their eyes. If they like the product and want it for themselves—and since there is

---

① close-up ['kləus ʌp] *n.* 特写镜头。
② demonstration [ˌdemən'streɪʃn] *n.* 示范,演示。
③ influencer ['ɪnfluəns] *n.* 影响者,意见领袖,红人。
④ fascinate ['fæsɪneɪt] *v.* 深深吸引;迷住。
⑤ a sense of belonging:归属感。
⑥ impulse buying:即兴购买,冲动购物。

a cool person recommending it，they probably do—they will make a purchase. Otherwise，it might be all out after the show is over and everyone else will have it but them.

For you，impulse buying means more sales，but in this case，also a boost in brand experience. New and returning customers will remain with the feeling of community and excitement[1] and will associate these emotions[2] with your business. The experience you provide is something that differentiates your brand from the rest and can make a customer pledge[3] their loyalty and return for more.

2.4　Build brand awareness

As mentioned，livestream shopping events are usually hosted by popular influencers or celebrities[4]. These public figures[5] have a loyal audience of followers that more than often are willing to take their word for it when they recommend products.

Associating your products with popular influencers can build brand awareness and make your business more popular among customers.

However，to make sure that the audience that watches live selling is more likely to become returning customers[6]，you have to choose your host very carefully. It has to be someone who is close to your industry or whose followers can directly benefit from your products. This way you can be sure that a reasonable percentage of the live shopping event visitors will find your brand interesting and will become returning customers.

2.5　Boost sales volume of underperforming products

Maybe you have been underselling products that are good，but for some reason they are not gaining enough popularity and are piling up[7] in your storage rooms. Live e-commerce can be a way to increase their sales volume.

The host can pay extra attention to the products you'd like to sell more of，and highlight their good qualities. Or you can add them to special packages available only for the duration of the e-commerce live event. In addition，mentioning that items are not that popular yet，and implying that the users who are online now can be among the first ones to possess them can make people feel like trendsetters[8]，and inspire them to buy.

Livestream shopping events give you an opportunity to speed up the selling process of items and boost your sales volume.This approach can deliver results much faster than

---

① 　excitement [ɪkˈsaɪtmənt] *n*. 兴奋,刺激;令人兴奋或激动的事。
② 　emotion [ɪˈməʊʃn] *n*. 情绪。
③ 　pledge [pledʒ] *v*. 许诺;保证。
④ 　celebrity [səˈlebrəti] *n*. 名人,明星。
⑤ 　public figure：公众人物,社会名人。
⑥ 　returning customer：回头客。
⑦ 　piling up：堆积,堆起。
⑧ 　trendsetter [ˈtrendsetə] *n*. 引领潮流的人。

other marketing strategies and can increase your revenue and free up[①] space in your storage rooms[②].

3　What makes a good livestream shopping host?

Good livestream shopping hosts should have a good sense for what they should be displaying based on the interactions with their followers. If a product does not work well with their personal brand, they will not showcase[③] such a product. Good hosts will put in hours of research on the products that they will showcase. Then, they will also start to create interest around a specific event well in advance by teasing images and special offers and interacting with their followers[④].

Text A 参考译文

跨境电子商务

1　什么是跨境电子商务?

跨境电子商务指的是向你所在国家地理边界以外的客户销售产品。它可能发生在企业和消费者之间(B2C)或两个企业之间(B2B)。

2　跨境电子商务的好处

2.1　扩大市场范围

跨境电子商务对卖家和品牌都有好处,因为可以进入新市场。无论你目前的销售额有多棒,通过面向更多未开发的市场开设在线店面,跨境销售都会飙升。

此外,还可以通过向数百万没有机会购买你的产品的潜在客户推广产品开拓新领域。

2.2　增加销售额和收入

许多企业主采用跨境电子商务最普遍的原因可能是这为他们增加销售额和获得更多收入打开了大门。通过将业务全球化,将其定位于更大的客户群。人们对你的品牌了解越多,对你的产品的需求就越高。

你添加到名单上的每一个国家都有可能代表着一条业务增长和收入增长的新途径。跨境电子商务可能是你的公司将收入提升到新高度所需的新生机。

2.3　全年需求

通过进入不同气候和季节的市场,你可以享受全年的持续需求。在同一个国家进行销

---

① free up：腾出,释放。
② storage room：库房,储藏室。
③ showcase [ˈʃəʊkeɪs] v. 展示(优点) n. 陈列柜。
④ follower [ˈfɒləʊə] n. 追随者,拥护者。

售的企业通常会受到相同季节、气候、场合等的限制。

不过，当你向国际市场销售产品时，你可以利用全年对产品需求的高峰。你的业务会受益于不同国家一年中不同时间发生的季节性激增及其天气条件。

2.4 品牌知名度

跨境电子商务的另一个突出优势是提高了品牌知名度。向其他国家的客户销售产品的商家在国际市场上获得了品牌知名度。

通过销售满足你所在国家以外客户需求的产品，你可以提高的品牌知名度和认可度，这有助于创建一个全球品牌。

2.5 竞争优势

许多公司从事跨境电子商务是为了在竞争对手面前获得竞争优势。你可能知道，如果你不填补市场上的空白，你的竞争对手就会填补。如果你的产品有机会打入国际市场，而你没有迅速抓住这个机会，其他人就会抓住机会。

这种销售方式的好处是获得了先发优势，这使你能够在竞争对手之前在潜在客户群体中建立强大的品牌知名度。在竞争中领先一步是至关重要的，而跨境电子商务可以让你做到这一点。

3 建立跨境电子商务战略的小贴士

3.1 研究本地需求

在进入国际电子商务市场之前，电子商务企业有必要了解国外市场的购买趋势。客户在网上有不同的价值观和购买习惯。企业有必要了解哪些商品可以跨境销售，哪些不能销售。

提供独特的产品并不能保证客户就会轻易购买。深入研究当地需求有助于跨境电子商务企业为目标国家的竞争做好准备。收集竞争对手的数据并洞察购买趋势和客户购买习惯，能帮助你与跨境客户建立融洽的关系。

3.2 分析国际竞争对手

为了建立强大的市场方法，电子商务企业必须分析其开展跨境电子商务活动的国际竞争对手。他们应该基于对跨境目标市场定价、沟通渠道和关键词术语的研究，优化市场进入策略。

3.3 发现潜在市场

分析哪种产品适合哪个市场，而不是试图一招包打天下。为此，电子商务企业需要检查目标国家的商业准则、文化、商业环境和这些市场的竞争情况。

3.4 确定并遵守目标国家的规章制度

一旦电子商务企业研究了当地需求并发现了潜在市场，它就应该明确该市场的规则和法规。每个国家都有一套电子商务企业必须遵守的贸易和商业准则。

每个国家都有不同的沟通方式，对产品和税收政策有不同的法律限制。例如，将植物材料、土壤和植物运往澳大利亚是非法的。埃及法律禁止进口烟熏鲑鱼。

无论服务、税费和收费如何,电子商务企业都应该对客户保持透明。这会在外国客户心目中建立对品牌的信任。

3.5 确保网站使用客户的语言

语言决定了电子商务企业与客户的联系程度。说当地语言有助于企业更接近客户,赢得他们的信任,增加销售额。大多数物流专家指出,客户不喜欢使用外语提供服务的商家。

电子商务企业可以将其网站翻译成当地语言,以获得买家的更多信任。可以选择语言是许多在线企业具有全球影响力的主要原因之一。如今,在线工具和平台使它们能够更容易地整合目标国家的所有母语。

3.6 向客户提供本地支付选项

除了语言之外,本地支付选项是赢得客户的另一个关键组成部分。当人们在购物车中看到外币时,往往会退出在线购物网站。

除了在客户中建立透明度和可信度之外,当地货币支付选项还可以减少对欺诈服务的恐惧。跨境电子商务企业可以为目标国家找到支付网关,并将其与网站整合。这减少了对购物车的丢弃,并最大限度地提高了销售额。

3.7 设置本地退货选项

因为退货成本高于产品价格,许多国际电子商务企业不提供本地退货选项。可以为跨境客户提供选择,让他们将购买的商品退回本地物流中心。这些本地退货选项对企业来说是一个很好的解决方案,可以帮助企业通过多种选择轻松吸引客户。

3.8 本地化产品数据

电子商务企业可以根据其跨境目标市场以多种方式定制其产品数据。他们可以设计适合 Facebook、Instagram 等渠道的产品数据。

除了满足新渠道的要求外,产品还必须与目标客户相关。例如,向美国受众发布适合法国客户尺寸的产品毫无意义。此外,电子商务企业应该确定其跨境目标市场中的重要假日,以提高销售额。

3.9 测试新的跨境市场

在进入新的跨境在线商务市场之前,电子商务公司对自己的产品进行测试是很重要的。他们应该考虑一次测试几个产品,而不是一次测试所有产品。这有助于他们在产品测试失败时以最小的损失退出市场。

跨境市场测试有助于企业更深入地了解目标市场,优化产品系列,帮助它们发现并调整关键信息,如定价、语言、沟通渠道等。这确保了它们的进入策略足够灵活,可用于进一步的电子商务业务运营。

附录 A 词汇总表

表 A-1 单词表

单词	音标	意义	单元
abandon	[ə'bændən]	v. 抛弃,舍弃,放弃	3A
absolutely	['æbsəlu:tli]	adv. 绝对地;确实地	9B
academic	[ˌækə'demɪk]	adj. 学术的,学院的,理论的	1A
accelerate	[ək'seləreɪt]	v. 加速,促进	7B
accident	['æksɪdənt]	n. 意外事件,事故	5A
accidental	[ˌæksɪ'dentl]	adj. 意外的	9A
account	[ə'kaʊnt]	n. 账号	8A
accountability	[əˌkaʊntə'bɪləti]	n. 责任,有义务	9B
accreditation	[əˌkredɪ'teɪʃn]	n. 鉴定合格	6B
accurate	['ækjərət]	adj. 精确的;精准的	8A
acquirer	[ə'kwaɪərə]	n. 发卡行,收单银行	5A
acquisition	[ˌækwɪ'zɪʃn]	n. 收购;获得;购得物	4A
actionable	['ækʃənəbl]	adj. 可操作的,可行动的	9B
activity	[æk'tɪvəti]	n. 活动,行动	4A
actor	['æktə]	n. 行动者,行为者	9B
ad	[ˌeɪ'di:]	n. 广告	3A
adequate	['ædɪkwət]	adj. 适当的,足够的	6B
adequately	['ædɪkwətli]	adv. 充分地,足够的	6B
adjust	[ə'dʒʌst]	v. 调整,调节	10A
adopt	[ə'dɒpt]	v. 采用	10A
advertiser	['ædvətaɪzə]	n. 登广告者,广告客户	9A
advice	[əd'vaɪs]	n. 忠告,建议	1A
affiliate	[ə'fɪlieɪt]	v. (使…)加入,接受为会员	1A
agent	['eɪdʒənt]	n. 代理人;代理商;代表;经纪人	4A
aggressively	[ə'gresɪvli]	adv. 侵略地,攻势地	6B
airfreight	['eəfreɪt]	vt. 空运 n. 货物空运费	6A

单 词	音 标	意 义	单元
alarm	[əˈlɑːm]	n.警报 vt.警告	9A
alleviate	[əˈliːvieɪt]	v.减轻；缓解	3A
ambiguity	[ˌæmbɪˈgjuːəti]	n.歧义；不明确，模棱两可	3A
ambitious	[æmˈbɪʃəs]	adj.有雄心的，野心勃勃的	1A
ammunition	[ˌæmjuˈnɪʃn]	n.军火，弹药	7A
ancient	[ˈeɪnʃənt]	adj.远古的，旧的	7A
animation	[ˌænɪˈmeɪʃn]	n.动画	1A
annually	[ˈænjuəli]	adv.一年一次，每年	5A
appreciate	[əˈpriːʃieɪt]	v.欣赏；理解，领会	3B
approachable	[əˈprəʊtʃəbl]	adj.可亲近的，可接近的	3B
appropriate	[əˈprəʊpriət]	adj.适当的	9A
assessment	[əˈsesmənt]	n.评估，估价	9A
asset	[ˈæset]	n.资产	9A
assistance	[əˈsɪstəns]	n.帮助；辅助；支持	4A
assure	[əˈʃʊə]	vt.保证，担保	2A
attachment	[əˈtætʃmənt]	n.附件	9A
attention	[əˈtenʃn]	n.注意，关心，关注	6A
attentive	[əˈtentɪv]	adj.周到的，殷勤的	4A
attitude	[ˈætɪtjuːd]	n.态度，看法，意见	2A
attract	[əˈtrækt]	vt.吸引 vi.有吸引力，引起注意	5A
attractive	[əˈtræktɪv]	adj.有吸引力的；引人注目的	5B
auction	[ˈɔːkʃn]	n.& vt.拍卖	6B
authenticate	[ɔːˈθentɪkeɪt]	vt.证明是真实的、可靠的或有效的	3A
authorise	[ˈɔːθəraɪz]	vt.批准	9A
auto-complete	[ˈɔːtəʊ kəmˈpliːt]	adj.自动完成的	3A
automate	[ˈɔːtəmeɪt]	v.使自动化	4A
automatically	[ˌɔːtəˈmætɪkli]	adv.自动地，机械地	2B
availability	[əˌveɪləˈbɪləti]	n.可用性；有效性	8B
avenue	[ˈævənjuː]	n.方法，途径	4A
awareness	[əˈweənəs]	n.知道，察觉	9A
background	[ˈbækgraʊnd]	n.背景；底色	3A

续表

单　词	音　标	意　义	单元
backing	[ˈbækɪŋ]	n. 援助,支持者,赞助者	6B
badge	[bædʒ]	n. 徽章;象征	3A
balance	[ˈbæləns]	n. 结余,余额,资产平稳表 v. 结算	1A
barrier	[ˈbæriə]	n. 屏障;障碍;界限	3B
base	[beɪs]	n. 根据地,基地,本部	7A
basket	[ˈbɑːskɪt]	n. 篮	2A
bidirectional	[ˌbaɪdəˈrekʃənl]	adj. 双向的	6A
biometric	[ˌbaɪəʊˈmetrɪk]	n. 生物特征	9A
blandishment	[ˈblændɪʃmənt]	n. 奉承,哄诱,甜言蜜语	1A
blog	[blɒg]	n. 博客;网络日志 v. 写博客	9B
boost	[buːst]	v. 使增长,推动;增强,提高	4B
botnet	[ˈbɒtnet]	n. 僵尸网络	9A
bottleneck	[ˈbɒtlnek]	n. 瓶颈	6A
boundary	[ˈbaʊndri]	n. 边界;界限;分界线	10A
breach	[briːtʃ]	n. 违背,破坏,破裂,裂口 vt. 打破,突破	5A
brick-and-mortar	[brɪk ənd ˈmɔːtə]	n. 实体店,传统的实体企业	2A
browse	[braʊz]	v. (在商店里)随便看;浏览	4A
burglar	[ˈbɜːglə]	n. 窃贼	9A
bypass	[ˈbaɪpɑːs]	vt. 绕过,迂回 n. 旁路	9A
calculability	[kælkjʊləˈbɪlɪti]	n. 可计算	2A
call	[kɔːl]	v. 调用	4A
cancellation	[ˌkænsəˈleɪʃn]	n. 取消,撤销;作废	4A
candidate	[ˈkændɪdət]	n. 候选人	7B
cardholder	[ˈkɑːdhəʊldə]	n. 持有信用卡的人,持有正式成员证的人,持卡人	5A
case	[keɪs]	n. 案例,事例	8A
cashflow	[ˈkæʃfləʊ]	n. 现金流	2B
casual	[ˈkæʒuəl]	adj. 漫不经心的;随便的;偶然的	3B
catalogue	[ˈkætəlɒg]	n. 目录	1A
certificate	[səˈtɪfɪkət]	n. 证书	3A
channel	[ˈtʃænl]	n. 渠道,通道	2A
character	[ˈkærəktə]	n. 字符	9A

续表

单　　词	音　　标	意　　义	单元
characteristic	[ˌkærəktəˈrɪstɪk]	adj.特有的,典型的 n.特性,特征	2A
chatbot	[tʃætbɒt]	n.聊天机器人	4A
check	[tʃek]	n.支票	1A
checker	[ˈtʃekə]	n.检测程序	9A
checkout	[ˈtʃekaʊt]	n.结账	3A
cheque	[tʃek]	n.支票	5A
chronological	[ˌkrɒnəˈlɒdʒɪkl]	adj.按时间排序的	8B
clerk	[klɑːk]	n.接待员,店员	4A
clickable	[ˈklɪkəbl]	adj.可点击的	3A
clickstream	[klɪkstriːm]	n.网站浏览记录;点击流	10B
code	[kəʊd]	n.代码,编码 v.编码	1A
collaboration	[kəˌlæbəˈreɪʃn]	n.协作	6A
collaborative	[kəˈlæbərətɪv]	adj.合作的,协作的	8B
collect	[kəˈlekt]	v.收集	8A
collection	[kəˈlekʃn]	n.收集,收藏品	1A
colossal	[kəˈlɒsl]	adj.巨大的	10B
combination	[ˌkɒmbɪˈneɪʃn]	n.结合(体);联合(体)	8B
comfort	[ˈkʌmfət]	n.舒适	4B
commission	[kəˈmɪʃn]	n.佣金,手续费;委托	1A
commitment	[kəˈmɪtmənt]	n.委托事项,许诺,承担义务	6A
commodity	[kəˈmɒdəti]	n.日用品	6B
compare	[kəmˈpeə]	v.比较	3A
competition	[ˌkɒmpəˈtɪʃn]	n.竞争者;对手;竞争,比赛	7B
competitive	[kəmˈpetətɪv]	adj.竞争的	6A
competitor	[kəmˈpetɪtə(r)]	n.竞争者	10A
compliance	[kəmˈplaɪəns]	n.依从,顺从	5A
component	[kəmˈpəʊnənt]	n.成分 adj.组成的,构成的	9A
composer	[kəmˈpəʊzə]	n.作曲家	7B
comprehensive	[ˌkɒmprɪˈhensɪv]	adj.全面的;综合性的	4A
compromise	[ˈkɒmprəmaɪz]	v.危及…的安全	5A
concept	[ˈkɒnsept]	n.概念;观念	8A

续表

单 词	音 标	意 义	单元
concern	[kən'sɜːn]	n.(利害)关系,关心,关注 vt.涉及,关系到	1A
concise	[kən'saɪs]	adj.简明的,简洁的	3A
conductor	[kən'dʌktə]	n.管弦乐队指挥;领导者	7B
confidence	['kɒnfɪdəns]	n.信心	9A
confident	['kɒnfɪdənt]	adj.坚信的,自信的;肯定的	9B
confidential	[ˌkɒnfɪ'denʃl]	adj.秘密的,机密的	9A
confidentiality	[ˌkɒnfɪˌdenʃi'æləti]	n.机密性	2B
confine	[kən'faɪn]	vt.限制;限定	10A
confirm	[kən'fɜːm]	vt.确定,批准	1A
confirmation	[ˌkɒnfə'meɪʃn]	n.证实,确认,批准	2A
confuse	[kən'fjuːz]	v.混淆,使困惑	3A
connectivity	[ˌkɒnek'tɪvɪti]	n.连通性	4B
conquer	['kɒŋkə]	v.占领;攻克	10A
considerable	[kən'sɪdərəbl]	adj.相当大的,相当多的	8B
consideration	[kənˌsɪdə'reɪʃn]	n.体谅,考虑	6A
consistent	[kən'sɪstənt]	adj.一致的;连续的	3A
consortium	[kən'sɔːtiəm]	n.社团,协会,联盟	6B
constantly	['kɒnstəntli]	adv.不断地,时常地	8A
construction	[kən'strʌkʃn]	n.建筑,建筑物	6B
consultant	[kən'sʌltənt]	n.顾问,商议者,咨询者	9A
consultation	[ˌkɒnsl'teɪʃn]	n.请教,咨询,磋商	7A
consumption	[kən'sʌmpʃn]	n.消费,消耗	7A
contactless	['kɒntæktləs]	adj.不接触的,无接触的	5B
context-sensitive	['kɒnteksts'ensətɪv]	adj.与内容相关的,上下文相关的	8B
contract	['kɒntrækt]	n.合同,契约	6A
contractor	[kən'træktə]	n.承包商	1B
contribute	[kən'trɪbjuːt]	v.增加,增进	3A
convenience	[kən'viːniəns]	n.方便	4B
conveniently	[kən'viːnjəntli]	adv.便利地	1A
conversation	[ˌkɒnvə'seɪʃn]	n.交谈,谈话	3B
conversational	[ˌkɒnvə'seɪʃənl]	adj.会话的,对话的	4A

续表

单　　词	音　　标	意　　义	单元
conversion	[kən'vɜːʃn]	n. 转换	3A
conveyor	[kən'veɪə]	n. 搬运者	7B
coordinate	[kəʊ'ɔːdɪneɪt]	adj. 同等的，并列的　vt. 调整，整理	7A
coordination	[kəʊ,ɔːdɪ'neɪʃn]	n. 协调，调和	6A
cornerstone	['kɔːnəstəʊn]	n. 基石，基础	4A
corporate	['kɔːpərət]	adj. 公司的；法人的	10B
corrupt	[kə'rʌpt]	vt. 破坏，损坏	9A
counter	['kaʊntə]	v. 抵制，抵消	9A
craft	[krɑːft]	v. 精心制作　n. 手艺，技巧	10B
creation	[kri'eɪʃn]	n. 创造	6A
creativity	[,kriːeɪ'tɪvəti]	n. 创造性，创造力	3B
credential	[krə'denʃl]	n. 凭证，凭据	9B
credibility	[,kredə'bɪləti]	n. 可信度，可信性	3B
cross-selling	[krɒs-'selɪŋ]	n. 交叉销售	8B
crucial	['kruːʃl]	adj. 至关紧要的	6A
crystal-clear	['krɪstl'klɪə]	adj. 清晰的	3B
cyber	['saɪbə]	adj. 计算机(网络)的，信息技术的	8A
database	['deɪtəbeɪs]	n. 数据库，资料库	2A
dazzle	['dæzl]	v. 使目眩，眼花；使惊叹	3B
decentralize	[,diː'sentrəlaɪz]	v. 分散	6A
decipher	[dɪ'saɪfə]	vt. 破译(密码)	5B
deface	[dɪ'feɪs]	vt. 损伤…的外貌(尤指乱涂、乱写)	2B
default	[dɪ'fɔːlt]	adj. 默认的　n. 默认值；缺省指令	3A
defence	[dɪ'fens]	n. 防御	9B
defenseless	[dɪ'fensləs]	adj. 无防御的，无保护的，不能自卫的	7A
definite	['defɪnət]	adj. 明确的，一定的	7B
demand	[dɪ'mɑːnd]	n. & v. 要求，需要	6A
demographic	[,demə'græfɪk]	adj. 人口(学)的；人口统计(学)的	1B
dependency	[dɪ'pendənsi]	n. 依赖，依靠	9B
deploy	[dɪ'plɔɪ]	v. 部署，调集	9B
description	[dɪ'skrɪpʃn]	n. 描述，说明	3B

续表

单　词	音　标	意　义	单元
desirable	[dɪˈzaɪərəbl]	*adj*.期望的,合意的,令人想要的	9A
destroy	[dɪˈstrɔɪ]	*vt*.破坏,毁坏,消灭	9A
destructive	[dɪˈstrʌktɪv]	*adj*.破坏(性)的	9A
detect	[dɪˈtekt]	*v*.发现;检测	8A
dial-up	[ˈdaiəl ʌp]	*v*.拨号(上网)	2B
diligent	[ˈdɪlɪdʒənt]	*adj*.认真的;勤奋的	9B
dimension	[daɪˈmenʃn, dɪˈmenʃn]	*n*.尺寸;维度	3A
directory	[dəˈrektəri]	*n*.目录	1A
disaffected	[ˌdɪsəˈfektɪd]	*adj*.不满的,不忠的	9A
disastrous	[dɪˈzɑːstrəs]	*adj*.灾难性的;极糟糕的	9B
disclosure	[dɪsˈkləʊʒə]	*n*.公开	6B
discuss	[ˌfleksəˈbɪləti]	*vt*.讨论,论述	5A
disguise	[dɪsˈɡaɪz]	*v*.假装,伪装,掩饰 *n*.伪装	9A
disrupt	[dɪsˈrʌpt]	*v*.使中断,使分裂,使陷于混乱	7A
disseminate	[dɪˈsemɪneɪt]	*v*.传播,散布	2A
dissolve	[dɪˈzɒlv]	*v*.消失,消除	2A
distract	[dɪˈstrækt]	*v*.分散注意力;使分心	3A
distraction	[dɪˈstrækʃn]	*n*.使人分心的事	3A
distributor	[dɪˈstrɪbjətə]	*n*.批发公司,批发商;分发者	1B
diversification	[daɪˌvɜːsɪfɪˈkeɪʃn]	*n*.多样化;多种经营	1B
download	[ˌdaʊnˈləʊd]	*v*.下载	2A
downstream	[ˌdaʊnˈstriːm]	*adv*.下游地 *adj*.下游的	6A
downtime	[ˈdaʊntaɪm]	*n*.停机时间,停工期	9B
dreadful	[ˈdredfl]	*adj*.可怕的	7B
drone	[drəʊn]	*n*.无人机	10B
duration	[djuˈreɪʃn]	*n*.持续时间;期间	8B
dynamic	[daɪˈnæmɪk]	*adj*.动态的	5B
e-commerce	[iːˈkɒmɜːs]	*n*.电子商务	1A
ecosystem	[ˈiːkəʊsɪstəm]	*n*.生态系统	4B
editable	[ˈedɪtəbl]	*adj*.可编辑的	3A
editor	[ˈedɪtə]	*n*.编辑器	1A

续表

单　词	音　标	意　义	单元
elevate	[ˈelɪveɪt]	v. 提升;提高	10B
emotional	[ɪˈməʊʃənl]	adj. 情绪的,情感的	2A
employ	[ɪmˈplɔɪ]	vt. 使用;雇用	1A
encompass	[ɪnˈkʌmpəs]	v. 包围,环绕	5A
encourage	[ɪnˈkʌrɪdʒ]	v. 鼓励	5A
encrypt	[ɪnˈkrɪpt]	v. 加密,将…译成密码	3A
encryption	[ɪnˈkrɪpʃn]	n. 编密码,加密	5B
enemy	[ˈenəmi]	n. 敌人,仇敌	7A
enforce	[ɪnˈfɔːs]	v. 强制执行;强迫	9B
engage	[ɪnˈgeɪdʒ]	v. (使)参与;吸引;引起(注意、兴趣)	8A
engagement	[ɪnˈgeɪdʒmənt]	n. 参与	4B
enhance	[ɪnˈhɑːns]	v. 提高,增强;改进	8A
enormous	[ɪˈnɔːməs]	adj. 巨大的;极大的	4A
ensure	[ɪnˈʃʊə]	v. 确保,确保,保证	9A
entertainment	[ˌentəˈteɪnmənt]	n. 娱乐	9A
entice	[ɪnˈtaɪs]	vt. 诱惑;怂恿	3B
entity	[ˈentəti]	n. 实体	6A
equitable	[ˈekwɪtəbl]	adj. 公平的,公正的	6A
essential	[ɪˈsenʃl]	adj. 本质的,实质的 n. 本质,实质,要素,要点	7A
establish	[ɪˈstæblɪʃ]	vt. 建立,设立,安置	5A
e-tender	[iːˈtendə]	v. 电子投标	6B
etiquette	[ˈetɪket]	n. 礼节	2A
excess	[ɪkˈses]	adj. 过度的,额外的	6B
exclusively	[ɪkˈskluːsɪvli]	adv. 排外地,专有地	5A
exhibit	[ɪgˈzɪbɪt]	v. 展览;表现	3A
expect	[ɪkˈspekt]	vt. 期待,预期,盼望,指望	5A
expense	[ɪkˈspens]	n. 费用,代价,损失,开支	1A
expensive	[ɪkˈspensɪv]	adj. 花费的,昂贵的	5A
expertise	[ˌekspɜːˈtiːz]	n. 专门技术,专门知识	1B
explain	[ɪkˈspleɪn]	v. 解释;说明…的理由	3B
exposure	[ɪkˈspəʊʒə]	n. 接触;泄露,暴露	8A

续表

单　词	音　标	意　义	单元
extensively	[ɪkˈstensɪvli]	*adv*.广泛地	8B
extol	[ɪkˈstəʊl]	*v*.赞美	1A
facility	[fəˈsɪləti]	*n*.设备,工具	1A
factor	[ˈfæktə]	*n*.因素,要素	2A
faithfully	[ˈfeɪθfəli]	*adv*.忠诚地,如实地	1A
fantastic	[fænˈtæstɪk]	*adj*.极好的;极大的;奇异的	4A
favorable	[ˈfeɪvərəbl]	*adj*.有利的,赞许的,良好的	1A
favoured	[ˈfeɪvəd]	*adj*.受优惠的,有特权的	6B
field	[fiːld]	*n*.区域,字段	3A
filter	[ˈfɪltə]	*n*.过滤器;筛选(过滤)程序	3A
fine-tune	[faɪn tjuːn]	*vt*.调整	1B
fingerprint	[ˈfɪŋgəprɪnt]	*n*.指纹,指印	4B
firewall	[ˈfaɪəwɔːl]	*n*.防火墙	9A
fix	[fɪks]	*v*.修复,修理	9B
flexibility	[ˌfleksəˈbɪləti]	*n*.灵活性,弹性,适应性	5A
flexible	[ˈfleksəbl]	*adj*.灵活的	6A
flourish	[ˈflʌrɪʃ]	*vi*.繁荣,茂盛,活跃	7B
fold	[fəʊld]	*n*.首屏	3A
folder	[ˈfəʊldə]	*n*.文件夹	9B
font	[fɒnt]	*n*.字体;字形	3A
forecast	[ˈfɔːkɑːst]	*n*.预报 *v*.预测	8A
forum	[ˈfɔːrəm]	*n*.论坛	6A
framework	[ˈfreɪmwɜːk]	*n*.构架,框架,结构	2A
fraud	[frɔːd]	*n*.欺诈,骗子;伪劣品,冒牌货	8A
fraudulent	[ˈfrɔːdjələnt]	*adj*.欺骗的,不诚实的	8A
freelancer	[ˈfriː lɑːnsə]	*n*.自由职业者	1B
frequency	[ˈfriːkwənsi]	*n*.频率,发生次数	6A
frictionless	[ˈfrɪkʃnləs]	*adj*.无障碍的	3A
fruition	[fruˈɪʃn]	*n*.享用,成就,实现	7A
frustration	[frʌˈstreɪʃn]	*n*.沮丧,挫折,失败	4A
fulfillment	[fʊlˈfɪlmənt]	*n*.完成;实现;实施;履行	10B

续表

单　词	音　标	意　义	单元
functionality	[ˌfʌŋkʃəˈnæləti]	n. 功能性	2A
fundamentally	[ˌfʌndəˈmentəli]	adv. 基础地,根本地	7A
furniture	[ˈfɜːnɪtʃə]	n. 家具,设备	6B
gather	[ˈɡæðə]	v. 收集,搜集	4A
generate	[ˈdʒenəreɪt]	vt. 产生,发生	2A
geographical	[ˌdʒiːəˈɡræfɪkl]	adj. 地理的	10A
gibberish	[ˈdʒɪbərɪʃ]	n. 无意义数据	5B
glitch	[ɡlɪtʃ]	n. 小过失,差错	3B
globalize	[ˈɡləʊbəlaɪz]	v. 使全球化	7A
graphics	[ˈɡræfɪks]	n. 图形	1A
groundwork	[ˈɡraʊndwɜːk]	n. 基础;基本原理	1B
guess	[ɡes]	v. & n. 猜测,推测	7B
hacker	[ˈhækə]	n. 电脑黑客	9A
halfway	[ˌhɑːfˈweɪ]	adj. 中途的,部分的,不彻底的 adv. 半路地,在中途,在半途	1A
handle	[ˈhændl]	v. 处理;应付	8A
handy	[ˈhændi]	adj. 容易做的;便利的	5B
harm	[hɑːm]	vt. & n. 伤害,损害	9A
harmful	[ˈhɑːmfl]	adj. 有害的	9A
harmony	[ˈhɑːməni]	n. 协调,融洽	7B
hassle	[ˈhæsl]	n. 困难的事情;麻烦的事情	3B
headline	[ˈhedlaɪn]	n. 标题 vt. 给…加标题	3B
hesitate	[ˈhezɪteɪt]	v. 犹豫;顾虑	9B
heuristic	[hjuˈrɪstɪk]	adj. 启发式的	9A
hijack	[ˈhaɪdʒæk]	vt. 劫持	9A
hinder	[ˈhɪndə]	vt. 阻碍	1A
hobbyist	[ˈhɒbiɪst]	n. 沉溺于某种癖好者	1B
honest	[ˈɒnɪst]	adj. 诚实的,正直的	2A
horizontal	[ˌhɒrɪˈzɒntl]	adj. 水平的	6B
huge	[hjuːdʒ]	adj. 巨大的	8A
hybrid	[ˈhaɪbrɪd]	n. 混合物	1B

续表

单　　词	音　　标	意　　义	单元
icon	[ˈaɪkɒn]	n . 图标	3A
identity	[aɪˈdentəti]	n . 身份；个性；一致	3A
ignore	[ɪɡˈnɔː]	v . 忽视；佯装未见	8B
imagination	[ɪˌmædʒɪˈneɪʃn]	n . 想象（力）	3B
impact	[ˈɪmpækt]	n . 碰撞，冲击，影响，效果	9A
implication	[ˌɪmplɪˈkeɪʃn]	n . 含意，暗示；牵连	9A
inadvertently	[ˌɪnədˈvɜːtəntli]	adv . 不注意地，无意地	9A
inbound	[ˈɪnbaʊnd]	adj . 到达的，入站的	6A
incentivize	[ɪnˈsentɪvaɪz]	vt . 以物质刺激鼓励	9B
incident	[ˈɪnsɪdənt]	n . 事件	9A
income	[ˈɪnkʌm]	n . 收入，收益，进款，所得	5A
inconspicuous	[ˌɪnkənˈspɪkjuəs]	adj . 不明显的，不显著的	3A
incorporate	[ɪnˈkɔːpəreɪt]	adj . 合并的，一体化的 vt . 合并	7A
increasingly	[ɪnˈkriːsɪŋli]	adv . 日益，愈加	6A
indication	[ˌɪndɪˈkeɪʃn]	n . 表明；标示	3A
inefficient	[ˌɪnɪˈfɪʃnt]	adj . 效率低的，效率差的	7B
infect	[ɪnˈfekt]	vt . 传染，感染	9A
influence	[ˈɪnfluəns]	v . 影响；支配	8A
influential	[ˌɪnfluˈenʃl]	adj . 有影响的	2A
inform	[ɪnˈfɔːm]	v . 了解；通知	10B
infrastructure	[ˈɪnfrəstrʌktʃə]	n . 基础组织	6A
in-person	[ˈinˈpɜːsən]	adj . 亲自的，本人的；现场的	3A
insight	[ˈɪnsaɪt]	n . 见解；洞察力	8A
in-store	[in-stɔː]	adj . 商店内的	3A
integral	[ˈɪntɪɡrəl]	adj . 基本的；必须的；完整的	8A
integration	[ˌɪntɪˈɡreɪʃn]	n . 综合	7A
integrator	[ˈɪntɪɡreɪtə]	n . 综合体，综合者	7A
interaction	[ˌɪntərˈækʃn]	n . 互相影响；互动	4A
interconnect	[ˌɪntəkəˈnekt]	vt . 使互相连接	6A
intermediary	[ˌɪntəˈmiːdiəri]	n . 中间人；媒介	1B
intrusion	[ɪnˈtruːʒn]	n . 闯入，侵扰	9A

续表

单　词	音　标	意　义	单元
inventory	[ˈɪnvəntri]	n.详细目录，库存，财产清册，总量	6A
investigate	[ɪnˈvestɪgeɪt]	v.调查，研究	2B
involvement	[ɪnˈvɒlvmənt]	n.包含	2A
iris	[ˈaɪrɪs]	n.虹膜	9A
irrespective	[ˌɪrɪˈspektɪv]	adj.无关的；不考虑的，不顾的	4B
irritant	[ˈɪrɪtənt]	n.令人烦恼的事物，造成麻烦的事物	9A
jargon	[ˈdʒɑːgən]	n.行话	5A
keystroke	[ˈkiːstrəʊk]	n.键击，按键	9A
keyword	[ˈkiːwɜːd]	n.关键字，关键词	8A
lag	[læg]	vi.滞后，落后	4A
lax	[læks]	adj.松弛的；松懈的；不严格的	9B
legislation	[ˌledʒɪsˈleɪʃn]	n.立法，制定法律	9B
letterhead	[ˈletəhed]	n.信头	2B
leverage	[ˈliːvərɪdʒ]	v.利用；发挥杠杆作用 n.杠杆作用；优势	10B
liaison	[liˈeɪzn]	n.联络	1A
likelihood	[ˈlaɪklihʊd]	n.可能，可能性	5B
link	[lɪŋk]	n.& v.链接	3A
linkage	[ˈlɪŋkɪdʒ]	n.链接	6A
litigation	[ˌlɪtɪˈgeɪʃn]	n.诉讼，起诉	9A
load	[ləʊd]	v.装载，加载	3A
localize	[ˈləʊkəlaɪz]	vt.使本地化，使局部化	10A
logistic	[ləˈdʒɪstɪk]	adj.物流的	7A
logistician	[ˌləʊdʒɪˈstɪʃən]	n.物流师	7A
logistics	[ləˈdʒɪstɪks]	n.物流；后勤	2A
logjam	[ˈlɒgdʒæm]	n.阻塞，停滞状态，僵局	7B
longevity	[lɒnˈdʒevəti]	n.长命，寿命	6B
loosely	[ˈluːsli]	adv.宽松地，松散地	6A
loyalty	[ˈlɔɪəlti]	n.忠诚，忠实	4A
lucrative	[ˈluːkrətɪv]	adj.有利可图的，赚钱的	1B
mainstream	[ˈmeɪnstriːm]	n.主流；主要倾向，主要趋势	10B
maintain	[meɪnˈteɪn]	vt.维护，维修	1A

续表

单　　　词	音　　标	意　　　义	单元
maintainability	[menˌteɪnəˈbɪləti]	n . 可维护性	7A
make-or-break	[meik ɔː breik]	conj . 不成则败	3A
malicious	[məˈlɪʃəs]	adj . 恶意的,有敌意的	9B
malware	[ˈmælweə]	n . 恶意软件,流氓软件	9B
mandatorily	[mændəˈtərɪli]	adv . 强制地,命令地	10A
manifold	[ˈmænɪfəʊld]	adj . 多种多样的;多方面的	9B
manufacturer	[ˌmænjuˈfæktʃərə]	n . 生产者,制造者,生产商	2A
manufacturing	[ˌmænjuˈfæktʃərɪŋ]	n . 制造业 adj . 制造业的	7A
margin	[ˈmɑːdʒɪn]	n . 利润,盈余	8B
marketer	[ˈmɑːkɪtə]	n . 市场营销人员	10B
material	[məˈtɪəriəl]	n . 材料;原料;布料	3A
maximize	[ˈmæksɪmaɪz]	vt . 最大化	10A
meaningless	[ˈmiːnɪŋləs]	adj . 无意义的,无价值的	5B
mentality	[menˈtæləti]	n . 精神,心理	7B
merchant	[ˈmɜːtʃənt]	n . 商人,批发商,贸易商,店主 adj . 商业的,商人的	5A
methodology	[ˌmeθəˈdɒlədʒi]	n . 一套方法;方法学;方法论	1B
military	[ˈmɪlətri]	adj . 军事的,军用的	7A
minimal	[ˈmɪnɪməl]	adj . 最小的,极少的	10A
mission	[ˈmɪʃn]	n . 任务	6A
mitigate	[ˈmɪtɪgeɪt]	vt . 使缓和,使减轻;使平息 vi . 减轻,缓和下来	8A
mobility	[məʊˈbɪləti]	n . 移动性;流动性	4B
module	[ˈmɒdjuːl]	n . 模块	2A
monitor	[ˈmɒnɪtə]	v . 监控	3B
mood	[muːd]	n . 情绪;语气	4A
mundane	[mʌnˈdeɪn]	adj . 平凡的,寻常的	3B
navigation	[ˌnævɪˈgeɪʃn]	n . 导航	3A
negligence	[ˈneglɪdʒəns]	n . 疏忽	5A
negotiation	[nɪˌgəʊʃiˈeɪʃn]	n . 商议,谈判	6B
newcomer	[ˈnjuːkʌmə]	n . 新来者,新手	1A
nicely	[ˈnaɪsli]	adv . 精细地	7B

续表

单　词	音　标	意　　义	单元
node	［nəʊd］	n. 节点	7A
non-compliance	［ˌnɒnkəm'plaɪəns］	n. 不兼容	9B
notice	['nəʊtɪs］	v. 注意到 n. 通知,布告,注意	1A
notification	［ˌnəʊtɪfɪ'keɪʃn］	n. 通知;通知单;布告;公布	3A
notify	['nəʊtɪfaɪ］	v. 通报	2A
novice	['nɒvɪs］	n. 新手,初学者	2A
obligation	［ˌɒblɪ'geɪʃn］	n. 义务,职责	5A
obstacle	['ɒbstəkl］	n. 障碍,障碍物	3B
obtain	［əb'teɪn］	vt. 获得,得到	1A
occasion	［ə'keɪʒn］	n. 场合	10A
occasionally	［ə'keɪʒnəli］	adv. 有时候,偶尔	7A
occupation	［ˌɒkju'peɪʃn］	n. 职业,占有	2A
offline	［ˌɒf'laɪn］	adj. 未联机的,脱机的,离线的	5A
offload	［ˌɒf'ləʊd］	v. 卸下,卸货	6B
omission	［ə'mɪʃn］	n. 冗长	5A
omnichannel	['ɒmnɪ'tʃænl］	n. 多渠道,全渠道	1B
omnipresent	［ˌɒmnɪ'preznt］	adj. 无所不在的	3A
online	［ˌɒn'laɪn］	n. 联机,在线式	1A
operation	［ˌɒpə'reɪʃn］	n. 活动;运行	10A
operational	［ˌɒpə'reɪʃənl］	adj. 操作的,运作的	7A
opinion	［ə'pɪnjən］	n. 意见	3A
optimal	['ɒptɪməl］	adj. 最佳的,最理想的	6A
optimization	［ˌɒptəmaɪ'zeɪʃən］	n. 最佳化,最优化	1A
option	['ɒpʃn］	n. 选项,选择权	1A
orchestra	['ɔːkɪstrə］	n. 管弦乐队	7B
ordinary	['ɔːdnri］	adj. 平常的,普通的,平凡的	9A
organizational	［ˌɔːɡənaɪ'zeɪʃənl］	adj. 组织的	4A
overlap	［ˌəʊvə'læp］	v. (与…)交迭	7B
packaging	['pækɪdʒɪŋ］	n. 包装	7A
painless	['peɪnləs］	adj. 愉快的,轻松的,不难的	1A
pallet	['pælət］	n. 草垫子;托盘;平台;运货板	7B

续表

单　　词	音　　标	意　　义	单元
paramount	[ˈpærəmaʊnt]	adj. 最重要的，主要的	10B
participant	[pɑːˈtɪsɪpənt]	n. 参与者，共享者	6B
participate	[pɑːˈtɪsɪpeɪt]	vi. 参与，参加，分享，分担	6B
password	[ˈpɑːswɜːd]	n. 密码，口令	5A
payment	[ˈpeɪmənt]	n. 付款，支付	1A
peer-to-peer	[pɪə tu pɪə]	adj. 对等的，点对点的 n. 对等网络	5B
penalty	[ˈpenəlti]	n. 处罚，罚款	5A
penetrate	[ˈpenətreɪt]	v. 渗透，进入	10A
pension	[ˈpenʃn]	n. 养老金，退休金	2A
perception	[pəˈsepʃn]	n. 理解，看法，见解	2A
performance	[pəˈfɔːməns]	n. 履行，执行；成绩；性能	6A
periodic	[ˌpɪəriˈɒdɪk]	adj. 周期的；定期的	9B
perpetrate	[ˈpɜː pətreɪt]	v. 犯(罪)，做(错事)，干(坏事)	9A
personalization	[ˈpɜː sənəlaɪzeɪʃn]	n. 个性化	4A
personalize	[ˈpɜːsənəlaɪz]	vt. 个性化	4A
persuasive	[pəˈsweɪsɪv]	adj. 有说服力的	3B
phishing	[ˈfɪʃɪŋ]	n. 网络仿冒，网络钓鱼	9B
pinpoint	[ˈpɪnpɔɪnt]	vt. 确定	4A
pipeline	[ˈpaɪplaɪn]	n. 管道，渠道	8A
pivot	[ˈpɪvət]	vt. 以…为核心	1B
plant	[plɑːnt]	n. 工厂，车间，设备	7A
platform	[ˈplætfɔːm]	n. 平台	4A
pleasant	[ˈpleznt]	adj. 令人愉快的；友好的	3A
plugin	[ˈplʌgɪn]	n. 插件	9B
pocket	[ˈpɒkɪt]	n. 衣袋，口袋	1A
policy	[ˈpɒləsi]	n. 政策；策略	3A
population	[ˌpɒpjuˈleɪʃn]	n. 人口	2A
pose	[pəʊz]	v. 形成，引起，造成	9A
position	[pəˈzɪʃn]	vt. 定位	10A
posture	[ˈpɒstʃə]	n. 态度；立场	9B
potentially	[pəˈtenʃəli]	adv. 潜在地	9A

续表

单　　词	音　　标	意　　义	单元
precaution	[prɪˈkɔːʃn]	n. 预防，警惕，防范	2B
predictability	[prɪˌdɪktəˈbɪləti]	n. 可预测性，预见性	2A
predictable	[prɪˈdɪktəbl]	adj. 可预言的	2B
preference	[ˈprefrəns]	n. 偏爱；优先权	5B
pre-selection	[pˈriːsɪˈlekʃn]	n. 预筛，预选	8B
presence	[ˈprezns]	n. 到场，存在	5A
prevalent	[ˈprevələnt]	adj. 流行的，盛行的；普遍存在的，普遍发生的	4A
principle	[ˈprɪnsəpl]	n. 法则，定律，原则；原理；观念；理由	2A
privacy	[ˈprɪvəsi]	n. 隐私	2A
privilege	[ˈprɪvəlɪdʒ]	n. 特权	9A
probability	[ˌprɒbəˈbɪləti]	n. 可能性，或然性，概率	2A
procedure	[prəˈsiːdʒə]	n. 程序，步骤，流程，手续	5A
profitability	[ˌprɒfɪtəˈbɪləti]	n. 获利（状况），盈利（情况）；收益性	10B
progress	[ˈprəʊgres]	n. 进程，进步，发展	2B
progression	[prəˈgreʃn]	n. 发展，进展	4B
prominent	[ˈprɒmɪnənt]	adj. 突出的	5B
promote	[prəˈməʊt]	vt. 促销，推销	1A
promptly	[ˈprɒmptli]	adv. 敏捷地，迅速地	2B
protect	[prəˈtekt]	vt. 保护	5A
provision	[prəˈvɪʒn]	n. 供应	6A
psychological	[ˌsaɪkəˈlɒdʒɪkl]	adj. 心理的；心理学的	3A
publication	[ˌpʌblɪˈkeɪʃn]	n. 出版；出版物	8B
publicize	[ˈpʌblɪsaɪz]	v. 宣扬	2B
purchase	[ˈpɜːtʃəs]	vt. & n. 买，购买	1A
puzzle	[ˈpʌzl]	n. 难题，谜	7B
qualify	[ˈkwɒlɪfaɪ]	v. (使)具有资格，证明合格	6B
query	[ˈkwɪəri]	n. 查询，询问	3A
quotation	[kwəʊˈteɪʃn]	n. 价格，报价单，行情表	6B
rank	[ræŋk]	v. 分等级；排列	10B
ransomware	[rænsəmweə]	n. 勒索软件	9B
rapport	[ræˈpɔː]	n. 友好关系；融洽，和谐	10A

续表

单　词	音　标	意　义	单元
rate	[reɪt]	v. 评估,评价	8B
ration	['ræʃn]	n. 定量,配给量,定量配给 v. 配给,分发	7A
rational	['ræʃnəl]	adj. 理性的;理智的	3B
reach	[riːtʃ]	v. 达到;到达;抵达;碰到,触及 n. 波及范围;影响范围	10A
react	[riˈækt]	vi. 起反应,起作用	7B
readability	[ˌriːdəˈbɪləti]	n. 可读性	3B
realize	['riːəlaɪz]	vt. 认识到,了解	7B
reciprocal	[rɪˈsɪprəkl]	adj. 互惠的,相应的	1A
recognise	['rekəgnaɪz]	v. 承认,识别,认可	9A
recognition	[ˌrekəgˈnɪʃn]	n. 承认,识别	1A
rectify	['rektɪfaɪ]	vt. 矫正,调整	2B
reed	[riːd]	n. 簧片	7B
register	['redʒɪstə]	v. 登记;注册	4B
registration	[ˌredʒɪˈstreɪʃn]	n. 登记,注册	3A
regular	['regjələ]	adj. 规则的,有秩序的,经常的	5A
regulation	[ˌregjuˈleɪʃn]	n. 规则,规章	9A
regulatory	['regjələtəri]	adj. 监管的	9B
relevant	['reləvənt]	adj. 相关的,有关的	1A
reliant	[rɪˈlaɪənt]	adj. 信赖的,依靠的	9A
removable	[rɪˈmuːvəbl]	adj. 可移动的	9A
rent	[rent]	vt. 租赁	1A
repetitive	[rɪˈpetətɪv]	adj. 重复的,啰嗦的	4A
replacement	[rɪˈpleɪsmənt]	n. 替换,更换;替代品,替换物	8A
replenish	[rɪˈplenɪʃ]	v. 补充	2B
representative	[ˌreprɪˈzentətɪv]	n. 代表	2B
reputable	['repjətəbl]	adj. 值得尊敬的,声誉好的	9B
reputation	[ˌrepjuˈteɪʃn]	n. 名誉,名声	2B
requirement	[rɪˈkwaɪəmənt]	n. 需求,要求,必要条件	5A
resonate	['rezəneɪt]	vi. 共鸣,共振	3B
respondent	[rɪˈspɒndənt]	n. 响应	4A

续表

单　　词	音　　标	意　　义	单元
responsibility	[rɪˌspɒnsəˈbɪləti]	n. 责任，职责	7A
responsive	[rɪˈspɒnsɪv]	adj. 响应的，做出响应的	6A
responsiveness	[rɪˈspɒnsɪvnəs]	n. 响应性	4A
restrict	[rɪˈstrɪkt]	vt. 限制，约束	9B
restricted	[rɪˈstrɪktɪd]	adj. 受限制的，有限的	2B
restriction	[rɪˈstrɪkʃn]	n. 限制；管制	10A
restrictive	[rɪˈstrɪktɪv]	adj. 限制性的	9A
retailer	[ˈriːteɪlə]	n. 零售商人	2A
retention	[rɪˈtenʃn]	n. 保留，保持	4B
retina	[ˈretɪnə]	n. 视网膜	9A
return	[rɪˈtɜːn]	v. & n. 退货	3A
revenue	[ˈrevənjuː]	n. 收入，收益	1B
revoke	[rɪˈvəʊk]	vt. 撤销，取消；废除	9B
revolutionize	[ˌrevəˈluːʃənaɪz]	vt. 彻底改革	10B
risk	[rɪsk]	n. 风险，危险；隐患 v. 冒风险	9B
rival	[ˈraɪvl]	n. 对手；竞争者 adj. 竞争的	10A
robust	[rəʊˈbʌst]	adj. 健壮的，耐用的，坚固的	7A
round-the-clock	[raʊnd ðə klɒk]	adj. 全天的，连续不停的	6B
satisfaction	[ˌsætɪsˈfækʃn]	n. 满意，满足	6A
satisfy	[ˈsætɪsfaɪ]	vt. 满足，使满意	2A
satisfying	[ˈsætɪsfaɪɪŋ]	adj. 令人满足的，令人满意的	6A
saturate	[ˈsætʃəreɪt]	v. 使充满，使饱和	4A
scare	[skeə]	v. 吓跑	5B
scenario	[səˈnɑːriəʊ]	n. 设想；可能发生的情况	9B
scheme	[skiːm]	n. 安排，配置，计划，方案 v. 计划，设计	5A
scramble	[ˈskræmbl]	vt. 把…搅乱	5B
script	[skrɪpt]	n. 脚本	4A
seamless	[ˈsiːmləs]	adj. 无缝的	5B
seamlessly	[ˈsiːmləsli]	adv. 无缝地	1A
search	[sɜːtʃ]	n. & v. 搜索	3A
security	[sɪˈkjʊərəti]	n. 安全性	3A

续表

单　词	音　标	意　义	单元
seduce	[sɪˈdjuːs]	vt.吸引,使入迷	3B
self-learning	[ˈselflɜːnɪŋ]	n.自学习(能力)	8B
self-service	[ˈself ˈsɜːvɪs]	adj.自我服务的;(商店)自选的;(饭店)自助的	4A
self-sufficiency	[ˌself səˈfɪʃnsi]	n.自给自足;自立	4A
sensory	[ˈsensəri]	adj.感觉的,感受的,感官的	3B
sequence	[ˈsiːkwəns]	n.次序,顺序,序列	7A
server	[ˈsɜːvə]	n.服务器	3A
settlement	[ˈsetlmənt]	n.解决,结算	6A
shape	[ʃeɪp]	v.塑造;决定…的形成	10B
share	[ʃeə]	v.共享,分享	3A
shopper	[ˈʃɒpə]	n.(商店的)顾客,买东西的人	3A
short-term	[ˌʃɔːt-ˈtɜːm]	adj.短期的	10B
shrewd	[ʃruːd]	adj.精明的	6B
significant	[sɪgˈnɪfɪkənt]	adj.有意义的,重大的,重要的	7A
significantly	[sɪgˈnɪfɪkəntli]	adv.重要地,有意义地	5A
single-sign-on	[ˈsɪŋgl saɪn ɒn]	n.单点登录	9B
skill	[skɪl]	n.技能,技巧	5A
skyrocket	[ˈskaɪrɒkɪt]	vi.突升,猛涨	10A
smartphone	[ˈsmɑːtfoʊn]	n.智能手机	4B
smooth	[smuːð]	adj.光滑的 v.使光滑	5B
snippet	[ˈsnɪpɪt]	n.小片,片断,摘录	1A
solid	[ˈsɒlɪd]	adj.可靠的;可信赖的	8B
solution	[səˈluːʃn]	n.方案	1A
sophistication	[səˌfɪstɪˈkeɪʃn]	n.复杂巧妙,高水平	9A
sortation	[sɔːˈteɪʃən]	n.分类	7B
span	[spæn]	v.横越,跨越	6A
spec	[spek]	n.规格;说明书	3B
specialist	[ˈspeʃəlɪst]	n.专家	9A
spectacular	[spekˈtækjələ]	adj.引人入胜的,壮观的	1A
speedy	[ˈspiːdi]	adj.快的,迅速的	5A
spend	[spend]	v.花费,消耗,用尽	2A

续表

单　　词	音　　标	意　　义	单元
spot	[spɒt]	v. 注意到	10A
spyware	[ˈspaɪweə]	n. 间谍软件	9A
stage	[steɪdʒ]	n. 阶段，时期	1A
standardize	[ˈstændədaɪz]	vt. 使标准化	4A
stark	[stɑːk]	adj. 刻板的，十足的 adv. 完全地	1A
stationery	[ˈsteɪʃənri]	n. 文具，信纸	6B
statistics	[stəˈtɪstɪks]	n. 统计学，统计表	7A
steer	[stɪə]	v. 控制，引导	2B
steward	[ˈstjuːəd]	n. 管家	2A
storefront	[ˈstɔːfrʌnt]	n. 店面	1B
straightforward	[ˌstreɪtˈfɔːwəd]	adj. 简单明了的	1B
straightforwardly	[ˌstreɪtˈfɔːwədlɪ]	adv. 直截了当地	6B
strategic	[strəˈtiːdʒɪk]	adj. 战略的，战略上的	6A
strategy	[ˈstrætədʒi]	n. 策略；部署	4A
streamline	[ˈstriːmlaɪn]	v. 使（系统、机构等）效率更高	2B
string	[strɪŋ]	n. 弦乐器	7B
strive	[straɪv]	vi. 努力奋斗，力求，力争	8B
stunning	[ˈstʌnɪŋ]	adj. 极好的	1A
subcategory	[sʌbˈkætɪgəri]	n. 子类，亚类	4B
submit	[səbˈmɪt]	vt. 提交，递交	1A
subsequent	[ˈsʌbsɪkwənt]	adj. 后来的，并发的	9A
subset	[ˈsʌbset]	n. 子集	9A
suggestion	[səˈdʒestʃən]	n. 建议	3B
suit	[suːt]	vt. 适合于 vi. 合适，相称	10B
suitable	[ˈsuːtəbl]	adj. 适当的，相配的	1A
superlative	[suːˈpɜːlətɪv]	adj. 最高的；最高级的；过度的 n. 最高级	3B
supervisor	[ˈsuːpəvaɪzə]	n. 监督人，管理人，主管人	7B
supplementary	[ˌsʌplɪˈmentri]	adj. 增补的，追加的	8B
supportable	[səˈpɔːtəbl]	adj. 可支持的，可援助的	7A
surge	[sɜːdʒ]	n. 汹涌；激增 v. 汹涌；激增；飞涨	10A
suspect	[səˈspekt]	v. 怀疑，猜想	9A

续表

单　　词	音　　标	意　　义	单元
sustainable	[sə'steɪnəbl]	adj. 可持续的	2A
sway	[sweɪ]	v. 摇摆	3B
swipe	[swaɪp]	vt. 刷(磁卡);偷盗,扒窃	5A
synchronize	['sɪŋkrənaɪz]	v. 同步	6A
synergistic	[ˌsɪnə'dʒɪstɪk]	adj. 协作的	7A
systemic	[sɪ'stiːmɪk]	adj. 系统的	6A
tactics	['tæktɪks]	n. 战术,策略	6A
tailored	['teɪləd]	adj. 订做的,剪裁讲究的	2A
target	['tɑːgɪt]	n. 目标;对象 v. 瞄准,面向	3A
task	[tɑːsk]	n. 任务,工作 v. 分派任务	7B
tax	[tæks]	n. 税,税款,税金 vt. 对…征税	6B
taxe	['tæks]	n. 税款	3A
telltale	['telteɪl]	n. 证据	7B
template	['templeɪt]	n. 模板	1A
template	['templeɪt]	n. 模板;样板	4A
tempt	[tempt]	vt. 吸引;使感兴趣 vi. 有吸引力	3B
territory	['terətɔːri]	n. 领域,管区,地盘;领土,版图	10A
testimonial	[ˌtestɪ'məʊniəl]	adj. 表扬的 n. 推荐信	3B
textile	['tekstaɪl]	n. 纺织品 adj. 纺织的	6B
thereafter	[ˌðeər'ɑːftə]	adv. 其后,从那时以后	1A
third-party	['θɜːdpɑːtɪ]	adj. 第三方的	1B
threat	[θret]	n. 威胁	9A
timeline	['taɪmlaɪn]	n. 时间轴,时间表	9B
tokenization	[təʊ'kɪnaɪzeɪʃn]	n. 标记化;令牌化	5B
traceable	['treɪsəbl]	adj. 可追踪的	8B
traditional	[trə'dɪʃnl]	adj. 传统的,惯例的	5A
traditionally	[trə'dɪʃənəli]	adv. 传统上	7A
transaction	[træn'zækʃn]	n. 交易,业务,事务	3A
transfer	[træns'fɜː]	v. 转账	5B
transmit	[trænz'mɪt]	vt. 传输,转送	5A
transparent	[træns'pærənt]	adj. 透明的;易懂的	10A

续表

单　词	音　标	意　义	单元
treat	[tri:t]	v.对待,处理	4A
trend	[trend]	n.趋势,倾向	8A
trigger	['trɪgə]	vt.引发,引起,触发	2B
Trojan	['trəʊdʒən]	n.特洛伊木马	9A
trustworthiness	['trʌstwɜː;ðɪnəs]	n.可信赖,确实性	10A
trustworthy	['trʌstwɜːðɪ]	adj.值得信赖的,可靠的	3A
turnover	['tɜːnəʊvə]	n.营业额,成交量	5B
unauthorized	[ʌn'ɔː;θəraɪzd]	adj.未被授权的,未经认可的	2B
unclutter	[ʌn'klʌtə]	vt.使整洁,整理	3A
undermine	[ˌʌndə'maɪn]	v.破坏,逐步减少效力	6B
undesired	['ʌndɪ'zaɪəd]	adj.不受欢迎的	9A
unique	[juː'niːk]	adj.唯一的,独特的,特有的	5A
uniqueness	[jʊ'niː;knəs]	n.唯一性,独特性	2A
unnecessary	[ʌn'nesəsəri]	adj.不必要的,多余的	6A
unpleasant	[ʌn'pleznt]	adj.使人不愉快的;讨厌的;不客气的	4A
unprotected	[ˌʌnprə'tektɪd]	adj.无保护的,无防卫的	9A
unregulated	[ˌʌn'regjʊleɪtɪd]	adj.无控制的,无调节的	9A
unsuccessful	[ˌʌnsək'sesfl]	adj.不成功的,失败的	10A
untapped	[ˌʌn'tæpt]	adj.未开发的,未利用的	10A
upload	[ˌʌp'ləʊd]	v.上载	1A
upstream	[ˌʌp'striːm]	adv.上游地 adj.上游的	6A
uptime	['ʌptaɪm]	n.(计算机等的)正常运行时间	9B
user-friendly	[ˌjuːzə'frendli]	adj.用户友好的	3A
user-generated	[ˌjuːzər-dʒenəreɪtɪd]	adj.用户创造的(内容),用户产生的	8B
username	['juː;zəneɪm]	n.用户名	4B
vague	[veɪg]	adj.含糊的,不清楚的	6B
valuable	['væljuəbl]	adj.有价值的;宝贵的	4A
variable	['veərɪəbl]	n.变量 adj.可变的,不定的	2A
various	['veərɪəs]	adj.不同的,多方面的,多样的	1A
vehicle	['viː;əkl]	n.交通工具,车辆,媒介物	2B
velocity	[və'lɒsəti]	n.速度,速率,迅速	6A

续表

单 词	音 标	意 义	单元
velvety	[ˈvelvəti]	adj. 天鹅绒般柔软的	3B
vendor	[ˈvendə]	n. 卖主	2A
vertical	[ˈvɜːtɪkl]	adj. 垂直的	6B
vet	[vet]	vt. 审查	9B
video	[ˈvɪdiəʊ]	n. 视频	3A
virtual	[ˈvɜːtʃuəl]	adj. 虚拟的,实质的	5A
virtue	[ˈvɜːtʃuː]	n. 优点,长处	1A
virus	[ˈvaɪrəs]	n. 病毒	9A
visibility	[ˌvɪzəˈbɪləti]	n. 可见度,可见性	6B
visible	[ˈvɪzəbl]	adj. 可见的;明显的	3A
void	[vɔɪd]	n. 空隙;空间	7B
volume	[ˈvɒljuːm]	n. 量	5A
vulnerability	[ˌvʌlnərəˈbɪləti]	n. 弱点,攻击	5A
vulnerable	[ˈvʌlnərəbl]	adj. 易受攻击的	9A
warehousing	[ˈweəhaʊzɪŋ]	n. 入库,仓库贮存,仓储配送	2A
website	[ˈwebsaɪt]	n. 网站	1A
well-crafted	[wel krɑːftɪd]	adj. 精心设计的	3B
wholesale	[ˈhəʊlseɪl]	adj. 批发的 adv. 用批发方式;以批发价 n. 批发	1B
widget	[ˈwɪdʒɪt]	n. 小器具,窗口小部件	3A
wireless	[ˈwaɪələs]	adj. 无线的	4B
wishlist	[ˈwɪʃlist]	n. 意愿清单,心愿单	3A
wishy-washy	[ˈwɪʃi wɒʃi]	adj. 软弱无力的;空洞无聊的	3B
withdraw	[wɪðˈdrɔː]	vt. 收回,撤销	6B
wizard	[ˈwɪzəd]	n. 向导	1A
woodwind	[ˈwʊdwɪnd]	n. 木管乐器	7B
workload	[ˈwɜːkləʊd]	n. 工作量	7B
workstation	[ˈwɜːksteɪʃn]	n. 工作站	7A
worm	[wɜːm]	n. 蠕虫病毒	9A

表 A-2　词组

词　　　组	意　　　义	单元
a bit of	一点，一星半点	3B
a bunch of	大量；一束；一群	4B
a combination of	…的组合	4B
a majority of	大部分	2A
a variety of	各种各样的	3A
a wealth of	大量的，丰富的	4A
according to	依照	6B
acquiring bank	收单银行	5A
ad placement	广告投放	4B
adapt to	适合	7A
Add to Cart	添加到购物车	3A
adhere to	遵循	9B
administrative cost	管理费用	6B
admission ticket	入场券	2A
advertising-based model	基于广告的模型	1B
after sales service	售后服务	8A
again and again	再三地，反复地	4A
all of a sudden	突然	7B
all year round	全年，一年到头	10A
apply for	请求，申请	5A
as a consequence	因而，结果	6A
as a whole	总体上	6A
as clear as possible	尽可能清晰	3A
at one time	同时；曾经	7B
at regular intervals	每隔一定间隔	9A
at the discretion of	随…的意见，由…自己处理	6B
at this point	此时此刻	8B
attract sb's attention	引起某人注意	6B
auto responder	自动应答器	4A
automation tool	自动化工具	10B
back order	延期交货，未交货，未交货订单	7B

续表

词　　组	意　　义	单元
back-door Trojan	后门特洛伊木马	9A
back-end code	后端代码	9B
background color	背景颜色	3A
bank transfer	银行转账	1A
base on	基于	7A
batch size	批量	7A
be aware of	知道	9A
be built into	被内置到…中	5B
be compatible with	与…兼容	5B
be configured to	配置为	9B
be essential to	对…必要的,对…非常重要	2B
be familiar with	熟悉	1A
be intended to be	规定为,确定为	6B
be interested in	对…感兴趣	6B
be likely to	可能	6B
be overwhelmed by	受不起,不敢当	2B
be prone to	有…的倾向,易于	9A
be ready to	预备,即将	1A
be responsible for	为…负责,形成…的原因	7A
be susceptible to	易受…感染的;易受…影响的	2B
be willing to	乐于	6B
bid against sb	(与某人)争出高价,抬价竞买	6B
bid on	投标承包(某项工程)	1B
big data	大数据	10B
big data-enabled technology	大数据支持技术	10B
biometric authentication	生物识别认证	4B
body language	身体语言,肢体语言	4A
brand awareness	品牌意识;品牌知名度,品牌认知度	10A
brand name	商标,品牌	2A
brand value	品牌价值	8A
brand visibility	品牌知名度	10A

词　　组	意　　义	单元
break ... down into	把…分为	1B
brick and mortar store	实体店	4A
building block	积木	7B
bullet point	商品五点描述;要点,卖点	3B
business climate	商业氛围	10A
business model	商业模式	2A
buyer-oriented e-marketplace	买家主导的电子市场	6B
by analogy with	从…类推,根据…类推	2A
calculate prediction	计算预测	8B
cash on delivery	货到付款,交货付现	2A
cater to	迎合,为…服务	2A
cease operation	停止运行	9A
chamber of commerce	商会	2B
chat box	聊天框	8A
checkout procedure	支付过程	2B
checkout wait time	结账等待时间	10B
cloud-based solution	基于云的解决方案	8B
come into play	开始活动;开始运转;投入使用	7A
commercial guideline	商业指南	10A
community-based model	基于社区的模型	1B
compete for	为…竞争	6B
competitive advantage	竞争优势	10A
competitive bidding	竞标,竞争出价	6B
competitive edge	竞争优势	8A
computing power	计算能力	8B
confirmation text	确认文本	3A
consolidate ... into	把…合并到…中	5B
content analysis	内容分析	8B
content-based and collaborative system	基于内容的协作系统	8B
contingent on	视…而定	3A
contribute to	促成;有助于	4B

续表

词　　组	意　　义	单元
conventional store	普通商店	2A
conversion funnel	转化漏斗	3B
conversion rate	转化率	3B
convert into	转化为	10B
coupled with	加上，外加	10A
credit card	信用卡	5B
cross docking	直接转运，直接换装，交叉配送	6A
cross-border e-commerce	跨境电子商务	10A
crowd out	挤出，推开，驱逐	1A
customer base	客户群	3A
customer behavior	客户行为	4A
customer behavior analysis	客户行为分析	10B
customer review	客户评论	10B
customer service	客户服务	4A
customer support service	客户支持服务	8A
customized recommendation	定制推荐	8A
cutting-edge design	最前沿的设计	2B
data analytic	数据分析	8A
data breach	数据泄露，资料外泄	9B
data privacy	数据隐私	9B
data set	数据集	8B
data-backed price management	数据支持的价格管理	10B
database tracking	数据库跟踪	8B
data-driven price management initiatives	数据驱动的价格管理计划	10B
deal with	处理，应付	8A
debit card	借记卡	2A
decision-making process	决策程序，决策过程	8A
delivery on payment	交货付款	2A
delivery route	交货路线，送货路线	8A
depend on	取决于；依赖于	3A
design template	设计模板	2B

续表

词　　组	意　　义	单元
digital content	数字内容	4B
digital media	数字媒体	2A
digital wallet	数字钱包	5B
direct selling	直销，直接销售	1B
direct shipment	直接运送	6A
dispose of	卖掉，转让，解决	6B
distribution center	配送中心	6A
drive out	消除	6A
drop shipping	工厂直接送货	2A
eat up	耗尽，吃光	4A
electrical grid failure	电网故障	9B
end user	最终用户	1B
endpoint protection	端点保护	9B
enterprise resource planning system	企业资源规划系统	10B
error message	出错信息	3A
essential sign	基本符号，重要标志	3A
face-to-face transaction	面对面交易	5A
facial-feature recognition	面部特征识别	9A
false alarm	假警报	9A
feature engineering	特征工程	8B
fee-based model	收费模型	1B
figure out	找出	10B
fill a gap	填补空白，弥补缺陷，弥合差距	10A
fill up	（使）充满；填充	8B
financial institution	金融机构	5A
financial risk	财务风险	5A
finished good	成品	6A
first impression	第一印象，初步印象	3A
first-mover advantage	先发优势	10A
fixed price	固定价格	2B
floor supervisor	领班；楼层主管	7B

续表

词　　组	意　　义	单元
foreign market	国外市场	10A
forward auction	正向拍卖	6B
forward position	前沿阵地	7A
free shipping	免运费	4B
from scratch	从零开始,从无到有,白手起家	2A
full page	整个页面;整版	3A
geographical location	地理位置	4B
gift card	礼品卡,赠卡	2A
global brand	全球品牌	10A
go for	适用于;选择,想要获得;喜爱	1A
government agency	政府机构	9A
hard disk	硬盘	9A
high end	高端	2A
high street	大街,主要街道	5A
high-contrast text	高对比度文本	3A
home page	主页	4A
hosting company	托管公司	1A
image recognition	图像识别	8A
image search	图像搜索	8A
impact on	影响;对…产生冲击	5B
impulse buy	冲动购买	5B
in advance	预先	7A
in line with	符合	7A
in order to	为了	3A
in practical terms	实际上	5A
in recent years	最近几年中	6B
in the first instance	首先,起初	2B
in the ultimate	到最后,终于	6A
individual preference	个人偏好	8B
information filtering system	信息过滤系统	8B
instant connection	即时连接	4B

词　　组	意　　义	单元
in-store pickup	实体店内取货	2A
intellectual property	知识产权	9A
internal policy	内部政策	3A
international market	国际市场	10A
interpersonal relationship	人际关系	4A
inventory management	库存管理,存货管理	8A
jumping-off point	起点,出发点	9B
keep up with	跟上	7B
knowledge base	知识库	4A
landing page	登录页面	9B
late payment	逾期付款	2B
lead time	订货至交货的时间	2B
legacy system	遗留系统,老旧系统	9B
live analytic	实时分析	10B
live representative	现场代表	4A
live up to	实践,做到	2A
local bank	本地银行	1A
local language	当地语言,本土语言	10A
local logistics center	当地物流中心	10A
local payment	本地支付	10A
local store	本地商店	1B
location tracking	位置跟踪,位置追踪	4B
log off	退出,注销	2A
long-term value	长期价值	10B
machine learning	机器学习	8A
main menu	主菜单	3A
making money	赚钱	2A
manual work	手工作业	8A
market share	市场份额,市场占有率	9A
market trend	市场趋势	10B
material handling	物料输送,原材料处理	7A

续表

词　　组	意　　义	单元
mathematical model	数学模型	8B
memory-based method	基于记忆的方法	8B
memory stick	存储条,存储棒	9A
Merchant Account Provider	商家账号提供商	1A
milestone payment	分期付款	6A
military science	军事学	7A
mini cart	迷你购物车	3A
minute by minute	全时;分分秒秒	6A
mobile banking	移动银行	4B
mobile device	移动设备	3A
mobile e-commerce	移动电子商务	4B
mobile payment	移动支付,手机支付	5B
model-based method	基于模型的方法	8B
modal window	模态窗口	3A
monthly fee	月费	5A
motor carrier	汽车运输	6A
multi channel support	多渠道支持	4A
multiple shop	连锁店,联营商店	2A
musical score	乐谱	7B
net value	净值	6A
network architecture	网络结构,网络体系	5A
network level	网络层	9A
non-handheld device	非手持设备	4B
ocean freight	海运	6A
old school	守旧派	7B
on the increase	增加	7B
on the plant floor	工厂车间层面	7B
on the spot	立刻,当场	4B
online backup	在线备份	9B
online merchant account	在线商家账号	1A
online payment	在线支付	5A

续表

词　　组	意　　义	单元
online retail marketplace	网上零售市场,在线零售市场	4A
online self-service tool	在线自助服务工具	10B
online shopping	在线购物,网上购物	2A
online shopping mall	在线购物中心,网上购物商城	5A
online shopping platform	网上购物平台	1B
online transaction	在线交易	2B
open source	开放源代码	2A
operational cost	运营成本	2B
operational process	运营过程;操作过程	10B
operational status	运行状态,运营状态	7B
optimum inventory level	最佳库存水平	10B
order confirmation	确认定单,证实定单	3A
order status	订单状态	3A
out-of-the-box shopping cart program	开箱即装即用购物车程序	1A
over and over	反复,再三	7B
overall cost	总值,全部成本	6B
pain point	痛点	3B
participate in	参加,参与,分享	6B
pay for	偿还,赔偿	2B
payment service provider	支付服务提供商	1A
payment system	支付系统	5B
peace of mind	安心,内心的宁静	7B
peak time	高峰期	7B
peer-to-peer payment	点对点支付	5B
penetration testing	渗透测试	9B
performance measurement	性能测定,工作状况的测定	6A
personal data	个人数据,个人资料	3A
personal identification number	个人身份号码	9A
personal information	个人信息	4B
physical distribution	实物配送,实物分销	7A
pick up	捡起;获得	1B

续表

词 组	意 义	单元
pick-to-light	光拣选系统	7B
pick-to-voice	语音拣选系统,声导选货	7B
popup window	弹出式窗口	3A
positive impression	正面印象	2A
postal money order	邮政汇票	2A
potential buyer	潜在买家	3B
potential customer	潜在顾客	10A
potential impact	潜在影响	9A
power surge	电涌	9B
prediction method	预测方法	8B
press release	新闻稿	1A
price list	价格表	9A
pricing point	价格点	6B
print out	(打)印出	2A
privacy policy	隐私政策	3A
private data	私人数据	8A
procurement contract	采购合同	6B
procurement cycle	采购周期	6B
product description	产品阐述,产品说明	3B
product detail page	产品详细信息页面	3A
product life cycle	产品寿命周期,产品生命周期	6A
product listing	产品清单	10A
product review	产品评论	3A
production facility	生产设备	6A
production logistic	生产物流	7A
profit margin	利润率	8A
prognosis model	预后模型	8B
progress bar	进度条	3A
project life cycles	项目生命周期	7A
promotional purposes	推广宣传目的	6B
protect from	保护	9A

续表

词　　　组	意　　义	单元
purchase history	购买历史记录	4A
purchasing habit	购买习惯	10A
purchasing pattern	购买模式	8A
push notification	推送通知	4B
quick view	快速查看	3A
raw material	原料	6A
real time	实时	2A
real-time analytic	实时分析	10B
real-time data	实时数据	10B
reciprocal links directory	互惠链接目录	1A
recommendation engine	推荐引擎	8A
recommendation platform	推荐平台	8B
recommendation system	推荐系统	8A
register as	表现为，显示出	6B
registration fee	注册费，报名费	6B
rely on	依靠，依赖	7B
request for bid	招标	6B
request for quotation	询价	6B
response time	响应时间	4A
return policy	退货政策	4A
return rate	退货率	3B
returns process	退货步骤，退货过程	3A
reverse flow	反向流动	7A
right away	马上，立刻	7B
role-based access	基于角色的访问	9B
round-the-clock support	全天候支持，连续不停地支持	2B
search box	搜索框	1A
search criteria	搜索条件	6B
search engine	搜索引擎	1A
search engines rank site	搜索引擎排名网站	2B
search for	搜索；查找	8B

续表

词　　组	意　　义	单元
search ranking	搜索排名	3B
second-hand equipment	二手设备	6B
security audit	安全监察,安全审计	9B
security hole	安全漏洞	9A
send out	放出	9A
sensitive information	敏感信息	5B
ship out	运出	7A
shopping cart abandonment	购物车放弃	3B
shopping experience	购物体验	4B
shopping mall	大型购物中心	2A
shore up	支撑,支持;加强	9B
short-term aim	短期目标	7A
sign up	注册,签约	1A
simulation software	仿真软件	7A
site optimization company	网站优化公司	1A
size chart	尺码表	3A
social media	社交媒体	3A
social proof	社会证明′	4A
software supplier	软件提供商	1A
sophisticated algorithm	复杂算法	8B
spam email	垃圾电子邮件	9A
square feet	平方英尺	7B
stand out	突出;超群	3A
stand out from	脱颖而出	8B
step up	行动起来;(使…)增加;(使…)加快速度	4A
stick to	遵守;保留;坚持	3A
strategic decision	战略决策	10B
strategic view	战略眼光	2B
supply chain	供应链	10B
swiped card transaction	刷卡交易	5A
symphony orchestra	交响乐团	7B

词　　　组	意　　义	单元
take account of	考虑	9A
take advantage of	利用	10A
take long	花费很多时间	2B
take on responsibilities	承担责任	7B
take steps	采取措施	9A
target customer	目标客户	10A
target market	目标市场	10A
targeted advertising	目标广告	10B
taxation policy	税收政策	10A
the turn of the century	世纪之交	7B
third-party distributor	第三方分销商	2A
track down	追踪	2B
track inventory	跟踪库存	10B
Trojan horse	特洛伊木马	9A
tune up	开始演奏；调音，定弦，调整，调节	7B
unauthenticated access	未经身份验证的访问	8A
unauthorized access	未授权的访问，越权访问	9B
unpatched software	未修补的软件	9B
upper hand	优势，上风，有利地位	3A
user behaviour	用户行为	8A
user forum	用户论坛	9B
value proposition	价值主张，价值定位	1B
vertically oriented business	面向垂直业务	1B
virtual online market	虚拟网络市场，虚拟在线市场	6B
voice recognition system	语音识别系统	8A
wallet system	电子钱包系统	1A
web design company	网站建设公司	1A
web shop	网络商店	2A
white paper	白皮书	7B
wire transfer	电汇	2A
with a view to	为了…，以…为目的	9A
zoom up	放大视图；推近	3A

表 A-3 缩略语

缩略语及原形	意 义	单元
2FA（Two-Factor Authentication）	双因素认证	9B
3PL（Third-party Logistics Provider）	第三方物流	6A
4PL（Fourth Party Logistics）	第四方物流	7A
AI（Artificial Intelligence）	人工智能	8A
APICS（American Production and Inventory Control Society）	美国运营管理学会	6A
B2B（Business to Business）	企业对企业	1B
B2B2C（Business to Business to Consumer）	企业对企业对消费者	1B
B2C（Business to Consumer）	企业对消费者	1B
B2G（Business to Government）	企业对政府	1B
C2B（Consumer to Business）	消费者对企业	1B
C2C（Consumer to Consumer）	消费者对消费者	1B
CD（Compact Disc）	光盘	9A
COFC（Container On Flatcar）	集装箱输送	6A
CRM（Customer Relationship Management）	客户关系管理	8A
CSCMP（Council of Supply Chain Management Professionals）	供应链专业管理委员会	6A
CSV（Comma Separated Value）	逗号分隔值	9B
CTA（Call To Action）	行动召唤	3A
CX（Customer Experience）	客户体验	9B
DoS（denial-of-service）	拒绝服务	9A
DRP（Disaster Recovery Plan）	灾难恢复计划	9B
DSD（Direct Store Delivery）	店铺直接配送	6A
DSS（Data Security Standard）	数据安全标准	5A
DVD（Digital Video Disc）	数字视频光盘	9A
EMV（Europay，MasterCard，Visa）	由 Europay、MasterCard 和 Visa 制定的智能卡标准	5B
FAQ（Frequently Asked Questions）	常见问题	3A
GDPR（General Data Protection Regulation）	通用数据保护条例	9B
GPS（Global Position System）	全球定位系统	4B
GSCF（Global Supply Chain Forum）	全球供应链论坛	6A
HIPAA（Health Insurance Portability and Accountability Act）	健康保险携带和责任法案	9B

续表

缩略语及原形	意　义	单元
ICP（Ideal Customer Profile）	理想客户特征	1B
ID（IDentity）	身份标识号码	4B
ILS（Integrated Logistics Support）	集成物流支持	7A
IMA（Internet Merchant Account）	因特网商家账号	5A
IoT（Internet of Things）	物联网	10B
IP（Internet Protocol）	网际互联协议	4B
KPI（Key Performance Indicators）	关键业绩指标	3B
NFC（Near Field Communication）	近场通信	5B
NPS（Net Promoter Score）	净推荐值,净促进者得分,口碑	10B
OECD（Organization for Economic Cooperation and Development）	经济合作与发展组织	9B
PC（Personal Computer）	个人计算机	9A
PCI（Payment Card Industry）	支付卡行业	5A
QC（Quality Control）	质量控制	7B
RFPs（Requests For Proposals）	需求建议书	1B
ROI（Return On Investment）	投资利润,投资回报率	10B
SaaS（Software as a Service）	软件即服务	8B
SCEM（supply chain event management）	供应链事件管理	6A
SCM（Supply Chain Management）	供应链管理	6A
SCOR（Supply-Chain Operations Reference-model）	供应链运营参考模型	6A
SEO（Search Engine Optimization）	搜索引擎优化	10B
SKU（Stock Keeping Unit）	库存单元,存货单元	7B
SSL（Secure Sockets Layer）	安全套接层	3A
TOFC（Trailer On Flatcar）	平车拖运	6A
UI（User Interface）	用户界面	3A
UX（User eXperience）	用户体验	3A
VPN（Virtual Private Network）	虚拟专用网	9A
VR（Virtual Reality）	虚拟现实	3A
WCS（Warehouse Control Systems）	仓库控制系统	7A
WIP（Work-In-Progress）	在制品	6A
WMS（Warehouse Management Systems）	仓库管理系统	7A

附录 B 电子商务新词的构成与词汇翻译

当今,电子商务具有极高的发展速度,产值增加幅度很大,与国外信息交流较多。其中,电子商务专业英语成为必不可少的媒介。由于电子商务涉及计算机、通信、网络、商务、金融及物流等多个方面,其专业英语新词呈现量多面广、含义复杂的特点。理解这些新词的构成并准确地用中文来阐释其意义是翻译的关键。

1 电子商务专业英语新词的构成方法

电子商务专业英语的新词中,与现有词汇完全没有联系的很少。绝大多数新词都是在现有词汇的基础上产生的,其构成方法有规律可循。

1.1 单词构成

在电子商务专业英语中,新单词的构成方法主要有以下几种:

- 新赋意义。通过给某个单词赋予新的、有电子商务专业英语特色的意义,使之成为专业单词,这是一种"旧瓶装新酒"的方法。如果不了解其在电子商务专业英语中的新意义,就会造成理解的错误。例如 quotation 在社交语境中为"语录""引言",而在电子商务专业英语中给它赋予了新的意思,即"报价单""行情"等。又如 acquire 的常用意思是"习得、获得",在电子商务语境中的意思是"购进、购买"。再如 logistics 的原意为"后勤",在电子商务中的意思是"物流",是一个专业性很强的词。
- 复合构造。这样构造的新词来自两个或多个现有的单词,由现有的单词组合在一起形成一个新词,如 banknote(钞票)、cardholder(持卡人)、storefront(店面)、wholesale(批发)、duty-free(免税的)及 outsource(外包)等。
- 派生法构词。词根就是一个单词最原始的"本体",不可以再拆分,是词的核心部分,词的意义主要是由它体现出来的。词根可以单独构成词,也可以彼此组合成词。词缀只能是黏附在词根上构成新词的语素,它本身不能单独构成词。派生法是英语主要的构词法,方法是通过给词根添加词缀构成新词,这样产生的词就被称为派生词(derivative word)。加上前缀的词,虽然意思改变了,但词性保持不变;相反,加上后缀的词,不但词义有些改变,词性也完全不同。例如,可以通过给词根加前缀 re 构成的词有 resell(转卖)、recall(召回),加前缀 ex 构成的词有 export(出口)、exchange(外汇),加前缀 un 构成的词有 undue(未到期的)、uncommercial(与商业无关的)及 undo(撤销)等,加后缀 er 构成的词有 bankroller(资助者)、retailer(零售商)、broker(经纪人),加后缀 or 构成的词有 distributor(经销商、推销商)、investor(投资者)及 vendor(销售商),加后缀 ment 构成的词有 payment(支付)及

management（管理）等。

- 拼缀法构词。对原有的两个词进行剪裁，各取其中的一部分，连成一个新词。例如，分别取出 communication（通信）和 satellite（卫星）的前 3 个字母 com 和 sat，拼接为 comsat（通信卫星）。又如，camcorder（摄像机）是 camera（照相机）与 recorder（录音机）的组合。

词组就是许多由单词组成的固定搭配。在电子商务专业英语中，词组广泛使用，其结构固定，专业意义明确。例如，acquisition price（购进价格）、digital order（数字订单）、electronic wallet（电子钱包）、online store（网上商店、电子店面）、online catalog（网上目录、在线目录）、payment card（支付卡）、payment option（支付方式选择）、sale volume（销售量）、trading partner（贸易伙伴）、supply chain management（供应链管理）、bank transfer（银行间转账）及 wire transfer（电汇）均是词组。

1.2 缩略语构成

缩略语可以有效提高信息含量，更加高效，符合网络时代有效传播的要求，因而在电子商务英语中广泛使用。缩略语具有明显的行业特色，不理解缩略语往往就不能理解整段文字的意义。

在电子商务专业英语中，缩略语的构成方法主要有以下几种：

- 首字母缩略。取各个单词的首字母组成缩略语。这种构成方法最为常见，是全部缩略语的基础和主体。例如，CA（Certification Authority，认证机构）、ASP（Active Server Page，活动服务器页面）、CRM（Customer Relationship Management，客户关系管理）、ERP（Enterprise Resource Planning，企业资源管理）、SET（Secure Electronic Transaction，安全电子交易）、RFO（Requests For Quotations，询问报价）以及 GATT（General Agreement Tariff Trade，关贸总协定）均是如此构成的缩略词。
- 首尾字母缩略。由某个单词的第一个字母和最后一个（或几个）字母缩略而成，例如 YD（Yard，码）、Rd（Road，路）、BK（Bank，银行）、ft（foot，英尺）、wt（weight，重量）、vr（voucher，记账凭证）及 gtee（guarantee，保证、担保书）等。
- 截割缩略。截去词的首部或尾部，留下的部分构成一个新词，例如 phone（telephone，电话）、App（Application，应用软件）、ID（IDentity，身份）及 ad（advertisement，广告）等。
- 转音缩略。将某个读音与数字相同的单词转换为数字，再进行缩略。例如，B2B（企业对企业）其原始形式为 Business to Business，将 to 转换为 two，再将 two 写为数字 2，最终缩略为 B2B。类似的还有 B2C（Business-to-Consumer，企业对消费者）、C2C（Consumer-to-Consumer，消费者对消费者）等。

2 电子商务专业英语词汇的翻译方法

电子商务专业英语词汇的翻译方法主要有直译、意译、音译和音义结合 4 种。

2.1 直译

直译即直接译出字面意义。直译法是一种最常用的方法，特别是在翻译复合词时，大都用直译法。直译法简单易行,便于理解。例如,把 checkout 翻译为"结账",把 term 翻译为"条款"。类似的例子有 instrument(票据、证券)、commission(佣金)、interest-free credit(无息信贷)、cash transaction(现金交易)、agent fee(代理费)、intermediate merchant(中间商)、quantity purchase(大宗订货)、after-sale service(售后服务)、capital surplus(资本盈余)与 shipping cost(运输费用)等。

2.2 意译

当一个英语词汇没有完全对应的汉语词汇或者按照其字面意思直接翻译不符合汉语的表达方式时,应该意译。通过某种转换,使用符合汉语习惯的词汇表达其含义,不拘泥于其字面意思。例如,将 brick-and-mortar store(水泥砖头商店)意译为"实体店",与"网络商店"相对应。

2.3 音译

音译即按照英语词汇的读音翻译为相应的汉语词汇。例如,将 cracker 翻译为"骇客"。因为 cracker 恶意破解商业软件,恶意入侵别人的网站,让人恐惧。如果翻译为"破解者、攻入者",既不形象也不生动。而汉字"骇"传神地表达了人们谈之色变的恐惧感。类似的翻译还有 e-mail(伊妹儿,电子邮件)、OPEC(欧佩克)与 Topology(拓扑)。

公司名称及产品名称的翻译通常采用音译,例如 Amazon(亚马逊)、Wal-Mart(沃尔玛)、Google(谷歌)、Cisco(思科)、Rolex(劳力士)、Coca-Cola (可口可乐)、Budweiser(百威)、Calvin Klein(卡尔文·克莱恩)、Nike(耐克)。

2.4 音义结合

音义结合即兼顾语音和词义,既取其义,亦取其音。例如,把 Internet 翻译为"因特网",取 Inter 之音、取 net 之义。类似的还有 Truly(信利)、Accord(雅确)、Fiyta(飞亚达)、Goldlion(金利来)及 Best Buy(百思购)。

电子商务的技术进步和商业模式创新都会带来新的专业英语词汇。应该根据其构造特点,依据专业背景知识,运用恰当的翻译方法,以专业化语言准确与贴切地翻译,在实现词义的对等或等效的基础上,追求传神与精妙,以期臻于信、达、雅的境界。

图书资源支持

感谢您一直以来对清华版图书的支持和爱护。为了配合本书的使用，本书提供配套的资源，有需求的读者请扫描下方的"书圈"微信公众号二维码，在图书专区下载，也可以拨打电话或发送电子邮件咨询。

如果您在使用本书的过程中遇到了什么问题，或者有相关图书出版计划，也请您发邮件告诉我们，以便我们更好地为您服务。

我们的联系方式：

清华大学出版社计算机与信息分社网站：https://www.shuimushuhui.com/

地　　址：北京市海淀区双清路学研大厦 A 座 714

邮　　编：100084

电　　话：010-83470236　010-83470237

客服邮箱：2301891038@qq.com

QQ：2301891038（请写明您的单位和姓名）

资源下载：关注公众号"书圈"下载配套资源。

资源下载、样书申请
书圈

图书案例
清华计算机学堂

观看课程直播